# Managing Financial Information in the Trade Lifecycle

# ELSEVIER WORLD CAPITAL MARKETS SERIES

## Series Editor: Herbie Skeete

The **Elsevier World Capital Markets Series** consists of books that cover the developments in the capital markets, as well as basic texts introducing the markets to those working directly or indirectly in the capital markets. Investors are more knowledgeable and demanding than ever before and there is a thirst for information by professional investors and those who sell and provide services to them. Regulators are demanding more transparency and new rules and regulations are being introduced constantly. The impact of competition means that markets are constantly changing and merging, and new instruments are being devised. This Series provides cutting-edge information and discussion about these and other development affecting the capital markets. Technology underpins and is driving innovation in the markets. Inappropriate technology or no technology can bring down even the soundest financial institution. This Series therefore also includes books that enable market experts to understand aspects of technology that are driving the markets.

Books in the Series include:

- *Managing Financial Information in the Trade Lifecycle* by Martijn Groot
- *MDDL and the Quest for a Market Data Standard* by Martin Sexton
- *Market Data Explained* by Marc Alvarez

**Series Editor Herbie Skeete** is a well known figure in the financial information industry having spent twenty-six years at Reuters. During his many senior positions with Reuters—most recently Head of Equities Content and Head of Exchange Strategy—Mr. Skeete has become recognized globally as an expert on exchanges and content issues. He is frequently asked to address conferences and to contribute to roundtable discussions. Mr. Skeete runs the exchange information publisher, Mondo Visione Ltd; edits the industry-standard *Handbook of World Stock, Commodity, and Derivatives Exchanges*, which celebrates its sixteenth edition this year; and operates the exchange information website www.exchange-handbook.com.

# Managing Financial Information in the Trade Lifecycle

## A Concise Atlas of Financial Instruments and Processes

Martijn Groot

AMSTERDAM • BOSTON • HEIDELBERG • LONDON
NEW YORK • OXFORD • PARIS • SAN DIEGO
SAN FRANCISCO • SINGAPORE • SYDNEY • TOKYO
Academic Press is an imprint of Elsevier

Academic Press is an imprint of Elsevier
30 Corporate Drive, Suite 400, Burlington, MA 01803, USA
525 B Street, Suite 1900, San Diego, California 92101-4495, USA
84 Theobald's Road, London WC1X 8RR, UK

**Library of Congress Cataloging-in-Publication Data**
Application submitted

**British Library Cataloguing-in-Publication Data**
A catalogue record for this book is available from the British Library.

ISBN: 978-0-12-374289-6

For information on all Academic Press publications
visit our Web site at www.books.elsevier.com

Printed in the United States of America
08   09   10    9   8   7   6   5   4   3   2   1

## Working together to grow
## libraries in developing countries

www.elsevier.com | www.bookaid.org | www.sabre.org

ELSEVIER    BOOK AID International    Sabre Foundation

# Table of Contents

# Foreword

**Bill Nichols**
**Program Director**
**Securities Processing Automation, FISD/SIIA**

The Financial Services industry has been characterized by high relative spending on systems and software technologies since these became available. According to most industry surveys, per capita spending on technology is considerably higher than in other industry segments, in some cases double or more.

Given that financial products lack "manufacturing friction"—there is no assembly line waiting for pre-manufactured components to be bolted together—the "arms race" for competitive advantage focuses on information advantages. But the dirty little secret of the industry is also tied to this lack of friction. Because markets absorb information quickly, any product, investment strategy, or service which has a true competitive edge derived from information or execution characteristics, or a combination of both, will lose that edge in a short timeframe, as other market participants react to the "new" competitive requirements.

So we have an industry landscape characterized by accelerating rates of change and adaption in terms of product offerings coupled with the same type of change profile in the mechanics by which these offerings are implemented—systems technology. These two factors are synergistic; ever-increasing complexity in instrument design and risk analytics are fed by increased availability of large data sets tied together in previously unworkable ways.

For practitioners in the Market Data world, whose mission in life is to make sure that the data is clean, reliable, accurate, and accessible from almost any conceivable perspective, there are other relevant factors as well. First, regulators are scrambling to keep up with and anticipate market developments. The complexity of regulatory requirements, especially across multiple jurisdictions, is a significant business issue for all involved. Next, the nature of the business requires multiple information sources and methods for combining them into a coherent view depending on internal or external customers' requirements. Here we run into the industry's dirty little secret, one that you won't find discussed much in the vast majority of books or articles about or for Financial Services practitioners. The secret is relatively simple:

*As a general rule, every system that was ever used to address a business process in a bank, brokerage firm, investment firm, or any of the related constellations of businesses that make up what we call the Financial Services Industry, is still out there. Either that piece of code or that piece of hardware (or both!) are still being used in operations, or the "new" system designed to replace it is shaped by how the first one was built.*

This complexity is a serious issue, especially for those tasked with maintaining, or migrating and moving forward these systems, and basically unaddressed in the existing literature until now; and are spotty at best. The publication in 1986 of the first version of David Weiss' book *After the Trade Is Made: Processing Securities Transactions* has been followed after a long silence by a plethora of new books touching on and around securities processing mechanics, but none sufficient as a guidance framework for those who do it for a living. Realistically, the field is changing too fast and both the data and the methods for dealing with the data ensure that most of the really good stuff stays locked up in training materials within firms. For the most part, by the time the material is no longer considered proprietary, it's out-of-date.

A corollary of the rapid rate of change in practice is the lack of a generally accepted framework which can serve as a "coordinate system" for industry discussions. Everyone talks about their piece of the puzzle, but putting together a consistent prototype of how different actors, their actions, competing goals, and interdependencies interrelate is something the industry has not yet sorted out.

Which brings us Martijn Groot's *Managing Financial Information in the Trade Lifecycle: A Concise Atlas of Financial Instruments and Processes*.

The title itself is pretty ambitious. Fortunately, Martijn pulls it off. He also goes a long way toward solving the framework issue. His approach is based on a combination of viewpoints, intersecting instrument and transaction lifecycles, and tying them together within a Supply Chain model borrowed (at least originally) from advances in Manufacturing and Operations Management. While not the only industry expert attracted to the Supply Chain approach, Martijn has done a masterful job of adapting it to the realities of Market Data practices. Here, for the first time, is a coherent descriptive framework that describes how the pieces fit together, why they need to be handled the way they are and what metrics and aspects of information quality can be used. It doesn't go into the mechanics of pricing and valuation for various instruments—that's not the point here, and there are plenty of other sources of information on that. There are other places where Martijn neatly draws the line and stays focused. If you need a concise overview of information management and the products and processes in the operations of the securities industry, including practical discussions related to trade-offs and legacy overhang, you now have it.

*This book is dedicated to my wife Annette
and my children Tim, Mila, and Daan*

.

# Series Editor's Preface

Herbie Skeete
London

Data management is not a glamorous area. I doubt whether you will find many children dreaming of a career in data management. However, whether in the rapidly expanding financial markets or in the competitive world of logistics, getting the correct number of cans of baked beans from warehouse to supermarket "just in time," management of data is of utmost importance in today's complex world of interlocking parts.

In the world of market data, a favorite saying of mine is that "Data is the very lifeblood of an organization." In providing a comprehensive and rigorous survey of the processes around the financial instrument lifecycle and how it is currently served by content providers, this book covers virgin territory.

Whilst not quite the *"Grey's Anatomy"* of data management, in dissecting the information supply train, Groot's *Managing Financial Information in the Trade Lifecycle* will become the standard work in the area of managing the financial information supply chain.

In addressing such topics as regulatory reporting issues, operational risk and the lifecycle of data from birth to retirement, the book provides key insights in industry developments that impact information sourcing and distribution. It carries impressively the huge amount of technical information which is inescapable in this area without forgetting either the real world legacy situations or the challenges of the present and changing landscape of the future.

If you are looking for insights on the key factors for choosing an information sourcing and distribution strategy, look no further; this is the book for you. To predict the markets, unfortunately, you will have to keep on tossing your lucky dice!

# Chapter 1

# The Changing Financial Services Landscape

## 1.1 Introduction

This book provides an overview of the challenges and best practices in financial content management. We will take the perspective of a financial institution as a series of systems and processes consisting of different steps and transitions that address various business problems. The business problems can be put under the umbrella of the transaction lifecycle—research, trades, and post-trade activities—and the financial instrument lifecycle—the birth, life, and demise of the raw materials of these trades. How are these business problems addressed? Through an information supply chain that transforms content as it flows through various stages where it is enriched, molded, or acted on. Why is all this taking place? To solve investment problems: Financial instruments are used to move money backward and forward through time.

We will discuss these three closely intertwined chained processes: the financial instrument lifecycle, the transaction lifecycle, and the information supply chain servicing these two cycles. Through a survey of the financial instrument lifecycle and the interplay between the information supply chain and the different processes in financial services, we will outline *what* key elements about information management are important *where*. We will discuss both content (i.e., descriptive information about the transactions and the instruments), as well as qualitative information on that content—*metacontent* if you like (descriptive information that qualifies content, e.g., speed, reliability). We will discuss different quality and service-level aspects of financial data such as speed, accuracy, retention and audit, and completeness and see that these can be key differentiators when it comes to the success of a financial process. This book provides an overview of financial instruments and processes and will discuss *what matters where* in the light of business and regulatory needs.

Looking at the instrument and transaction lifecycles and the information supply chain serving these lifecycles, we will observe that separating these processes and knowing what you need where and when allows you to design and manage your processes in a much better way. Whether it is in quantitative modeling to price products or assess risks, information issues are consistently and persistently at the top position of charts of issues. Data are unreliable, hard to find, expensive, generally perceived to be of dodgy "quality" however defined, or just simply unavailable.

## 1.2 Historical Perspective and Current Industry Landscape

The following are some of the major industry themes when describing the current financial industry information management landscape:

- The *volume* of information to be processed has skyrocketed. This is due not only to growth of the available financial product universe, but also to changes in trading strategies and execution venues. The order size has decreased, and the number of messages (requests for quotes, indication of interest) for each transaction has increased.

- The *complexity* of products has increased. On the one hand, risk has become a continuum which could be sliced, diced, blended, and bundled. Financial products can be "built to order" for counterparties rather than sold out of inventory. However, sometimes residual risk is hard to price, and the information discrepancies between two counterparties and different levels of sophistication still mean that frequently risk ends up where it is least understood—regulation on customer protection and reporting notwithstanding.

■ The *lag* between the moment of the transaction and moment of settlement is shrinking. A lengthy settlement time brings risk into the process. The longer this lag, the larger the potential outstanding balance between counterparties and the higher the settlement risk (the money at risk). The pressure is on settlement risk to decrease. Both the introduction of a middleman (a central counterparty that clears the trades) and a shortened cycle between trade and exchange of cash and product address this.

■ *Competition* on cost for the plain vanilla products combined with a search for higher margin in complex products puts two different pressures on processes: that of a low per unit cost combined with a need for flexibility to accommodate more intricate structures.

■ *Increased regulation* to make markets and market participants more transparent: This has resulted in pre-trade (reporting of quotes and indications of interest) and post-trade (reporting of transactions) transparency requirements. Together with increased scrutiny of the quality of information processes, the granularity of the reporting on market, credit and operational risk, and the scrutiny on client take-on ("Know Your Customer") and client behavior (e.g., Anti-Money-Laundering controls), this has caused compliance and risk departments to balloon and has put further pressure on processes and procedures.

The first wave of automation was aimed at cheaply processing the standard, plain vanilla products. These products were mostly aimed at solving investment problems: i.e., companies that needed money through equity or debt funding or somewhere in between. At that time, the market for derivatives was tiny or nonexistent. With greater volatility and instability of the financial system came the need to *price* and subsequently *trade and transfer* various types of financial risk. This caused an enormous flurry of financial product innovation. When new product lines such as interest rate swaps began to appear in the 1980s, this led to architectures of local (also called *decentral*) systems around the mainframes. Different applications with separate business logic were needed to accommodate the proliferation of products. However, it has become apparent that the content needed to operate these applications and that makes their outcome valuable suffers from this very decentralization. All too often information that enters a processing application arrives late, faulty, or incomplete. Similarly, many applications require similar data. Discrepancies in input cause havoc downstream when it comes to reconciling transactions and when aggregate financial reports need to be made. We will discuss the issue in more detail later in this chapter, but part of the reason is the blending of information and business logic. Each application has its own storage that often independently sources information. Added to this is that all too often these stores have been tweaked frequently to allow for variations in the products they are supposed to handle.

## 1.3 The Instrument Lifecycle

New instruments are being created to fulfill funding, investment, and risk transfer needs. The lifecycle of a financial product covers many stages, with different players active at every stage. Conception and creation of instruments take place at exchanges, at product development groups in banks, at origination departments in banks that are the middleman between corporate funding needs and investors, and bilaterally between professional counterparties and financial institutions. Instruments are traded on stock exchanges, on crossing networks, and over the counter. Trading is facilitated by central markets such as exchanges, by dealers or market makers who quote prices and act as the counterparty, and by brokers who play the middleman role and seek to line up two counterparties to a transaction. Asset servicing basically covers the maintenance of instruments, such as handling corporate actions, e.g., splits and dividends and proxy voting. Prime brokers offer various services to hedge funds by the investment banking community. The services can include securities lending, custodial services (the two activities can be grouped together under the term *asset servicing*), financing positions, and sometimes software/analytics solutions, e.g., for portfolio optimization and risk management. These services mean that it is much simpler to run a fund: You can concentrate on the front-office aspects of it. Eventually, instruments retire through expiration (futures and options), maturity (bonds), or delisting (equity).

## 1.4 The Transaction Lifecycle

Financial transactions come about through reconciling different needs (investing needs, hedging needs) or different opinions on value (trading). The transaction lifecycle covers a pre-trade, trade, and post-trade phase. Pre-trade covers research and price discovery, whereas post-trade covers clearing and settlement, reporting, and custody of the assets. Various departments are involved.

Pre-trade includes research departments, both very specific and short term (creating direct trade ideas, e.g., *cheap/dear* or relative value analysis of bonds to determine which bonds are relatively cheap or expensive, looking at correlation patterns for hedge portfolios), as well as longer term (an economic bureau to look at macroeconomic data, a credit department that determines internal credit ratings for companies) for the banking business. Post-trade is basically the back office: the correct administration and fulfillment of the transactions done in the front office. Reporting is done through the finance and risk management functions. Custody is often a separate business or is outsourced.

## 1.5 Customer Focus or Product Focus

These two cycles intertwine: Pre-trade research often leads to the creation of custom instruments for specific investors or investor groups. In the case of over the counter (OTC) derivatives, the start of the transaction and instrument lifecycle coincide, since every trade is a new, unique bilateral contract. The information industry services the needs of decision making at every stage. Behind the provision of information (research, streaming data, and corporate actions) to people and applications that need to act on it, there is often a lengthy supply chain with content being enriched, derived, bundled, and validated at different stages (see Figure 1.1).

## 1.6 Flow and Bespoke Business Models

The trend to automate processes and information flows is continuing. The basis for competition is either efficiency in processing (pure commoditized product) or distinguishing yourself by offering special products or services. In operations management, a distinction is made between a *customer solutions* and a *standardized products* concept of offering products and services. The customer solutions product concept includes characteristics such as customization, product focus, low volume, complexity, and high margin. This would, for instance, include OTC derivatives in the case of financial products. The standardized product concept includes characteristics such as a high level of standardization, process focus, high volume, relative straightforwardness, and low per unit margin. This would, for example, cover foreign exchange and cash equity in the financial markets. In this case, automation is often the only way to reduce the marginal cost/unit cost and thus to increase or at least defend the margin institutions make on this business.

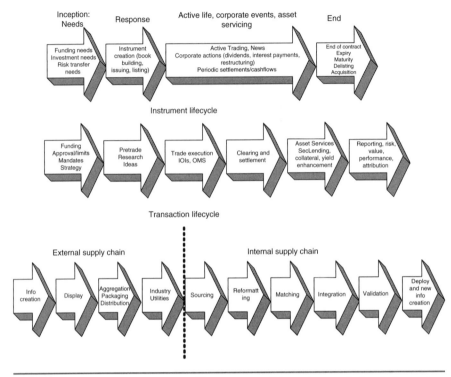

**Figure 1.1** The instrument and/transaction lifecycles and the information supply chain

These different processing models in the transaction lifecycle can be also summarized along the dimension illustrated in Table 1.1.

The harder to price and process also means the higher the margin. Risk management and back office can also add a lot of value in the *customer solutions* products, for example, in easy settlement. For the *standardized products*, they would be seen as pure cost centers and managed on cost per transaction.

In reality, the distinction between these two processes is not always clear-cut in the financial markets. First, many customer solutions will include or be based on standardized products, such as customized baskets or derivatives on a vanilla underlying. Second, the organization of a bank is also often not based on this product and process distinction, but on client segments and a high-level financial markets division. An institution's departments could be split across, for example, equity and equity derivatives and fixed income. An institutional investor or corporate treasurer will need both plain vanilla bulk products such as foreign exchange, deposits, or equities, as well as tailored

**Table 1.1**  The Two Different Processing Products

| Customer Solutions | Standardized Products |
| --- | --- |
| Low volume | High volume |
| High margin | Low margin |
| Difficult price discovery, competition on flexibility/service | Transparency, competition on cost |
| OTC model, brokers | Exchanges, direct access to execution venues |
| Complex | Simple |
| Customization focus, product focus | Process focus |
| Little automation | High degree of automation |
| Fragmented and incomplete content products | Many content providers of necessary information |

OTC derivative solutions. Within these departments, the different products are related from a pricing, information sourcing, and risk perspective, but may be fundamentally different in processing. (For example, a cash equity, single stock future, and customized call warrant are all in the same department.) The lack of a sound information architecture hurts both processing models.

A trader increasingly has to be able to provide value-add as product commoditization erodes margins, and activities that used to be value-add become commonplace and automated. In the standardized products business, the key metric is *cost per transaction*. Higher costs chip away at an already-eroded margin. Discrepancies in data can lead to errors in settling or executing the trade. Since the degree of automation is very high for these products, breaks that require manual attention are very costly. In the customer solutions markets, the key differentiator is product innovation and proper valuation of complex structures. In information terms, this comes down to access to various categories of traditionally separately handled information (e.g., blending currency, credit, and commodity risk requires high-quality market data, research information, and in the case of credit, insight into full exposure and legal structure) which cannot be accomplished in a model where different product lines are handled independently. It requires a holistic view of information with links between the various categories (holding and subsidiaries, issuer and issues, instrument with market data of all the execution venues, and so on). Content providers have in some cases failed to keep up with the demand for new information from the financial institutions, thereby opening the door to

| | 1960s | 1970s | 1980s | 1990s | 2000s |
|---|---|---|---|---|---|
| **Business Drivers** | Relatively stable world | Floating currencies | Deregulation Basel I | Value at Risk reporting framework | Basel II, MiFID, hedge fund explosion |
| **Financial Products** | Stocks and bonds | MBS, currency options, equity options, financial futures | Interest rate swaps, CMOs | More exotics, credit derivatives | Emerging markets, Exotics |
| **Technology and vendor products** | Start of FSI automation, mainframes, end of ticker tape era | Minicomputers, more and more software companies | PCs, more and more "Decentral systems", RDBMS, spreadsheets, Bloomberg terminals | Internet, middleware, XML, low latency race | |

**Figure 1.2**   Some key developments that drove application and content product proliferation

new entrants. In Figure 1.2, we provide a historical overview of some key changes that drove software applications and content products in the financial services industry.

## 1.7 The Typical Information Architecture

If you look at the typical architecture of a bank or investment manager, you will notice what appears at first sight to be an enormous mess. Unfortunately, at second sight, it still often remains a mess. Many streams of information come in at various locations in a process, sometimes multiple times. Multiple conversions take place as content needs to be moved from one processing place to another. Reconciliation applications have been put in place with no other function than to control the damage. Occasionally, haphazard attempts have been made to bring order to this jungle by putting in middleware or a data backbone. Typically, political or technological problems have prevented not only completion of these initiatives, but even their fruition to a stage where they actually reduce some of the chaos. If this were a diagram of a factory floor, the amount of waste would be unacceptable, and the operations manager would probably have been fired a long time ago. In many cases, the fact that things have not broken down completely is testimony only to the power of Excel and the ingenuity of countless ad hoc reconciliation actions by desktop users. We call this situation *high entropy*, and a resemblance with the second law of thermodynamics presents itself when analyzing this situation.

Frequently, content lies hidden across the whole enterprise like a set of Easter eggs carefully hidden in the backyard. This seems an absurd situation because this information would otherwise be the basis of informed trading and investment decisions. When linked together, the various nuggets of data would complement one another, and overall quality and insight would be increased. Why does this situation of inaccessible and fragmented data persist? Why are data often buried and inaccessible? How can the value of data be unleashed?

Reasons for this include the use of disparate formats, the use of different identifiers to pinpoint a certain instrument or client, technological challenges in extracting and combining information, and—last but not least—the decentralized and often not clearly defined functional ownership of data. Typically, information is owned on a departmental basis, so the equity department, fixed-income department, and treasury department would all guard their own data stores even though there is overlap between the data they keep—for example, information on issuers and customers.

Many acronyms have been coined for the strategy of creating a dedicated function to manage data. They include CDM (centralized data management) and EDM (enterprise data management). More creative have been the names for the persons in charge of such an initiative; they are alternately termed CDOs (Chief Data Officers) or Data Czars. These strategies and persons have a number of challenges that confront them. Whether the roles are that of a driver that controls budgets or a policeman who tries to maintain the law will vary by institution.

Typical spaghetti architectures lead to a vicious cycle (see Figure 1.3). A lack of trust in data quality will lead people to think that it pays to be in control of the data. Budget holders will therefore continue to invest in local repositories and content products, thereby exacerbating the situation.

A large financial services institution may have many thousands of applications. This means that the great bulk of the IT budget goes toward maintaining applications that often use obsolete technologies and that no longer fulfill the user's requirements. Worse, most of the applications integrate on a peer-to-peer basis with dozens of other applications, leading to a vast number of connections and potential failure points.

We will see that there are many reasons for this descent into chaos which make it almost into a natural law like the second law of thermodynamics:

- Political reasons. Institutions are often organized by client segment, by geography, and typically also by product line (treasury, equity markets, fixed income, credit). Each outfit wants to control its own destiny and

The Data Jungle

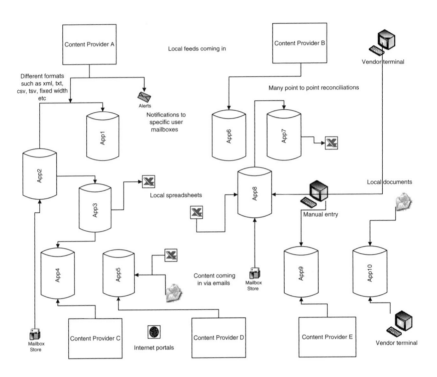

Local stores, embedded data models, local feeds, manual entry, duplication, complex cross references

**Figure 1.3**  Typical spaghetti architecture

wants to decide where its budget on applications and content goes. Because time to market is often critical, the focus of front-office decision makers can be short-term oriented. Frequently, a solution is put in place with little consideration for the architectural implications or the cost of maintaining it in the future. In addition, nobody wants to depend on somebody else's application to fix the problem. Therefore, it is typically easier to add a small application or content feed that you control than to be dependent on someone else.

- Content licensing issues. Many vendors of content are, of course, aware of the office politics of their clients and will use this knowledge to their advantage. Furthermore, no content vendor will want to sell everything at once, so there is a tendency to license content at the lowest organizational unit.

A department has a problem and budget. The budget can fix a particular problem, and the issue is solved. The fact that there may be 10 other departments with similar problems is overlooked or, when it is recognized, internal (time to market) and external (enterprise-license-averse vendors) complications often prove to be insurmountable problems.

■ The content industry lacks standardization. Vendors think up their own formats and often their own identification and product classification codes. This complicates the integration problem. This cross-reference problem is exacerbated by the prevalence of local codes, different standards, and reuse of some codes, which leads to ambiguity.

■ Embedded data models in (legacy) applications. Applications embed their own proprietary data models and data stores, which makes integration very complex. To bring order to this architectural jungle, information and business logic need to be separated. The information supply chain needs to deliver quality content about each stage in the instrument lifecycle to those points in the transaction lifecycle where that content can be acted on. All too often information, business logic, and presentation are welded together. The reason for this is straightforward: Dependence on other parties to provide information adds a risk for the vendor.

■ There are many specific needs at the department level. Product proliferation has been enormous, and the reality is that in many cases pricing, processing, and modeling of certain complex financial products have become so specialized that many niches in content and applications have been created. This means that a diversified institution has a choice between buying multiple products and services externally or having a very large internal IT and business analysis department. The last option cannot always solve the problems because vendors can offer products with the required business logic for certain niches faster and cheaper. This leaves the job of integrating all these products and content services to the local IT department or systems integrator. To them falls the often unappreciated task of whipping data into shape, molding and massaging it to fit into often arcane formats, welding it to heterogeneous architectures, and also interpreting and repairing it.[1]

■ Many institutions have heterogeneous architectures. One reason for this is the time-to-market pressures which cause institutions to buy applications that do not run on hardware they already have. Although integration products are available to address this situation, this has led to increased cost and a higher hurdle for integration.

■ Obviously, the knowledge about specific content and business logic is concentrated in the hands of the users. As financial products have diversified along the dimensions of credit, interest rate, equity market, currency, and commodity risk, it is very hard to set up a centralized department with the required budget and staff to service these various users.

Typically, additions to the IT and content infrastructure of a financial services institution (FSI) lead to locked-in costs that are very hard to get rid of. Without drastic measures, most IT budgets will only go up, since the vast bulk of the budget is spent on maintaining the current infrastructure. Perversely, this also means that the only new developments which can be funded are precisely the short-term tactical extensions which only add to the chaos.

## 1.8 Consequences and Costs

Is the lack of a sound information architecture a problem? The answer to this question comes down to cost, and in the end, there are not many institutions that will be able to continue to afford such an architecture. A company has to speak with one voice; one arm needs to know what the other arm is doing. When it is hard to take an inventory, to take stock of what content is present where within an institution, consistency becomes very difficult. Many practitioners in financial services complain about data issues. Some of the top complaints are about the following topics:

- Flexibility
- Ability to select
- Standards
- Timeliness
- Accessibility
- Arcane formats
- Data model extensibility and the speed and ease with which new products can be added
- Linkages, e.g., between issue and issuer, between different listings of an instrument, between different entities in a corporate legal structure
- Lineage/audit
- Historical data
- Discrepancies between various local stores

The costs of this situation are essentially threefold:

- *Direct recurring costs* in maintaining and reconciling separate information flows, employing staff to keep track of them and operate redundant products and services. The percentage of transactions that fails to settle may lie between 2% and 5%. Note that this 2%–5% can take a much bigger slice of the trading profits, so the exceptions management process needs to be automated.

- *Costs through higher operational risks.* These costs vary from failed transactions and subsequent claims to higher capital charges for increased operational risk. In the case of transactions, costs can range from interest charges or other claims in case of failed settlements to potentially large amounts when the underlying entity in, for example, a credit derivative is not unambiguously identified. Under Basel II, banks have to set aside regulatory capital to cover their operational risks, and the Advanced Measurement Approach allows them to use their own data on these kinds of losses. This means that lower losses have the added-on benefit of a lower amount of regulatory capital set aside. Other costs of faulty processes can include a higher multiple of the bank's Value at Risk number, another component of the regulatory capital.

- *Opportunity costs.* The spaghetti architecture described previously does not scale: It is very costly to add new product capabilities to it. Furthermore, when a new product or service requires multiple information streams, this is costly to achieve. Complex instruments and hybrids typically need to tap into multiple databases to collate all the information required. Paradoxically, the spaghetti situation that arose partly because of time-to-market pressures means that time to market for new products is very long. Products aside, client information is also often fragmented in a spaghetti architecture. This means that there is the opportunity for better service, helping client retention.

Fragmented data storage and processing causes problems for the optimal execution of the business functions around financial instrument lifecycle management:

- This leads to a very lengthy and costly supply chain which is error prone. Many controls need to be built into it to guarantee a certain quality.
- Simultaneously, demands for quality go up, both because of business as well as regulatory reasons. To add to this, lower latency requirements plus increases in product types and volumes put further strain on the current information supply chain.

- The nature of the content products currently available combined with lack of standards is preserving that state. (See also Chapter 3 conclusions.) Content products need to be able to supply their content in a more accessible way, from an identification point of view and a technical point of view, and also to be able to "cut" their products to a user's needs (viz. portfolio products).

- Different quality requirements by different types of business functions within the instrument/trade lifecycle complicate the problem.

- Easier and faster access to information is one of the largest, mostly untapped productivity improvement opportunities left to financial institutions. Very frequently, two sets of identifiers are cross-referenced in an Excel spreadsheet within one institution. Often a company is losing significant amounts of time and money because of data quality issues. If data constraints in the sense of trust in an access to information could be eliminated or at least greatly reduced, the potential gains would be massive.

- Information becomes valuable only when it is acted on. This seems almost too trivial to mention, but in reality valuable pieces of information are often marooned in an isolated system, user, or indeed entire department.

But how big is the problem really? What does it cost the industry? If we look at some industry numbers, the total number of applications is in the thousands if you just count third-party products, let alone internally built software. There are many hundreds of content products, many big ones and many niche players. Surveys show that most institutions keep multiple independent stores.[2] Estimates on poor-quality data vary widely, partially due to difficulties and inconsistencies in defining quality: "quality variances ranging between 4 and 30 percent, including missing issues, missing data elements, inconsistent coding and mismatching data values."[3] Annual data management costs for large firms have been estimated between $238 million and a staggering $1,242 million.[4]

## 1.9 Outline of This Book's Chapters

Chapter 2 provides an overview of the lifecycle of a financial instrument, discussing the various stages in the life of an instrument from conception to retirement. We will also discuss the financial markets, different market models, main instrument types, and descriptive standards in this chapter. Chapter 3 discusses the information supply chain behind the content used by financial institutions in their decision making and reporting. We will see that this supply chain covers many stages from information creation down to final consumption. Each step is discussed alongside an assessment of the changing dynamics of the supply chain. A survey of the landscape for financial data content is provided, dividing data into different categories depending on where it is sourced from. Different roles in this market, such as creators, aggregators, redistributors, and so on, are discussed together with an assessment of different distribution and sourcing models, including developments around data pooling and hub models. Chapter 3 also discusses the various categories of content and different sourcing and distributing aspects of these different content types.

The approach of viewing all information management issues in terms of a supply chain to power the instrument and transaction lifecycle may appear to be overly mechanistic, but these abstractions help to clarify the issues. The function of different data types in the processes that define a financial services institution's business is the topic of Chapter 4. Here, we will offer a taxonomy of the main processes within the transaction lifecycle and what the important criteria are in information management terms. We will also cover use cases reflecting various stages in the transaction lifecycle. Whereas Chapter 2 discusses the instrument lifecycle and Chapter 3 the information supply chain, Chapter 4 focuses on the transaction lifecycle. We will discuss the main stages in the trading process from pre-trade research to custody and reporting and analyze the main types of applications and information needs at each stage. We will see that it is not just the content that differs, but just as importantly the quality and metadata aspects that differ at different stages in the transaction lifecycle. Consider these simple examples: For a trading infrastructure, speed is paramount; for a financial reporting process, you want completeness and accuracy; for best execution reporting, you want complete transparency and lineage showing what price has been selected out of the available quotes. Chapter 5 dissects data quality aspects, including speed, accuracy, consistency, authentication, transparency, synchronicity, and relevance in greater depth, and discusses key performance indicators (KPIs). It defines criteria for success and also shows where it can go disastrously wrong. It provides a framework for balancing these various dimensions of financial content with cost and business requirements. We will end with an appraisal of the current state of the financial services landscape and provide recommendations on infrastructure and content management.

Many industry groups clamor for and promote data standard and common data models, instrument and venue taxonomies. Yet inertia often remains, since existing formats and systems are incredible sticky and costly to replace. Also, the "if it ain't broke, don't fix it" mentality of staff in operations still prevails. But this is not so much the question. The processes may not be "broke," but they definitely are leaky and erode and chip away at profit margins.

In the case of implementing data standards, there is an understandable reluctance to be the first. The first industry player to implement a new standard will hardly benefit. That institution bears all the risk and cost of implementing first yet has *no one* to talk to using this standard although there may be benefits internally of deciding on a standard into which a lot of thought has gone. So, we need a tipping point. Regulators are reluctant to prescribe specific standards, leaving this to the industry to resolve. In cases in which critical mass has been reached (for example, ISO 15022 in certain parts of the corporate actions processing chain and FIX in pre-trade information), the efficiencies and pay-off have been high.

At the end of the day, financial information management should understand the requirements and service different parts of the transaction lifecycle. It should accomplish a full understanding of the content needs and of the information supply chain for the various stages in the instrument and transaction lifecycle. Adequate metrics and reports should give insights into the state of the business. Questions such as "Where are we?" "What are we doing?" "Where can we go wrong?" should be easily answered. The information supply chain should hold up under regulatory scrutiny and provide a foundation for business growth.

## Endnotes

[1] Ironically, this has spawned a separate application market in itself: that of enterprise system integration, middleware, ETL ("extract, transform, load") products.

[2] See, for example, surveys from A-Team Group. "The majority of respondents maintain between four and six security master files, with one third of them maintain [ing] up to three and 9% maintain[ing] a challenging 10 or more securities master files." *Source:* A-Team report "Static Data Becomes Dynamic," www.a-teamgroup. com.

[3] EDM council metrics; see www.edmcouncil.org.

[4] See "Operational Risk & Reference Data, Costs, Capital Requirements & Risk Mitigation." A.D. Grody, F.C. Harmantzis, G.K. Kaple, February 2007.

# Chapter 2

## The Instrument Lifecycle: The Life and Times of Financial Instruments

### 2.1 Introduction

In this chapter we will describe the lifecycle of financial instruments, taking the analogy of a biography covering all events from origination ("birth") to maturity, delisting, or expiration ("death"). We start by describing the reasons to issue instruments and why investors would be buying or selling them. This is followed by a discussion of the different types and a classification of financial instruments. We will use various perspectives to look at financial products and look at different methods to lend order to the often bewildering array of

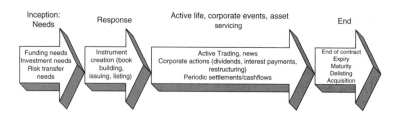

**Figure 2.1** Instrument lifecycle

products and terms by reviewing the main data standards created to model and classify them.

We will then discuss the context in which instruments are bought and sold: financial markets and venues of trade, such as exchanges and alternative trading systems. We will describe the issuing and creation process of financial products, including the fixing of terms and assignment of unique identifiers. After this, we will describe the various categories of players that have an interest in financial products and will stress their different roles and perspectives. In Section 2.8 we will discuss the interdependencies between various financial products considering the relations between different products and markets. We will discuss common drivers behind instrument value, correlations between markets, and the role of benchmarks.

Corporate actions are the topic of Section 2.9, "Ups and Downs Throughout an Instrument's Life," which include not only events that originate at the instigation of the issuing company, but also other events that materially impact the share value, such as news, (class action) lawsuits, and so on. In Section 2.10 we will continue the metaphor of a biography of a financial instrument by discussing how financial instruments come to their end. We will see that although this can be a happy or unhappy ending depending on your perspective, generally the ending is predictable (see Figure 2.1).

Throughout this chapter, common themes will be the perspective of *processing*, the level of and scope for automation, the consequences of information and identification problems in this processing, the relation between different types of content, and the steps in the instrument lifecycle, plus the differences in trading, processing, pricing, and reporting of these various product types.

## 2.2 Enter the Protagonist: The Financial Instrument

Many new financial instruments are issued every day. The original purpose of financial instruments was to act as transfer channels for funds between investors and businesses. Businesses needed money, investors needed returns. This could take the form of *all-equity financing* (giving the investor a stake in the business and a stake in the distributed profits through dividends) or *all-debt financing* (a loan whereby the investor would be paid interest and the principal). Intermediate (mezzanine) forms of financing including convertible bonds, preferred stock, and subordinated debt were all somewhere in the middle. Although there were variations on this theme, these were essentially the choices.

The purpose of financial instruments has expanded from funding to risk diversification. Although certain derivatives and insurance contracts have been around for centuries, the increased volatility in the financial system introduced in the 1970s set in motion an explosion of product development. This started in the 1970s with the first exchange-traded equity options and financial futures contracts, gathered momentum in the 1980s with interest rate swaps, and exploded in the 1990s with more structured products such as CMOs and credit derivatives.

All these products are not so much about satisfying funding needs but rather about risk transfer. To some extent, these products are traded between professional market participants, but a benefit has also been that corporate treasuries have many more tools at their disposal to manage business risk factors such as inflation, currency risk, interest rate risk, plus commodities and even macroeconomic numbers. There are many uncertainties in life, some of which companies want to deal with, some of which companies want nothing to do with. These products have helped corporates and financials to have more choice, plus the ability to make choices on what their core business is: the risk factors to which they actively seek exposure because they know better than anyone else how to manage them.

Financial instruments used to exist to move money through time backward and forward. Although the occasional crash still instills some modesty into the best of financial engineers, instruments can be tailored to client profiles and to an investor's needs and objectives and current portfolio. Many types of exposure can now be priced and traded, and products can often be tailor-made against an investor's portfolios and desired exposure. We have entered the era of mass customization of financial products thanks to the easy and cheap availability of exposure to many risk drivers and advances in software and hardware power to blend these risk factors and price the composite result. We can look at the total landscape of financial products in different ways:

- *Reason for creation.* What are the interests of the various parties that create products?
- *Processing and data perspective*—for example, by looking at the predictability of cash flows, both in terms of amount as in terms of timing. Where are

the bottlenecks? What are the thorny, unique identification and information management issues that impede automation and scaling of the process?

■ *Market players' perspective.* Who is buying, and who is selling different financial products?

First, let's discuss why anyone would create a financial product. Reasons can include addressing funding needs, creating new sellable product to get commissions, dealing with internal reasons, and attracting new clientele. We will discuss these various reasons in the following text.

Instruments created for *funding purposes* can be for businesses to fund, for example, capital expenditure and for banks, for example, to fund positions in financial instruments. We can distinguish between two types of funding. The first type is money market funding, which is short-term funding—for example, through the issuance of certificates of deposit, commercial paper, and through repurchase agreements ("repos"). A security is sold now, and repurchase for a future date is agreed simultaneously. The second type is capital markets funding. This happens through public bond issues, equity issues, or private placements. In the case of origination of a bond, a business or government wants money at the lowest possible interest rate. The bank that arranges the issue will be compensated on a percentage fee and rewarded on the basis of the amount of money raised and on the price at which this was achieved. A risk is that of *underwriting* the bond, promising placement of a certain amount, in case markets turn. In case of an Initial Public Offering (IPO), a company wants to sell shares at the highest possible price. The lead managing bank gets a percentage fee of the total deal amount. If the IPO does not do well, the bank can lose money because it has bought some part of the shares itself through underwriting the deal and because it may be expected to support the price for some time after the issue.

Creating *new product* is often a way to gain commissions. For example, in the case of securitization, a new financial structure is created by packaging a set of bonds, putting them into an *Special Purpose Vehicle* (a legal entity set up for the sole purpose of carrying these assets) and selling off various portions of the packaged structure again. Similarly, many investment funds are created. The fund manager charges a percentage management fee plus potentially a performance fee. If the fund does well, the investment manager will do double well: In case of good performance, the manager receives a performance fee, but the fund will also attract new money, leading to a higher management fee. As this business easily scales (generally, the cost of managing $20 billion USD is far less than twice the cost of managing $10 billion USD), this is an attractive proposition.

To be seen as an *attractive and innovative counterparty*, many over the counter (OTC) exotic derivatives are created. Banks that can tailor products to specific needs for clients and that are willing to make a market in unusual risk factors can cement the client relationship and attract other business while charging a sound margin. Similarly, innovative retail structures are created. Institutions that are first with a certain product—for example, a turbo, warrant, click fund, reverse convertible—can attract additional retail business to their branches. Just as banks and other financial institutions, other market players such as exchanges also have to remain attractive to do business with. To attract liquidity and support other products, exchanges maintain an active set of options and futures contracts. Sometimes exchanges launch new products to secure the attractiveness of the overall venue. In many cases the financial institution will already have data connections to the exchange and a relationship with the clearing party, meaning that the additional cost to process these products will be low. Products can also be part of a *branding* or *marketing strategy*, establishing the organization as a leader in the field—for example, an index in a certain product set such as UK Gilts or commodities.

Other reasons for financial products are internal reasons such as *balance sheet management*. This is a driver in particular for banks. Loans that are on the balance sheet carry a credit risk charge. This charge was 8% of risk-weighted assets (loans to governments carry a 0% weighting; loans to companies carry the full 100% weighting) but has now become more refined under the Basel II Internal Ratings-Based Regime. Due to this charge, there is an incentive to move these loans off the balance sheet of a bank onto the balance sheet of a company that does not fall under the Basel rules, such as an insurance company. So, in the same way that a certain tax regime drives retail financial product development (e.g., types of mortgages, savings and investment products), so does regulation drive wholesale product development. This process is called *regulatory arbitrage*.

Against the background of various reasons for creation, several trends over the past decades have caused enormous proliferation in product types. Three of the main trends behind this product proliferation are derivative product development, securitization, and the emergence of structured finance.

Derivatives have taken an enormous flight. Let's consider an imaginary company with a mix of equity and debt financing on the balance sheet. You could own a share in it, or you could own part of the debt. In the past, these were basically the options available to investors seeking exposure to this company, sometimes augmented with some mezzanine options such as subordinated debt, preferred shares, or convertible bonds. Nowadays, you can buy or sell options on the equity or trade a future on the price of the share through single stock futures. Furthermore, you could trade a credit default swap on the company or be involved in trading derivatives on products that drive the share price, e.g., commodities such as base metals, power, oil, and so on, and impact the share price. You could include shares of this company in a basket together with other companies and then create warrants on this basket or create a fund that tracks a certain index of which this stock is part. Advances in financial engineering[1]—the procedures of blending and pricing risk drivers—as well as software and hardware developments have made this mass customization possible. Derivatives have come into existence on the foreign exchange, interest rate markets, credit markets, commodity markets, on natural phenomena and on macroeconomic figures.

Securitization is about selling future cash flows. Newly created products are secured (collateralized) by direct cash flows from receivables or by other financial products such as mortgages or bonds. These instruments can be secured by money coming in from mortgages, student loans, credit card receivables, and so on. One of the drivers behind this is to free up regulatory capital for the banks by redistributing credit risk volume off the banks' balance sheet.

Securitization started relatively simple with *passthroughs*, instruments that directly passed on the cash flows received from the collateral. Through structured finance, the risk in these packages has been graded and sliced up. Indeed, structured finance is the business of bundling and unbundling cash flows. It is concerned with pooling together a large number of bonds or mortgages, for example, and then redistributing the cash flows over different tranches catering to different investors.

## 2.3 Types of Financial Products

### 2.3.1 INTRODUCTION

The total number of securities including equities and government, corporate, and municipal bonds runs in the multiple millions. Add exchange-traded derivatives such as options and futures, and the number expands significantly. Add OTC derivatives where the distinction between a trade and an instrument is blurred, and the number is essentially infinite. To lend some order to financial products, industry groups and market practitioners have created many taxonomies of financial products. A basic distinction within financial products is that between securities which are instruments that represent ownership such as stocks and bonds versus commodities and derivatives which are either bilateral contracts or represent physical goods such as copper, oil, and soy. The variety and pace of product innovation combined with the often unique needs of investors for which products are tailor made are such that any list that claims to be exhaustive will be out of date very quickly.

Rather than giving a complete overview of all possible product types, we will cover the variety of financial products according to one of the more commonly used public classification schemes: that of the Classification of Financial Instruments (CFI).[2] The CFI classification has been designed to group financial products in a uniform and consistent way. It includes codes for financial product types to facilitate electronic processing. The first character of the CFI code indicates the category and is the highest level of classification. The categories are as follows:

- Equities (E)
- Debt instruments (D)
- Entitlements (Rights) (R)
- Options (O)
- Futures (F)
- Others/Miscellaneous (M)

We will discuss the most common product types within each category. It is not the aim of this book to go into detail regarding how to price each of these products. Instead, we will give a characterization of each of the various types and focus on keying and processing issues at various steps in the instrument and transaction lifecycle.

Apart from the CFI code classification, many content providers have their own product classification, typically reflected in the way their products are structured and sold. An example of this is the Bloomberg yellow key classification corresponding to the high-level classification within the Bloomberg database.[3]

Instruments are also often portrayed through a *stacked* model, moving from underlying physical goods owned by legal entities, to securities that represent claims or ownership on those entities, to derivatives with indices and currencies as cross-vertical pillars (see Figure 2.2).

The CFI code is used around the world; many countries started to allocate CFI codes during the 1990s.[4] The use of the CFI code is skewed toward exchange-traded products where trade volumes are typically larger and where processing has been more automated. Within the CFI classification, many derivative instrument types are grouped together under the "Miscellaneous" category. We will discuss classification schemes that have been set up specifically for OTC derivatives later in this section.

A useful categorization of financial instruments, both in terms of processing as well as for risk measurement, is looking at the *cash flows*. We can evaluate

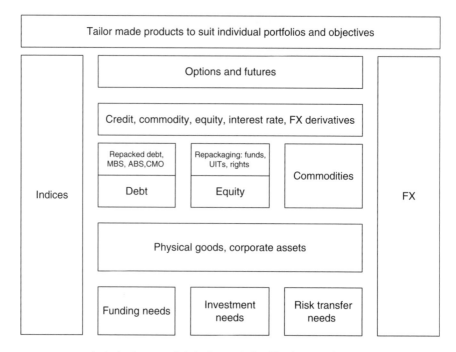

A stacked approach to instrument classification, or a "needs"
driven approach with cross functional pillars on either side for
currency conversion and benchmarking purposes.
We move up from needs to physical, to securities, to repackaging,
derivatives, options and futures and tailor made goods.

**Figure 2.2**  Landscape picture of financial product families

the incoming and outgoing cash flows along two criteria: the certainty as to
when they will occur and certainty as to the amount. Typically, the purchase
of a security is associated with one initial outflow against a future cash flow
stream representing, for example, dividends, coupon payments, and the
redemption in case of a bond. The only occasions in which there are
subsequent cash flows are as a result of corporate actions when, for example,
a rights issue is used to purchase additional stock or is needed for fees or services on the securities such as custody charges. In many derivative contracts, on
the other hand, such as futures, forward rate agreements, and interest rate swaps,
there will normally be no initial cash flow, but a periodic settlement of the balance
of the contract instead. In Table 2.1, we show examples of instruments according
to the various natures of the cash flows associated with the instruments.

The frequency of the cash flows can vary from daily (e.g., to keep up the
maintenance margin for exchange-traded futures and options) to once in 30
years for a 30-year zero coupon bond. This has big consequences for the work

**Table 2.1**    Cash Flow Characteristics of Different Instrument Types

| Cash Flow Size | Sample Instruments | Cash Flow Timing | Variance Depends On |
|---|---|---|---|
| Fixed by contract | Deposits, bonds | Fixed, e.g., annually or semi-annually or one-off (zero bond) | Credit default, settlement errors |
| Fixed by contract | Puttable bond | At holder's discretion | According to put schedule |
| Fixed by contract | Callable bond | At issuer's discretion | According to call schedule |
| Fixed, some flexibility in contract | Complex bonds where the coupon is dependent on other factors, e.g., business performance, price of commodities | Fixed | Contingent on contractually defined (external) events or factors |
| Variance according to dividend policy/ AGM decisions | Common stock | Fixed | Company performance, dividend policy change |
| Depending on price differential of asset with regard to benchmark at one point in time | Options, warrants, swaps | Fixed | Performance of reference or of underlying asset |
| Depending on price differential of asset with regard to benchmark averaged out over time | Asian options, exotic options | Fixed | Performance of reference or of underlying asset |

(Continued)

**Table 2.1** (*Continued*)

| Cash Flow Size | Sample Instruments | Cash Flow Timing | Variance Depends On |
|---|---|---|---|
| Bandwidth within contractual minimum and maximum | Retail structured products, certain clickfunds | Fixed | Performance of reference or of underlying asset |
| Depending on price movement of a group of underlying products | Basket products, first-to-default, worst case, Passport options | According to contractual resettlement | Performance of reference or of underlying asset |
| Zero upfront, then periodic, direction depending on market | Interest rate swap, FRA | Periodic, e.g., quarterly | Market dependent |
| Zero upfront | Future | Initial margin payment, after that potentially daily maintenance margin depending on market movement | Market dependent |

needed to process it. If you hold a bond or deposit, you can book the accrued interest as revenue. If you hold a more complex instrument, you have to start making assumptions as to when and indeed if a cash flow will appear. Also, if cash changes hands on a daily basis, e.g., in keeping up maintenance margin, that means processing the exchange's margin call on a daily basis. An assessment of the likelihood of and probability distribution of the size of future cash flows is part of the pricing and risk management of the product. Reflecting their primary purpose of risk transfer, many OTC derivative products are cash settled periodically instead of the underlying being delivered. Calculating the exact amounts due hinges on accurate administration of all the terms and conditions of the transaction.

Note that there are differences in quoting conventions for various financial products. In Table 2.2, we present some examples.

This also has repercussions for data management because different quote types for different products need to be interpreted in different ways. Sometimes information which is assumed to be understood is not included in the quote—for example, the "big number" in foreign exchange quotes. When EURUSD is quoted, the bid/ask quote of 1.3612–1.3614 could be summarized as 12–14. The practice of quoting prices in fractions (1/32, 1/64) has for the most part disappeared, but many local peculiarities remain, such as the quoting of share prices in pennies rather than pounds on the London Stock Exchange, as well as idiosyncrasies in quoting conventions for certain currencies.

In the subsections that follow, we will discuss the main CFI product families. We will provide examples of common data fields needed to describe each of these product classes.

### 2.3.2 EQUITY INSTRUMENTS

The first category in the CFI classification scheme is Equity. Equity means direct ownership of a corporation in the form of shares. That corporation

**Table 2.2**   Different Quoting Conventions

| Sample Product | Quoting Convention |
| --- | --- |
| Equity | Price per share |
| Bond | Percentage of nominal value, e.g., 94.10% without accrued interest |
| Currency option | Volatility of the at-the-money option |
| Money market future | 100 minus implied deposit rate |
| Forward rate agreement (FRA)* | Forward interest rate |
| FX Forward | Offset in 1/10,000 or 1/100 depending on the currency priced |
| Credit Default Swap | Basis points for premium, e.g., 57 for a 0.57% premium. |

*Except for Scandinavian (NOK, DKK, SEK) FRAs, which are typically quoted as 100 – forward interest rate.

can be a normal business or can be a trust or mutual fund: in other words, a legal entity whose business is to invest in financial products such as shares, bonds, or money market products.[5]

We can distinguish between a large set of types of equity; there are various shades of gray between bonds and equity where the grade of guarantee of periodic cash flows differs. The differences are typically in whether or not the dividend is guaranteed, the order in which share types are eligible to receive dividends, conversion characteristics, and level of voting rights. Common types include the following:

- *Normal Shares or Common Stock.* These include voting rights for decisions put to the shareholders and will receive dividends when declared. The dividends can be annually, semi-annually, or quarterly. Some mutual funds that hold many shares pay out monthly. Some shares will not pay dividends; see the discussion of mutual fund styles later.

- *Depository Receipts.* These are used to accommodate investment into the company's stock through exchanges in foreign countries. Depository receipts are issued by a depository bank and represent shares (can be one but can also be a fraction higher or lower than one) in a foreign company. These depository receipts can be either sponsored or not. In the case of unsponsored depository receipts, the depository bank has to buy a sufficient number of original shares as collateral. When a depository receipt is sponsored, the issuer selects the depository bank.

- *Preferred Shares.* Preferred shares are similar to normal shares but receive a guaranteed amount of dividend when funds are available. They thus jump the queue for capital distribution. Voting is sometimes restricted. In the case of cumulative preferred shares, dividend accrues when it cannot be paid out, and as soon as sufficient funds for distribution are available, the holder receives the accumulated amount.

Often special shares have been issued by the company to increase the level of control it has over its own direction. Examples are golden shares held by a management-controlled entity such as the company's pension fund or by the government in the case of a privatized company. These shares hold veto rights on shareholder decisions. Other examples include shares with extra voting rights and the separation of the outstanding shares in "class A" and "class B" shares. In the latter case, class A shares offer more voting rights than class B and are typically under the control of the company's management. In some countries it is common to trade certificates of stock instead of the stock itself. In those cases an investor holds only a certificate that will receive any dividends or other capital distributions. Voting rights, however, remain at a trust office that holds the actual shares. Thus, voting rights on these certificates are typically controlled by the company's management or board of directors. Instead of to the general public, shares can also be issued to selected groups of investors through *private placements*. Within the United States, such securities are called *144A securities*, and the investors must be Qualified Institutional Buyers. Regulatory requirements on disclosure of information are typically lower in these cases because the investors are more sophisticated and do not require the same level of protection as the general public.

*Private equity* refers to the holdings of a company that is not listed on a stock exchange. Instead of being traded on a public market, in this case larger chunks of a company are exchanged via bilateral deals. This term is often used in conjunction with *venture capital* although that is more aimed at investing in companies at an early stage of their lifecycle.[6] When an institution is engaged in selling chunks of a company or another security to individual investors instead of via a public process, we call this *private placements*. Common information elements of equity are shown in Table 2.3.

From a processing perspective, cash equity is a very high volume and highly automated business. Trade sizes range from very small retail trades to large institutional block trades that can be many times average daily volume. To a large extent, the equity market colors the general public's perception of the financial market although it is just one of the many financial markets.

Apart from shares in a "normal" company, there are also many investment vehicles. The purpose of these funds is to pool money from many different

**Table 2.3**  Common Equity Descriptive Fields

| Field Name | Meaning |
|---|---|
| Identifier | A code that uniquely identifies the equity, possibly together with the trading venue |
| Listing | Identifying the particular market |
| Company name | Legal name of the issuer |
| Last dividend | Gross amount of last dividend paid out |
| Market capitalization | Total value of all outstanding shares |
| Free float | The percentage of shares that freely trade in the market |
| Ex dividend date | Date after which the stock is traded without the right to the last dividend |

investors and to invest that collectively so as to receive economies of scale, benefit from professional fund management, and so on. Many funds also invest in products and markets that are harder to access for (retail) investors, thus giving the general public more choice as to what markets to invest in. There are many different names in circulation for these types of vehicles; the naming depends on the jurisdiction of the country. Examples of these kinds of funds are as follows:

- *Mutual Fund.* This can mean slightly different things in different jurisdictions. Typically, a distinction is made between a *closed* and an *open-ended* fund. In an open-ended fund, new shares can be issued more or less continually, and investors can always buy additional units of the fund. The price of these mutual funds will be in accordance with the net asset value of the holdings they have. Closed-end funds, on the other hand, have a fixed number of units and will trade more like regular shares. In this case the value is not just a function of the holdings of the fund, but also of the supply-and-demand mechanics.

- *Exchange-Traded Funds.* These funds are listed on an exchange and are thus easy to buy and sell. Examples are funds that track a certain index such as the funds that track the Dow Jones ("Diamonds") and Standard & Poor's indices ("SPDRs") in the United States.

- *Unit (Investment) Trust.* This is a collective investment vehicle typically found in the United Kingdom and jurisdictions with similar law. A unit trust can also refer to a group of securities that are purchased at the same time on the basis of a certain trading strategy or investment idea. They are held until the trust matures, which can be a couple of years or longer.

- *Hedge Funds.* Whereas mutual funds have been set up for the general public, hedge funds aim at high net-worth individuals. They are not listed, often closed end, and typically investors cannot quickly liquidate the units they have in the fund. Funds can have different liquidity profiles depending on their investments. If they invest in infrastructure projects, it can take very long to exit; if they invest in blue chip equities, it may be very easy to exit quickly. Since these funds are not open to the general public, investors in hedge funds are supposed to be fairly knowledgeable and regulation is lighter, analogous to the situation for 144A securities. The hedge fund market has exploded, and many thousands of hedge funds are around. The name *hedge fund* is misleading because hedge funds are by no means a homogeneous "hedging" group; their trading styles and risk profiles differ enormously. In some sense, hedge funds represent the decoupling of the proprietary trading function from the bank. Hedge funds have lent new impetus to a buy-side that used to employ predominantly "buy and hold" long-term strategies. Hedge funds have given investors the ability to seek exposure to the returns of trading strategies formerly usually found in sell-side trading floors.

■ *REIT.* A Real Estate Investment Trust is a company investing in real estate. Typically, these vehicles do not have to pay corporate income taxes under certain conditions, e.g., when they distribute 90% or more of their income to the investors. Public REITs can be listed on stock exchanges.

The mutual fund market has developed enormously both to cater to investors' different tastes and for marketing reasons to develop many different products giving investors access to many markets and risk profiles. A lot of flavors of funds invest in, for example, certain products (bond, equity, futures), certain industry sectors (pharmaceuticals, energy), and certain regions (East Asia, Latin America, Europe). Apart from this, a whole set of funds has been set up to cater to specific investor types, e.g., to address a specific risk profile (e.g., a certain mix of equities and bonds) and to address specific investment horizons. Apart from funds with these specific mandates, there are also "total return funds" that have a broader mandate. These are similar to hedge funds, but for retail clients. These are all consumer products, and there is a lot of branding and marketing around this.[7] And then there are also funds of funds—a fund whose investments are made in other funds. This may be an attractive spreading of risk, but the extra layer normally translates into double fees. All these fund types are actively managed; i.e., a portfolio manager is paid to make investment decisions and to select from the total set of products that are available under the mandate of the fund.

This can be contrasted with tracker funds such as ETFs whose sole aim is to mimic a specific index as closely as possible. For example, a Eurostoxx 50 tracker will invest in the Eurostoxx 50 in the same proportion as the composition of the index. When the index composition changes, the fund will follow the index. The benefit from these funds is that costs (expressed in *TER*, total expense ratio) are a lot smaller. Costs are low because investment decisions are automatic, the holdings are predictable, and the fund also can make money by lending out its securities. Given the number of mutual funds and fees that have to be deducted, it is statistically impossible for them to all outperform their respective indices. Large issuers of trackers include Barclays Global Investors' iShares. These are becoming more popular, as the management fee that is charged to holders of mutual funds is creeping steadily upward. Whereas a TER of 0.5% to 1% is common for fixed-income funds, for equity funds it will generally be between 1% and 2%, depending a bit on the market the fund invests in. Funds investing in the stock markets of the European Union or United States will have relatively low

TER compared to funds investing in the stock markets of East Asia or Latin America, which will experience higher trading, settling, and custody costs. In many cases TERs have significantly crept up in the past decade, perhaps reflecting larger infrastructure, processing, and compliance costs.

Apart from the themes such as geography or product, funds can also be categorized according to their investment styles and size of the companies invested in. For example, a fund can invest in companies with relatively small, medium, or large market capitalization. A fund also can invest in rapidly growing companies or companies that pay regular dividends. A very useful classification is that of Morningstar, one of the major fund-rating companies.[8]

### 2.3.3 DEBT INSTRUMENTS

In any kind of debt instrument, an issuer has borrowed money from the lender, the holder of the debt instruments. In exchange for lending money and taking on the credit risk (the risk that the borrower does not pay back the loan), the lender is compensated, for example, through receiving regular *coupon payments* or through receiving a higher sum at repayment date than was originally lent. The repayment sum is called the *redemption price* and can be higher than the *issue price*. The final payment date when the principal is repaid is called the *maturity date*. Bonds can be *bearer bonds*, meaning whoever has the bonds has the claim, or they can be *registered bonds*, meaning a register with names of bond holders is kept.

### *Issuer Characteristics*

Bonds and other debt instruments can be classified in various ways. One way is to look at them in terms of issuer category. The issuers can be national governments, local governments, or government-associated institutions such as lower level governments, including provinces, states, municipalities, and counties, or government-sponsored entities such as regional development corporations. In these cases there is often some kind of guarantee delivered by the national government. As long as a national government issues bonds in its own currency, the credit risk is nonexistent because the national government can always print extra money to repay the lender. Other types of issuers are supranationals (e.g., the World Bank, the European Investment Bank). Government-associated agencies that issue large amounts of asset-backed securities include U.S. agencies such as the Federal National Mortgage Association (FNMA, or "Fannie Mae"), Government National Mortgage Association (GNMA, or "Ginnie Mae"), Federal Home Loan Mortgage Corporation (FHLMC, or "Freddie Mac"), and Small Business Administration (SBA).

Apart from the government and government-related institutions are the corporate issuers. These bonds are called *corporate bonds*. They are further subdivided according to the credit rating of the instrument and according to the industry sector. Corporate bonds with a credit rating below BBB are called *junk bonds* or more affectionately *high yield bonds* to refer to the relatively high coupon rate. Of course, these bonds are only high yield when the issuer does not default.... One concern of bondholders will be the anticipated inflation because inflation will eat away at the principal. Therefore, there are also *inflation-protected bonds.*

Most Organization for Economic Cooperation and Development (OECD) countries issue government bonds, and the major currencies have large corporate bond markets. The introduction of the euro in the European Union stimulated the development of the European corporate bond market. Credit ratings are discussed at length in Section 3.5.5.

## *Repayment Characteristics*

Another way to look at bonds is how the investor is compensated for taking on the risk. There are *straight* bonds, which basically pay a fixed annual or semi-annual coupon and repay the principal at the maturity date of the bond. The price of the bond in the secondary market will fluctuate with the prevailing interest rate. If interest rates go down after the issue of the bond, the bond will become more valuable as it returns an above-market interest rate. Conversely, if interest rates go up, the bond will decline in price. The total return of the bond, i.e., the interest rate plus any capital appreciation, is called the *yield*.

Another type of bond is a *floating-rate note*. Here, the coupon rate is tied to a prevailing benchmark rate and is normally expressed as a spread against this rate. An investor will, for example, get the London Interbank Offered Rate ("Libor") plus 50 basis points every 6 months and the value of the reference rate as of the date of the coupon payment is used. Normally, the principal is repaid at the end of the life of the bond; this is called a *bullet bond*. If, on the other hand, the principal is repaid gradually during the life of the bond, we call it an *amortizing bond*. A bond which does not pay any interest but in which the investor is compensated by payment of an amount higher than the issue amount is called a *zero bond*. The coupon payments can also be in currency other than the principal amount.

## *Optionality*

Some bonds contain extra features to tune them to the needs of the borrower or the target lender market. These are normally in the form of options to the lender or the borrower. In a *callable bond*, the borrower has the option to repay the bond early at certain dates or date intervals. This feature will allow the borrower to benefit from falling interest rates, giving the option to refinance at a lower rate. A *call schedule* contains the set of call dates with their associated call prices. Normally, a call price will be a bit higher than the original amount to compensate the borrower. In a *puttable bond*, the lender has the option to put the bond to the borrower, demanding early repayment. This feature will allow the lender to benefit from rising interest rates in case there is no secondary market available.

In *convertible debt*, the option to exchange the outstanding notional amount of the bond into shares of the issuing company is included. In this case, a conversion price and conversion time are part of the bond characteristics. If the price of the stock exceeds the conversion price, the convertible bond will begin to trade more and more like the stock itself.

Optionality elements complicate the pricing of bonds because they lend an element of unpredictability to it. They can, however, make the bond more attractive to certain lenders who believe they will benefit from the option. The coupon rate for a convertible bond will, for example, be lower than that for a bond of the same issuer and the same characteristics without the conversion option.

### Other Financing

Apart from issuing bonds, there are many alternative ways of fulfilling—usually shorter term—financing needs such as bank loans. Bank loans are essentially bilateral loan agreements tailored to a specific situation, and the amounts can be lower. The pricing of these credits is the realm of the classic banking business. Bank loans are often tailored to a particular lender with many covenants to help protect the bank; "covenants" in a bank loan are similar to "terms and conditions" for a public debt issue. Often many *credit enhancements* are written into a bank loan agreement, as banks will always try to secure a loan whichever way they can. These can include *seniority* provisions, the pledging of *collateral*, and the inclusion of *triggers*. Seniority refers to the place the lender has in claiming the assets of the borrower in case of a bankruptcy. Senior debt means a relatively early place in the queue; subordinated debt refers to a relatively low rank, typically just before the claims of the equity holders. Collateral means pledging other assets such as financial instruments, real estate, or equipment as security against the loan. Credit triggers are events such as a rating downgrade, which can imply early repayment.

Bank loan information for the secondary market is collated by several data vendors including Reuters and Markit. Other financing provisions a bank can provide to its clients are contingent financing, that is, standby facilities and guarantees. This gives the borrower the assurance that funds can be drawn upon when necessary. These kinds of products also include guarantee products such as a *letter of credit.*

## Maturity: Short-Term Versus Long-Term Financing

Another way to look at bonds is at their term. The issuers of loans seek financing for different periods. Bonds can vary in length from a few years to perpetual bonds. Medium-term notes are often a few years up to 10 years in length. Many governments issue longer dated debt, up to 30 years and more.

Short-term financing varies from literally overnight to 1 year. In this case we have a number of different instruments:

- *Deposits.* These simple cash deposits are also sometimes called *CDs*, or *certificates of deposit.*
- *Repurchase Agreements or "Repos."* In this case underlying assets are sold and repurchased at a higher rate; the securities repurchased basically serve as collateral for a short-term loan. A bond loan is related to a repo, but a difference is that the bond in the bond loan is used for some operational purpose such as cleaning up a failed-to-deliver. The term of a repurchase agreement can vary, but most common is the overnight repo; it can also be open. Third-party repos are commonly used to reduce the risk associated with transfer of these securities. In this case a neutral third party handles both the cash and securities/collateral. We will discuss this at more length in Chapter 4 in the discussion on asset services.
- *Bankers' Acceptances.* This short-term paper is issued by a nonfinancial institution and guaranteed by a bank.
- *Commercial Paper.* This very short-term debt paper can be issued by larger corporations. These short-term instruments are used for *money market funding* as opposed to medium term notes (MTNs) and bonds which are referred to as fulfilling *capital markets funding* needs.

Other common criteria to categorize the bond market include by currency, e.g., the USD bond market, the GBP bond market, and categorization of debt instruments by the specific project they finance (for example, infrastructure finance). Debt issues against these kinds of projects often have coupons and repayment schedules that in some way depend on success of the project. They are secured by the anticipated cash flows of the project.

## Structured Products

One of the major trends in product development for the financial markets has been in structured products. Generally, in a structured product, a pool of assets (bonds, mortgages, credit default swaps, etc.) is created and put in a separate legal entity. This separate entity is called a *Special Purpose Vehicle* (SPV) and issues instruments which are secured by the assets in the pool. Part of the reason for this development has been regulatory drivers: It costs banks money to have assets on their balance sheets because they have to set aside capital for solvency reasons.

Typically, a structured product is sliced up into different sections called *tranches*. Each tranche has separate credit characteristics. For example, consider a $100 million structured product secured by 100 high yield bonds of $1 million each. Five tranches with a size of $20 million each can be issued against this pool of bonds. Any losses that are incurred in the portfolio because of default will first be given to tranche one; when tranche one is extinct, tranche two will start to incur losses, etc. This means that tranche five will have a very high credit rating, and tranche one will not. Lower ranked tranches will either have very high coupons or will not be issued and remain on the books of the issuer.[9] Higher ranked tranches will have low coupons.

The pool of instruments can also be *overcollateralized*, meaning, for example, $110 million worth of bonds to back $100 million of securities issued by the SPV. This is done to achieve a higher credit rating for the highest tranches. Structured products can be created out of pools of mortgages (mortgage-backed securities, or MBSs, or collateralized mortgage obligations, or CMOs), credit card receivables, student loans, car loans, and so on. Unlike MBSs, the underlyings here are not insured by a government or a government-sponsored entity. Mortgage securities can be either *passthroughs*, where the cash flows received from the mortgages are directly relayed to the investors, or CMOs, where an SPV sits in the middle with the possibility of structuring and creating different tranches. In a collateralized debt obligation (CDO), the pool of assets consists of bonds, loans, or other fixed-income products. In a *synthetic* CDO, the bonds are replaced by credit default swaps. Typical structured product information is shown in Table 2.4.

Mortgage bankers facilitate the issuance of mortgages. These mortgages are sold to a dealer who creates pools and structures MBSs. While the mortgages are still being processed, pools can already be traded, sometimes for months. These are called *to be announced* (TBA) pools. In a TBA trade, the pool properties are defined, but the pool is not yet populated by actual mortgages. Yet the characteristics of the pool are sufficiently known and understood for it to be traded. Eventually, the actual instruments will be delivered against the TBA instruments by the mortgage banker, after which the dealer defines the contents of the pools. *Allocation* refers to the process in which the dealer fills the TBA pools with actual mortgages.

**Table 2.4** Common Structured Product Descriptive Fields

| Field | Meaning |
|---|---|
| Agency name | Name of the agency that issues the structured product |
| Pool number | Number of a mortgage pool |
| WAC | Weighted average coupon of the contents of the pool |
| WAMA | Weighted average maturity of the contents of the pool |
| WALA | Weighted average loan amount of the contents of the pool |
| CPR/PSA | Indications of prepayment rate, i.e., the rate in which the mortgages in the pool are expected to be prepaid. |

## *Bond Pricing*

A bond price is typically expressed as a percentage of the notional. It can also be priced according to the yield which represents the net annual return to the investor if the instrument is held to maturity. Sometimes the yield for corporate bonds is expressed as an add-on to the yield on risk-free government bonds. This add-on is called the *credit spread*. Other measures that are often used in the fixed-income context are *duration*, which is a measure of sensitivity of bond prices to changes in the prevailing interest rate, and *convexity*, which is the second order sensitivity to the interest rate.

Issuers have become more creative in issuing debt instruments where the payments are tied in some way to the performance of the business that is funded, e.g., tied to earnings or tied to specific business drivers such as prices of commodities that are important to the business (e.g., crude oil, copper, steel). This also includes performance bonds and nonrecourse loans. In *nonrecourse* debt, the loans are secured by collateral. When the borrower defaults, the lender can seize the collateral, but if that is not sufficient to cover the loss, the lender cannot go after the borrower for more compensation, hence nonrecourse. The exposure of the lender is hence capped by the value of the collateral. *Payment in kind*, or PIK, bonds pay additional bonds in lieu of cash interest. In the case of *performance bonds*, a bond is issued to one side of the contract to guarantee against the failure of the other side. This is a guarantee or insurance product. We see more and more blending of insurance elements with structured finance. Examples of structured finance products where there is an element of insurance include *Constant Proportion Portfolio Insurance* and *Constant Proportion Debt Obligations*.

Apart from equity and debt, there are *hybrid securities* which display characteristics of both product types. Preferred shares are sometimes seen as hybrid because they are debt-like in the sense that they pay a fixed coupon; seen that way, they are akin to perpetual bonds. However, legally they are common stock because they could contain normal voting rights and come behind bond holders in the event of a bankruptcy. Common data elements of a bond are listed in Table 2.5.

Just like equity, bonds are securities. They have long been given unique identifiers such as ISIN and CUSIP codes by the national numbering agencies. Although they have derivative characteristics, structured products settle very much like corporate bonds and are also assigned codes by the national numbering agencies.

### 2.3.4 OPTIONS

Options is the first category of derivative products in the CFI classification. An option is the right but not the obligation to buy or sell a certain product

**Table 2.5** Common Bond Descriptive Fields

| Field | Meaning |
|---|---|
| Maturity date | Date on which the principal of the bond is repaid |
| Payment frequency | Frequency of coupon payments, e.g., annually, semi-annually, quarterly |
| Yield | Return on the bond when purchased and held until maturity assuming cash flows can be reinvested at same rate |
| Coupon rate | Contractual interest rate on the bond |
| Daycount basis | Basis on which accrued interest is calculated, e.g., 30/360, ACT/365, etc. Generally, a daycount basis consists of interpretations of the length of the month and of the year. In the 30/360 case, each month is assumed to last 30 days. In 30/360, interest accrued over January–February would together constitute 1/6 of the yearly interest due. In the case of ACT/ACT, the actual number of days is used both for the month and for the year (so 366 days for leap years). |
| Rating | Credit rating assigned to the bond by a particular rating agency |
| Call schedule | Combination of time intervals and call prices |

at a fixed price at or during a certain time. The right to buy at a certain price is called a *call option*. The right to sell at a certain price is called a *put option*. The value in options lies in the fact that a price for future purchase can be secured today by buying a call or put. A *call* option will become more valuable as the price of the underlying asset goes up; a *put* option will become more valuable as the price of the underlying asset goes down. The price at which the asset can be bought or sold is called the *strike price*. Options can be used both as (portfolio) insurance products or as highly speculative instruments.

The terminology of options includes the following phrases. A call option is *in the money* if the strike price is lower than the current price of the underlying; i.e., it is worth something if exercised right now. Similarly, a put option is in the money when the strike price is higher than the current price of the underlying. An option is *at the money* if the strike is the same as the underlying. If an option is not at the money or in the money, it is said to be *out of the money*. The level of being in or out of the money can be scaled to a percentage level by dividing the strike price by the underlying. This is called the *moneyness* of the option. An at the money option has moneyness of 100%, an out of the money call where the strike is 10% higher than the current price has moneyness of 90%, and so on.

Combinations of call and put options with different strikes and/or maturity dates into one trade are known under different names. Following are some examples:

- *Straddle.* The purchase (or sale) of both call and put options on the same underlying with the same strike and same maturity. The buyer will benefit from a strong move either way; the seller bets on stability (low volatility).

- *Strangle.* Similar to the straddle but buying call and put options that are both out of the money. A very strong move in the underlying will benefit the buyer.

- *Spread strategies.* Trades with multiple options that differ in strike price or expiry date. A *bull call spread* involves buying a call with low strike price and selling a call with high strike price. A *calendar spread* involves options that are similar but for their expiry date.

Options are traded both on exchanges and over the counter. The underlying can be practically anything. Common underlying products are individual stocks, stock indices, foreign exchange, interest-rate-related products (bond option, swaption, cap, floor, collar), and futures. Exchange-traded options contain standardized terms such as the number of underlying shares for a stock option, the expiry calendar, a set of available strikes, as well as rules and procedures on what happens in exceptional cases such as a merger of the underlying, large dividends, spin-offs, and stock splits. OTC options can be tuned to the buyer's exact strike price and expiry date needs and more closely matched to their exposure. From a processing perspective, there will be more often special and complicating provisions.

If you are selling (or *writing*) options, you will receive the *option premium* or the price of the option. In return for this, you run a risk that you will have to deliver the underlying at a price lower than the prevailing market price (in case of writing a call) or that you will have to purchase the underlying at a price higher than the prevailing market price (in case of writing a put). To insure against this risk, the clearinghouse associated with the exchange on which the option is listed will want the writer of the option to maintain a margin account. The margin will have to be maintained and will reflect the amount to which the writer is exposed at that moment. In the case of *covered call writing*, where the writer of the option already owns the stock, this is not necessary. The margin account will typically pay interest.

A key concept associated with options is that of *leverage*, i.e., scaling the exposure to a certain price driver. In the case of a direct investment into cash instruments, the leverage would be one; i.e., if the cash instrument (equity, bond) changes 10% in price, the value of the investment also changes 10%. If the exposure is leveraged, this can be magnified into 20%, 30%, etc. In the case of options, the metric for leverage is called *delta*; this is one of the "option Greeks." See also Chapter 4 for a section on analytics and risk measures. On the downside, it also means that down movements can wipe out the entire investment. See Table 2.6.

There is a very large variety of option types apart from the plain vanilla call and put. These are collectively referred to as *exotic options*, and various flavors in the various option terms are explained here:

**Table 2.6** Common Option Descriptive Fields

| Field | Meaning |
|---|---|
| Call/Put indicator | Indication of the type of the option |
| Expiry date | Date on which the option expires or can be last exercised |
| Underlying | Reference to the underlying product |
| Strike price | Contractual strike price |
| Exercise type | Specification of time periods at which the option can be exercised |

- Unlike a call or put option, a *chooser option* gives the option holder some time to decide whether it will be a call or put.

- Some options may be exercised only at a specific date, the *expiry date*. These are called *European options*. Options that may be exercised continually up to and including the expiry date are called *American options*. Options that can be exercised at multiple points in time before the expiry date but not continuously are called *Bermudan options*. In some cases, exercise is contingent on the underlying security price touching a certain price point; these are called *barrier options*. One popular type which shares some characteristics with a barrier option is a *turbo* or *speeder*. These highly leveraged products are issued by a bank where the investor buys exposure to a certain underlying with a certain lever (higher than 1). Exposure is bought with the turbo premium together with borrowed money from the bank. In case of adverse price movements, the underlying is sold by the bank when a certain price point called the *stoploss* point is reached.

- A *digital* option (also called binary option) either pays a certain amount or nothing, based on the price level of the underlying at maturity.

- *Quanto* options are options on assets in another currency; the exchange rate risk is taken away by fixing the exchange rate.

- For *path-dependent* options, it is not just the final price point that is important but also the path that was taken during the life of the option to get there. Examples are *average rate options* in which the payoff depends on the average price during the life of the option and a *lookback option*. In the latter case, the option holder can select the strike price from the price range over the life of the option, i.e., the lowest price in the case of a call, the highest price attained for a put.

- In *multiple asset* options the underlying consists of multiple products. An example is a *passport* option, which is an option on the performance of an entire trading account. If the account makes a profit, that goes to the option holder. In case it makes a loss, the passport option insures the option holder against that loss.

- The underlying can be different things. If the underlying is another option, we call it a *compound option*. If the underlying is an interest rate swap, the option is called a *swaption*—that is, the right to enter into a swap. The swaption has two flavors: a *payer swaption* or *receiver swaption*. The name indicates the rights with regard to the fixed leg. In the case of a payer swaption, the buyer has the right to enter into a swap paying the fixed leg, and in the case of a receiver swaption, the buyer has the right to enter into a

swap receiving the fixed leg. Caps, floors, and collars are all options where
the underlying product is an interest rate. A cap effectively locks in a maximum interest rate. The seller pays the difference between an exercise rate and
reference interest rate, if the reference rate exceeds the exercise rate. In case
of a floor, the seller pays the difference if the reference rate is below the exercise rate. Caps could, for instance, be used by variable rate borrowers to cap
their funding costs. A combination of a cap and floor is a collar effectively
confining the interest rate to a certain price band. A variable rate borrower
can, for instance, sell a floor (setting a minimum interest rate that is to be
paid) and use this premium to buy a cap (setting a maximum interest rate
that is to be paid), making this is a zero-cost construction.

Most of the exotic options are typically catered for specific investors and
are custom products you will not find on an exchange. Options have become
widely available since they were introduced on the Chicago Exchange in
1973. The introduction of the Black Scholes pricing formula around the same
time made for consistent and transparent pricing in these markets, which
established liquidity even though the model made many assumptions. In Europe, the first options exchange was the European Options Exchange (EOE),
which started in Amsterdam in 1978.

Options identification is not as straightforward compared to the previous CFI
types discussed. They do not typically get coded by national numbering agencies,
and some of the coding schemes devised previously cannot cope with the number
and variation of options. In the United States, this is addressed by the Options
Symbology Initiative from the OPRA.[10] Lacking an identification standard, an
option has to be identified by a series of descriptive elements such as exchange,
identifier of the underlying asset, call/put indicator, strike price and expiry date,
which makes linking and matching different options much more difficult. In the
case of OTC options, as the number of terms can be very high, these instruments
often require manual intervention in processing unlike standardized exchange-
traded contracts. OTC options are also more difficult to price, and information
needed for revaluation often relies on in-house pricing models.

The set of options on the same underlying is called an *option series*. Information on the option series is often condensed into a *volatility smile* or *volatility surface* to create a market snapshot. We discuss this in more detail in Chapter 4.

## 2.3.5 FUTURES

The second category of derivative products in the CFI classification is Futures.
The key characteristic of futures is that this concerns the trading of a product

*now* for settlement at a *future* date. Unlike options, futures are not a right, but an *obligation* to buy or sell a product at a certain future date. Similar to options, futures can be on almost any underlying. Futures markets have long been established in agriculture where farmers could lock in a price for their produce. These are often called *soft commodities* and consist of futures on soy, grain, livestock, rubber, potatoes, and so on. However, there are also major futures markets in energy products (coal, crude oil, natural gas, jet fuel), base metals (zinc, copper), and precious metals (gold, palladium). The number of futures contracts on different underlyings continues to grow.

The demand for commodity futures comes from both speculators and from businesses that either produce these commodities or require them for their production. As such, the use of futures can be part of their normal planning or treasury operations as well as part of strategic planning. For example, shipping companies can use futures to lock in prices of crude oil, power plants can buy coal, the chemical industry can sell plastics, and so on. The reason for this is that otherwise companies would be exposed to a lot of volatility in commodity prices. These prices are exposed to a very large set of risk factors that combine such diverse items as the following:

- Event risk
- Cash flow risk
- Basis risk
- Legal/regulatory risk
- Op risk
- Tax risk
- Geopolitical/macro and weather risk

The political situation frequently determines the relative rarity and supply risks that impact the price. In addition, price volatility is caused by fundamental factors such as supply and demand, macroeconomic data, and weather, as well as financial factors such as technical trading, the number of speculators, and market imperfections. Some commodity prices are correlated with the business cycle, whereas others are not.

Apart from commodity futures, there are futures markets in many other product types. We discuss the most important ones here:

- Futures on equity indices (S&P500) and single stocks. There are also mini-futures which make these futures markets more accessible to retail investors. The owner of the index has to license the use of its index products to the futures market. Futures on specific stocks, *single stock futures*, are a more recent phenomenon; their use was previously restricted to limit the short selling of equities.

■ Apart from agricultural futures, there are also futures on the weather. These are futures on Heating Degree Days (HDD) or Cooling Degree Days (CDD). The Heating Degree Days statistic takes all days when temperatures topped 18 degrees Celsius. It takes the number of degrees above 18 and adds them. So 2 days with 19 and 20 degrees Celsius temperature leads to an HDD number of 3. The Cooling Degree Days statistic takes all days when temperatures remained below 18 degrees Celsius. It then adds the differences between the actual temperature reached and 18. So 3 days with 4, 15, and 17 degrees leads to a CDD number of 18. Futures on CDD and HDD multiply these numbers with a dollar amount. These kinds of futures are part of weather derivatives; see also the discussion of the CFI category "Miscellaneous" later in this chapter.

■ Futures on interest rate products. A short-term interest rate future would be, for example, the Eurodollar futures contract at the Chicago Mercantile Exchange. A longer term interest rate future is a bond futures contract such as the Eurex Bund future. A difference between short- and long-term interest rate futures is the nature of the underlying. In case of short term, this is, for example, a 3-month USD or EUR deposit; in the case of a bond future, this is typically a synthetic bond, and multiple physical bonds are eligible for delivery. In this case the cheapest available bond is called the *Cheapest to Deliver*.

■ Apart from all the exchange-traded futures products, there are also over the counter futures products which are very similar to futures, mostly in foreign exchange and in interest rates. The benefit of OTC products is that they can be tuned to the needs of a particular investor. Examples are an FX Forward, which is an agreement to buy or sell a currency in the future at a certain price. A variation is a Non Deliverable Forward (NDF), where the difference between the contracted price and prevailing spot rate is settled. Another example is a Forward Rate Agreement (FRA), which is an agreement to lock in a certain interest rate in the future. The seller will compensate the buyer in case the interest rate has moved adversely for the seller. The quoting convention for FRAs is, for example, 3X6 or 6X12. The first case means the interest rate locked in commences in 3 months and lasts until 6 months from now. The second case means that the interest rate locked in commences in 6 months and lasts until 12 months from now. In the first example, the price of a 3-month deposit is locked in, and the second example locks in the price of a 6-month deposit.

The set of commodities on which futures markets are made is expanding. More recent additions to futures include plastics such as the polypropylene and the linear low density polyethylene contracts on the London Metal Exchange.[11] On the other hand, the number of different grades of, for example, fuels is so large that only a number of products have active futures markets. Therefore, it is necessary in data models to show explicit links and correlations between different products and to look at the whole group within a commodity complex. For example, there is a large set of grades of oil, only a couple of which have a forward market (e.g., WTI and Brent Crude). Often you need to proxy the physical with one of these grades, or you have products sitting between two other products. For example, ethanol is the middle product in the market between oil and sugar.

Similar to options, a margin account has to be kept. Unlike options, it has to be kept regardless of whether you are buying or selling a future because both parties can be exposed to adverse price movements. The exchanges on which futures are traded are more consolidated than, for example, equity exchanges. The reason is perhaps that the assets underlying these contracts are needed everywhere—e.g., everybody needs coal and oil funding, whereas equity exchanges traditionally have had local companies as a captive client base for listings. Common data elements of futures are shown in Table 2.7. In Table 2.8, we list a number of sample contracts.

Nonfutures financial products are also referred to as *cash* or *spot* products, so, for example, cash equity for equity here and now instead of in the future.

**Table 2.7**  Common Future Descriptive Fields

| Field | Meaning |
| --- | --- |
| Expiry date | Last trading day of the future |
| Delivery specifications | Detail on product quality/grades and other description that is eligible for delivery |
| Exchange | Name of the exchange on which the future trades |
| Tick value | Dollar value associated with one tick price change in accordance with future contract specifications |
| Type | Type of underlying, e.g., money market, bond, plastics, metal, energy |

**Table 2.8** Example Future Contracts

| Contract | Description |
|---|---|
| Eurex Bund Future | Notional bond issued by Federal Republic of Germany with maturity between 8.5 and 10.5 years. Contract value is 100.000 EUR or 100.000 CHF. |
| CME Eurodollar Future | Underlying is a 3-month deposit with principal value of $1M. Minimum fluctuation is $25. |
| Nymex Light Sweet Oil Contract | Trades in units of 1,000 barrels. Delivery point is Cushing, Oklahoma. Minimum price fluctuation is $0.01 per barrel or $10 per contract. |
| CME S&P500 future | Value is $250 times the S&P 500 index. Minimum fluctuation is $0.10 in the index value or $25 in the contract value. |

## 2.3.6 RIGHTS

Rights are identified by the CFI as a separate product type although they are closely related to the equities and also to the options category. Generally, rights constitute the option to purchase shares at a certain (preferential) rate. Types of rights include *subscription rights* and *warrants*.

Subscription rights are issued to current shareholders instead of or in conjunction with a dividend. They are distributed proportionally to the holdings of an investor. Subscription rights can usually be separately traded on the exchange where the shares themselves are listed. These rights can be either *renounceable*, meaning they can be detached from the shares and sold to someone else, or *nonrenounceable*.

Rights are normally traded for a limited time and, similar to the case of corporate actions, the dates surrounding them—such as ex data and last trading date—have to be clear for processing, and owners of the stocks that incur the rights have to be informed in a precise and timely manner.

Another type of right is a warrant, which is essentially a call option on company stock. Unlike normal call options, warrants are issued by the company that also issued the underlying shares; when warrants are exercised, new shares are issued. Warrants are often attached to a preferred share or to a corporate bond as a sweetener and can also be detached.

Apart from these warrants that a company issues on its own stock, another type of warrant is called a *naked* warrant. These warrants are called "naked" because they are issued without an accompanying bond. They are financial products normally issued by banks on, for example, a basket of stocks. They are also called *covered* warrants; the companies that issue the shares have nothing to do with them. Settlement of these products is normally in cash. A large number of these warrants have been issued with different themes such as industry sector warrants on sectors such as pharmaceuticals and energy.

## 2.3.7 MISCELLANEOUS

At the start of the instrument type discussion, we mentioned that the CFI standard was set up with exchange-traded products in mind. The Miscellaneous category includes anything not covered under any of the other types and includes a large variety of instrument types.

Many other products start to become available, and more and more different types of exposures have become tradable. Drivers that have contributed to the extraordinary flowering and branching out of new financial structures in the last decades include the following:

- Deregulation has led to new markets and many companies can trade products that they either were not allowed to trade or that did not exist in the first place.
- More competition among banks to distinguish themselves from their peers through product innovation.
- A more volatile business climate that fostered demands from corporations and investors.
- Advances in quantitative finance, risk management, and computing power that made sure these often complex products could be priced and managed.

Most of the products classified under the Miscellaneous section in the CFI standard are derivatives. Derivatives have allowed for the creation of markets for distinct pieces of risk—e.g., credit, foreign exchange, interest—and therefore allow for a proper pricing and transfer mechanism for this risk. Derivatives can be used to hedge away exposure that is not desired or to leverage exposure to other risk factors. For example, credit default swaps can reduce concentration risk in a bank's loan book. Of course, derivatives have to be used wisely; as with every product, it helps if you know what you are buying.

In any case, exposure to these kinds of products (as with all products) needs to be carefully monitored.

The most common financial product not discussed so far is the *swap*. In a swap, two parties swap two sets of returns. Typically, a fixed return is swapped against a more uncertain return. For example a variable interest rate is swapped against a fixed interest rate, or a fixed return is swapped against the return of a stock index, a property portfolio, or the return of a commodity.

Interest rate swaps were one of the first widely traded OTC derivatives. The International Swaps and Derivatives Association (ISDA) was first set up as the International Swap Dealers Association in 1985. Swaps quickly became popular because they allow for active interest rate exposure management, and they quickly attracted a large corporate client base.[12] In an interest rate swap, a fixed interest rate is swapped against a variable interest rate (normally, an index such as Libor plus a certain spread). At the inception, the contract is worth nothing; as the market level of interest rates change, net payments will be made periodically (e.g., quarterly). A swap is made on a certain *notional amount,* which in the case of a plain vanilla interest rate is not exchanged. There have been many innovations and variations developed since then, both on the types of underlying that are swapped, as well as in the swapping structure. Other common swap types and variations include the following:

- *Interest Rate Swap Variations.* Several variations on the plain vanilla interest rate swap were discussed in the preceding paragraphs. They include a floating-for-floating exchange when both cash flows are floating—say, a Libor and a non-Libor rate. These kinds of swaps are called *basis swaps.* When the interest rates also refer to two different currencies, we talk about a *cross-currency swap.* In a *constant maturity swap*, the floating rate is reset to a fixed asset; this asset has a maturity that has a fixed offset as of the date of the reset date, so it will extend beyond the life of the swap. In a *rollercoaster swap*, the underlying notional can change—for example, it can be seasonal—to tune the payments to the exposure of the buyer. In an *extendible swap*, the swap includes the option for one party to prolong the life of the swap.

- *Commodity Swap.* In a commodity swap, two parties can exchange a variable commodity price (such as the spot market price for oil) against a fixed price for the commodity, or they can exchange, say, the return on a commodity index against Libor + spread.

- *Equity Swap.* In an equity swap, the return on a particular equity, a basket of equities, or more commonly an index is swapped against Libor + spread.

■ *Total Return Swap*. Again, the return on an underlying asset is swapped against a fixed rate. The difference is that in this case the return of the underlying asset will also include all the capital gains or losses on the underlying asset.

■ *Longevity Swap*. This type of swap can be used for pension funds, life insurance, and reinsurance companies. Here, the underlying assets are mortality figures. So the projected annual mortality rate at the start of the life of the swap is exchanged with the realized mortality rate of a certain reference population. This swap is part of a set of longevity derivatives that also include *longevity bonds*.

■ *Variance* or *Volatility Swap*. In a variance swap, the payout is calculated as notional multiplied by (realized variance – strike variance level). So again, a floating volatility (realized) is swapped against a fixed level (the strike level).

■ *Property Swaps*. Here, the return on a real estate portfolio is swapped against, for example, a Libor + spread rate or against the return on a property index.

Apart from these kinds of swaps, many other derivatives on underlyings such as weather (apart from the HDD and CDD futures, derivatives on wind speed and precipitation have come up), power, property, and macroeconomic numbers (e.g., GDP) have come up. An important class of products which is classified under the Miscellaneous category in CFI is *credit derivatives*.

Credit derivatives transfer (part of) the credit risk of an underlying instrument. They can, for example, include insurance against the default of a bond or certain payments tied to certain *credit events* such as the downgrade of a company or bond issue by a rating agency or the failure to make an interest payment. A common type of credit derivative is the *credit default swap* in which a *protection buyer* pays a premium on a certain notional to the *protection seller*. In exchange, the buyer will receive a payment when a certain credit event occurs. Single-name credit default swaps are traded on thousands of companies. Note that there is no clear cut in credit between structured products and credit derivatives—a synthetic CDO is a new instrument collateralized by a pool of CDSs—and to some extent the CFI high-level classification imposes an artificial distinction.

As products have become more exotic, they tend to have moved further and further away from the capabilities of the content and processing infrastructure that was set up to deal with more traditional, more vanilla instrument types. There have been identification issues—for example, unclarity on the full legal name of the underlying credit of the CDS—and difficulties in settlement where a longer settlement lag has translated into larger risk. We will discuss ramifications on clearing and settlement of these products in Chapter 4.

Lastly, we can also include cash in various currencies (FX) as a product type in the Miscellaneous category.

### 2.3.8 INDICES

There are many indices around the world, either created by the exchanges or by other companies. Famous creators of indices are MSCI Barra, Dow Jones, and the FTSE Group.

The number of available indices has exploded, and they cover every possible geography, marketplace, asset type, or investment theme. Indices proxy and summarize markets, and products around indices offer easy access to various markets.

Although they are not financial products in themselves, they are the basis for many derivatives (e.g., options and futures on the S&P 500 index) and also for tracker funds. For this, index providers have to license their indices to the companies that offer these tracker funds and contracts. They are also widely used by mutual funds and other investors as benchmarks for their own performance and as beacons in the overall market. They must therefore be investable and replicable. Some indices have given investors easy access to exposure that was previously more costly to obtain, such as commodities and volatilities.[13]

Indices can be calculated in different ways. The major distinction is between *price-weighted* (weighted sum of the component prices) or *capitalization-weighted*. In the latter case, the weight assigned to the constituent depends on its market capitalization, so larger companies weigh more. In this case there is also a distinction between full weighting (i.e., weighing the entire 100% of the company) or only taking the market capitalization as represented by the free-float part. The *free-float* part is the publicly traded bit of the company, which can be less than half the total number of shares outstanding. Another way to compute an index is to have it *volume-weighted*. In this case, shares qualify for inclusion not by market capitalization but by average traded volume.

A dividend-adjusted index is adjusted upward when a constituent stock pays a dividend, also called a *total return index*. The index divisor has to change when the basket of stocks is updated to preserve the index value.

In a *bond index*, the various constituent bonds could be weighted by the amount of each bond outstanding. This is similar to stock market indices where the constituents are weighted by market capitalization. The total return variant of a bond index would take the coupon payments into account. Every index will have rules for inclusion and exclusion of constituents which would be applied periodically, e.g., annually.

The older indices were designed to be overall barometers of the market and included the 30, 100, 250, etc., largest companies in the market. Examples are the DJIA, Nikkei 225, FTSE 100, CAC 40, and DAX. Other indices aim to highlight the performance of a certain section—e.g., the Financials, Telecom, Energy, Commodities—or focus on certain types of stocks such as high dividend-paying stocks. More recently, we have seen more thematic indices, e.g., indices that summarize performance of socially responsible investing. A lot of research goes into the creation of new topical indices, for example, selecting the constituents from a potentially large set of contenders by checking their figures and also their business practices, say, in the case of a socially responsible investment index.

A few examples of stock indices are listed in Table 2.9.

Index data has become more and more important. Needs for this information include providing clarity on the index methodology and on the constituents and their weights, as well as timely information on all changes in, for example, composition, corporate actions policy, dividend rules, and other adjustments. Index data have to be provided in real time so that responses can be immediate and can be closely tracked. On the other hand, historical data on the index are needed to be able to benchmark fund performance over the years.

**Table 2.9**  Example Stock Indices

| Index | Calculation and Reset Methodology, Inclusion Criteria |
|---|---|
| Nikkei 225 | Price-weighted index for the Tokyo Stock Exchange. Constituents reviewed annually. |
| DJIA | Price index of the New York Stock Exchange with 30 constituents. The sum of all component prices is divided by a divisor. This divisor is reset from time to time, to generate the value of the index. |
| FTSE100 | Started in 1984 with a value of 1000. Constituents are the 100 largest listings on the London Stock Exchange by market capitalization. |
| NASDAQ100 | Contains 100 of the largest companies on the NASDAQ, excluding the financial services companies. Weights are based on market capitalization. |

The index needs to be replicable and transparent because it is the basis for a lot of trading strategies or the benchmark for many investment products, including ETFs, warrants, and tracker products.

## 2.4 Financial Markets

### 2.4.1 INTRODUCTION

Financial instruments need a home, a place in which they can be exchanged and traded and where investment ideas can be implemented. These places are called the *financial markets*. Financial markets can be quite abstract: No physical goods are traded, but instead titles to companies or obligations or contracts change hands in large sizes. Participants do not actually have to meet, and deals can be struck in a split second. An open and transparent market is in the interest of the general public and explains why exchanges—just like financial institutions—are also regulated.

### 2.4.2 MARKET TYPES

There are different ways to look at the many different financial markets. Typical classifications of markets include the following:

- *Primary* markets (where new issues are sold to investors) or *secondary* markets (where existing issues are traded). For example, there is a primary market for U.S. government bonds. This concept of primary versus secondary primarily holds for securities, i.e., instruments issued for funding needs. It is not really applicable for derivatives, which are essentially bilateral contracts and are always created from scratch whenever a transaction takes place.
- *Over the counter* (OTC) and *exchange* markets. The difference is that exchanges are organized places of trade, and OTC is more of a peer-to-peer model. Exchanges trade standardized products, and typically a clearinghouse or central counterparty acts as the buyer for every seller and the seller for every buyer, thus taking away the settlement risk; whereas in OTC trades, there is exposure to the credit risk of the counterparty. Frequently, larger stocks are listed on multiple exchanges, and there would be a distinction between the exchange of *primary* listing and other listings.
- Classification on instrument type, foreign exchange markets, commodity markets, credit markets, interest rate markets, and equity markets.

■ Classification based on *market model*, i.e., the procedure that is used to arrive at transaction prices. These can be fixings, periodic auctions, continuous auctions, and so on.

The formerly clear-cut division between OTC and exchange markets is blurring. There are a number of reasons for this, including the following:

■ In OTC markets, we also see product standardization as product volumes increase. Industry bodies such as ISDA are driving standardization of terms and legal framework.

■ Exchanges are creating new products in the areas of credit and foreign exchange, which were historically the domain of brokers. Exchanges are doing this as part of their business development, also to remain competitive and to make these kinds of products available to the retail investor.

■ The central counterparty model of a clearinghouse which was always inextricably linked to an exchange is also introduced into OTC markets. Examples include the Continuous Linked Settlement (CLS) Bank, which is owned by a large number of banks and provides intra-day settlement of foreign exchange transactions. Clearinghouses such as LCH.Clearnet and DTCC also provide Central Counterparty services for OTC products such as swaps, credit derivatives, and repos.

■ Regulation erodes monopoly positions that exchanges enjoyed in some jurisdictions, allowing trades to be executed elsewhere. Due to ongoing consolidation in the financial services industry, often liquidity of a certain product is concentrated in fewer than a dozen players. These players can form consortia themselves and pool their liquidity off exchange.

■ Many retail products or products aimed at high net-worth individuals are created by banks using OTC derivatives and are sometimes listed on an exchange. This includes, for example, funds that have a target end date where the investment strategy and derivatives used are in line with that target end date.

■ Often exchanges have established alternative trading venues aimed at professional market participants. An example is the EuroMTS platform for euro-denominated government bonds.

Consequently, the question of whether to choose OTC or exchange for a product requires a lengthier answer nowadays, although really exotic always means choosing OTC. Product innovation continues to be concentrated on the OTC side, but exchanges are following. On the settlement side, clearing services are introduced for OTC products.

## 2.4.3 VENUE TYPES

A regular market such as an exchange will have a *rule book* that describes all procedures and which governs the operation of the market. This will include, for example, when to suspend trading because of price movements, when to delist a company because it breaks exchange rules, what the listing requirements are on solvency and information disclosure, and so on. OTC markets have no rule book, but an analogy is the common legal framework (e.g., the ISDA master agreement) that sets down the terms and law under which these OTC trades take place. Within a specific stock exchange, there are sometimes also different market segments. There is the normal market for established companies, but many exchanges also have a "hatching" market for smaller, less established companies. A sample market for "fledging companies" includes the alternative investment market (AIM), which is part of the London Stock Exchange.

Traditional exchanges have undergone a lot of change. There have been many alternative trading venues. Partially as a result of this, exchanges have demutualized and moved from member-owned cooperative societies to regular corporations, often public companies listed on their own trading system. Meanwhile, concentration among market participants has led to cost-cutting pressure. An increasingly smaller number of players is responsible for an increasingly larger chunk of the total daily volume. On the technology front, there has been a trend for financial markets to go electronic and to move away from open outcry system. In Europe, this has long been the case; in the United States, it is a more recent phenomenon.

In the past, stock exchanges were closely tied to a national economy. This is no longer the case. Exchanges are consolidating and are competing for liquidity and for listings. Because the regulatory landscape in terms of listing requirements and disclosure requirements differs from country to country, there is not often a level playing field. Perhaps in the future we can expect trade venue regulation to also become an international affair, the same as bank solvency requirements.[14]

Apart from traditional exchanges, there can be different organized marketplaces to trade on, such as Alternative Trading Systems (ATS). They include the following:

- *Systematic Internalizers.* This is a term introduced by the Markets in Financial Instruments Directive (MiFID) regulation in the European Union. It defines the practice of internalization, i.e., crossing orders on a financial institution's own book without the orders going to the exchange.

This happens on both sides of the Atlantic. In the United States, these internal order books are called *dark pools of liquidity*; in the European Union under MiFID, there will be disclosure requirements on these transactions. Firms that acts as Systematic Internalizers are also obligated to publish firm quotes in liquid shares up to standard market size.

■ *Multilateral Trading Facility.* Under MiFID, this can be either a regulated market (i.e., a market operated with instruments admitted through a listing process) or a market run by an investment firm.

■ *Electronic Communication Networks (ECNs).* These computerized trading systems exist outside regular markets, initiated by financial deregulation in the United States. Many of the ECNs have been bought by the larger exchanges in recent years. In crossing networks such as Posit, a price is submitted with the order, and crossing takes place a couple of times per day. Unlike exchanges, there is no price discovery process here. See also Chapter 3 for information disclosure and content licensing issues around this topic.

There has always been a need for alternative execution methods to deal with large-size orders. When it comes to information, the size of an order may be as valuable as the price. In the case of larger sizes, you do not want to expose the size, since you will just give everyone an option to trade against you. Used to control the information, leakage alternative procedures, whether called *upstairs trading* or *block-crossing networks*, have been around for a long time.

### 2.4.4 BIRTH AND EVOLUTION OF A MARKET

Another interesting way to look at markets is by their maturity. Typically, product innovation starts with investment banks identifying a need for a new offering in the course of dealing with their customers and subsequently creating a product. As this happens more often, typically an index is born, created by the largest dealers to have a common point of reference. After this, transactions can be structured, benchmarked, and priced against the index, whether it is a credit index or property index. If the market develops further, we tend to see standardization of deal terms and the emergence in any case of a "plain vanilla" version of the product. A legal framework will be drawn up covering standard terms and applicable law. At this point, exchanges can also start to think of introducing the products because retail clients will want direct access to these products. Possibly banks will come up with targeted products for their clients against the index. As the market and liquidity develop further, there will be more and more possibilities of price discovery. Transparency of the marketplaces will go up. Processes will become more standardized, and more data will become available to fuel them.

### 2.4.5 AN EXAMPLE OF MARKET EVOLUTION: TRADABLE CREDIT

A good example of this market development process is credit. Historically, issuer credit had been inferred from the equity and bond markets. Credit derivatives started to be traded in the late 1990s. These were mostly single-name CDSs. The market started as purely OTC, which drove a need for reference data, especially around identification of the underlying credit. Index families such as itraxx and CDX were created in the early 2000s as a family of CDS index products.[15] Market data provision developed rapidly through the services of Markit. Price discovery possibilities were vastly improved as many data providers started to carry information on the product(s). Deal terms became standardized with the 2003 ISDA credit derivatives definitions. This meant that risk management became easier, and many vendors of trading systems, risk systems, portfolio management, and settlement systems included capabilities to handle the products in their offerings. As the market grew, it began to support more research and press, such as trade publications around it. Standardization helps a market grow. The number of players increased, and processes became more standardized because of the introduction of standard identification to identify CDSs, the RED code, and because of clearing services for CDS, e.g., offered by the DTCC deriv/serv service.[16] Exchanges including NYSE Euronext, CME, and Eurex are launching their own credit products, opening up this exposure to new audiences and the general public. Increased liquidity will first lead to evaluated pricing services and ultimately to real-time data. In the end, the commoditization of products and corresponding reduction of margins will lead to the creation of new products. (See Figure 2.3.) In Table 2.10, we summarize the various stages and characteristics of market development.

### 2.4.6 MARKET MODELS

The function of a market is to create a price. How does the price discovery process work? How does a transaction price come about? How are two parties of the trade brought together? This is defined by the *market model* used by the specific trading venue. The suitable market model greatly depends on the maturity of the market.

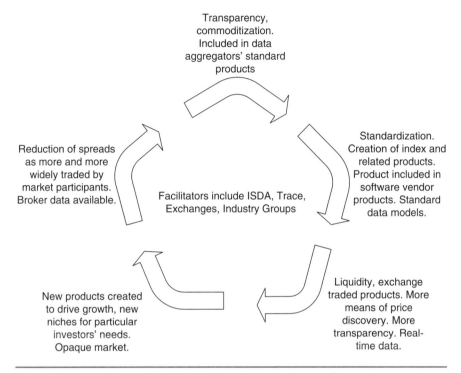

Transparency,
commoditization.
Included in data
aggregators' standard
products

Reduction of spreads
as more and more
widely traded by
market participants.
Broker data available.

Standardization.
Creation of index and
related products.
Product included in
software vendor
products. Standard
data models.

Facilitators include ISDA, Trace,
Exchanges, Industry Groups

New products created
to drive growth, new
niches for particular
investors' needs.
Opaque market.

Liquidity, exchange
traded products. More
means of price
discovery. More
transparency. Real-
time data.

**Figure 2.3**    Evolution of a marketplace and continuous innovation

Some products lend themselves more naturally to a certain trading model or way of execution of trades. For example, cash equity seems to be well suited to an exchange because the main market is the secondary (i.e., post IPO) market; for fixed income, there is much more of a buy-and-hold by pension funds, so this is more of an OTC market. It is not so much professional versus retail, although the access to an exchange for retail individuals is easy; this also explains probably the mini sizes of some future contracts, e.g., the baby S&P 500 futures contract. The average trade size on an exchange is much smaller compared to OTC.[17] You do not do a swap on $1,000, but you may want to buy $1,000 worth of stock options or stock.

Apart from the OTC/Exchange distinction, there are more flavors. Within OTC, there can be brokers who can sit in the middle (possibly two brokers, one acting for each side of the trade). Within exchanges and alternative trading systems, there are different trading models, such as quote driven and order driven. Following are the most common market models:

■ *OTC Model.* The over the counter model simply means that two parties find each other with or without the help of brokers and negotiate the

**Table 2.10** Stages of Market Development

| Market Sophistication Level | Characteristics | Examples |
|---|---|---|
| One-offs, customized deals | No index available, separately structured deals, no standardization on deal terms | Reinsurance deals, e.g., weather derivatives |
| One-offs, index exists | Benchmark can be included in standard terms, pricing off the benchmark, more common understanding in value | Property derivatives |
| Highly standardized, illiquid | Typically, a price fixing once or multiple times per day | Illiquid stocks |
| Highly liquid | Open to retail clients, smaller order size | Cash equity/blue chips |

terms of a transaction. Deal terms can be custom, although in practice there is often a legal framework in place to cover, for example, settlement terms.

■ *Fixing.* This means that the major dealers of a product come together and determine the price at which they will buy and sell. This can be once per day or multiple times per day. An example is the London gold fixing in which the five participating firms determine the price of gold twice per day.

■ *Auction.* Here, securities are simply auctioned off, either to the highest bidder or, for example, for new U.S. treasury bills through a Dutch auction.

■ *Quote-Driven Trading System.* In a quote-driven system, there will be an interdealer market; dealers make a market by quoting financial products. Clients relay buy and sell orders through their brokers, who execute them with the dealers, so dealers participate in every trade. Examples are the currency and bond markets.

■ *Order-Driven Trading System.* In an order-driven system, clients relay orders through brokers who put them in the central order book. Dealers who trade for their own account can also enter orders into the order book. In the order book, buy and sell orders are matched.

■ *Continuous Hybrid Model*. This is a common market model on exchanges. Here, there is a limit order book together with market makers who are obligated to quote prices for the traded securities. This is the way many stock exchanges work.

■ *Crossing Network*. Clients can submit buy or sell orders with a price, and the orders are crossed at certain fixed times with regard to a benchmark price obtained from another (transparent) trading venue.

■ *Single Price Auction*. To determine the open or close price of an exchange, separate procedures are used, such as a single price auction. This is also used to resume trading after the market in the instrument has been suspended because of, for example, large drops.

Some of the market models discussed are presented schematically in Figure 2.4.

The terms *pre-* and *post-trade transparency* are often used. Pre-trade transparency refers to the speedy disclosure of quotes and orders, and post-trade transparency refers to the speedy disclosure of actual trade prices and sizes. In the context of exchange data, the terms *level 1* and *level 2* data are also used. Generally, the term *level 1 data* refers to the current price or last trade price together with the current best bid and offer. The term *level 2 data* gives a more comprehensive picture of the current market conditions and includes the order book for order-driven markets or all dealer quotes for quote-driven markets.

The type of market model has great consequences for the types and amount of data available. Not every market model leads to the same disclosure of this information. In order-driven markets, there is an order book to disclose, for example, the five best bid and five best offer prices. This is an indication of the *market depth*. In quote-driven markets, there are all the dealer quotes to disclose.

# 2.5 The Birth of a Financial Instrument: The Process

## 2.5.1 INTRODUCTION

In the preceding section, we discussed the different types of markets; in this section, we will discuss how instruments end up there. Instruments can be born into an established market according to clear procedures (e.g., a new government bond, a new equity) and walk a well-trodden path, or they can be the first new species. In this section, we will start by outlining a number of types of "birth" and will discuss the accompanying data and standards process as far as it exists.

We distinguish between different types of birth of instruments including the following:

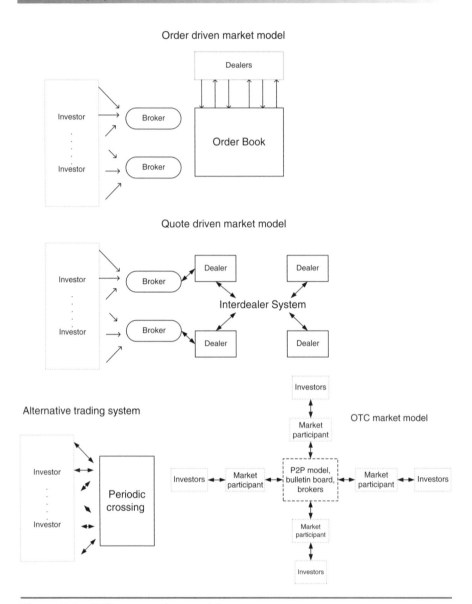

**Figure 2.4** Different market models

- New issues of bonds and equities.
- Calendar births. Exchange-traded futures and options are created regularly on the basis of a predictable product creation schedule. This needs to be reliable because investors will want to roll over contracts.

■ New structures, new derivatives. Banks can think up new structures (e.g., correlation swaps) for their clients, and exchanges can introduce, for example, a new future contract on a new underlying or wholly new products. New exchanges can also occur.

■ New indices, unit trusts, and funds are launched which cover certain markets, asset types, or investment themes.

■ Instrument change through either political events such as the introduction of a new currency (e.g., the euro), disappearance of a currency (e.g., the Slovenian crown), or change of currency regime, or the introduction of new product because of increased market maturity. This case can include the introduction of fixed-income derivatives as liquidity of the currency deposits increases and as a bond market develops in the currency. Currencies can then develop FRAs, futures, or a swap market.

Obviously, these different types of births correspond to various degrees of complexity in processing and data issues. Unique codes play a role and can greatly facilitate the automation of the transaction lifecycle. New currencies and curves require changes to the basic setup of systems in financial institutions. For new securities and new funds, the bank also faces marketing and compliance challenges. They have to decide who to offer these funds, but also who would and should be allowed to trade them.

The birth process of securities and derivatives is very different. Securities are tied to an issuing company and represent to a varying extent a claim on the assets of a corporation. Derivatives are contracts which can either be one to many—i.e., if they are standardized products created by an exchange and cleared through a central counterparty—or one to one—i.e., bilateral contracts in the case of OTC derivatives.

## 2.5.2 ISSUING SECURITIES

The issuing of equities normally requires the creation of a prospectus which informs prospective investors of the company. Different jurisdictions have different demands on the prospectus. Unlike a bond, an equity is normally listed on one or more exchanges. The competition between exchanges has meant a competition to attract new listings. The new issues of today can be the blue chips of the future, so for any stock exchange, it is vital to attract new listings.

Unlike derivatives, both bonds and equities are normally allocated identification numbers by the national numbering agency. The most common

**Table 2.11** Example Numbering Agencies

| Country | National Numbering Agency | NSIN |
|---------|---------------------------|------|
| Japan | Tokyo Stock Exchange | SICC |
| France | Euroclear France | Euroclear code/ direct ISIN |
| United Kingdom | London Stock Exchange | Sedol |
| Canada | The Canadian Depository for Securities Ltd | CUSIP |
| Germany | Wertpapier-Mitteilungen | WKN |
| United States | Standard & Poor's—CUSIP Service Bureau | CUSIP |
| Italy | Ufficio Italiano dei Cambi | Direct ISIN |

international code is the ISIN code.[18] ISIN codes consist of a two-letter country code, a nine-character security identifier that is alphanumeric, and a check digit. The nine-digit number is the national security identifier number (NSIN), and is issued by the local National Numbering Agency. Typically, NSINs are converted to ISIN codes by prefixing the ISO country code, padding the left-over space with zeros, and adding a check digit. Table 2.11 presents a list of the national numbering agencies of the G7 countries.

In addition to NSIN codes, exchanges normally use mnemonics, called *tickers*, to designate listed instruments. The exchange itself is also the subject of a standard, either ISO 10383 or the market identification code (MIC). There are currently around 400+ MIC codes in existence spread over 131 different countries.[19]

### 2.5.3 PUBLIC INSTRUMENT IDENTIFIERS

Identifiers that came out of an ISO standard, i.e., the ISIN, have long been established and are broadly in use for equities, indices, listed funds, and to some extent bonds. In some markets, ISIN codes are also assigned to futures and options.

The ISO process cannot keep up the pace of product development and the tradable universe, and occasionally a new standard is created for a new product type. This happened with the identification of the underlying company/entity in the case of credit derivatives where, after some ambiguities, Deutsche Bank, JPMorgan Chase, and Goldman Sachs introduced the reference entity database (RED) and assigned a unique code to the underlying of each single-name CDS. Markit took over this code and management of it, and since the early 2000s, it has become widely distributed by other vendors.

There are limits to what identification schemes can key. To identify a complex OTC—the other extreme—the complete contract terms can be required because every transaction is a unique contract.

### 2.5.4 PROPRIETARY INSTRUMENT IDENTIFIERS

Apart from public identifiers such as the ISO standards, there are also proprietary standards which are in common use. One of the more common ones is the Reuters Identification Code (RIC), which we consider here as an example. The RIC way of encoding is a combination of intuitive mnemonics and conventions that you have to know about. An RIC includes the following common elements:

- Frequently, a combination of a ticker, a dot, and an exchange code. The exchange code is Reuters' own coding, e.g., AAH.AS for ABN AMRO trading on Euronext Amsterdam.

- Convention for OTC instruments with a combination of ISO currency codes and acronyms or tickers to denote instrument types, e.g., D for deposit, O for option. There can be generic RIC codes as well as RIC codes that display the quote from a certain provider; e.g., EUR3MD= would be the generic RIC code for a 3-month EUR deposit, and EUR3MO=ABC would be the quote for a 3M currency EURUSD option from market maker ABC.

- Indices are often preceded by a dot, e.g., DJI, the Dow Jones Industrial Average.

- Logical groups of RICs are called *chains* and are preceded by the # sign. They could denote a group of RICs including, for example, all those on the run treasury bonds, all the constituents of a certain stock index, and so on.

- Logical conventions; e.g., 1 postfix denotes the front future contract, the first one to expire.

Because the content products in which information is delivered by a vendor are sometimes keyed with a proprietary identifier, it is no surprise that institutions have tended to make use of this identifier in their own systems. There are, however, intellectual property rights that need to be adhered to, and the owner of the proprietary code needs to allow permission for its use.

Apart from the NSIN codes and tickers, financial institutions often use internal identifiers. Sometimes a bank has its own product classification and uses instrument keys that reflect this. Other reasons include that it may be a legacy of older systems or that not all traded products receive ISIN codes. Some rules of thumb on creating an identifier are that it should

- Have a clearly defined format (you should know whether it is numeric, alphanumeric, etc.);
- Be human readable;
- Contain check-digit or other error-correcting code;
- Be unambiguous;
- Have sufficient future capacity. Relabeling or changing the format normally has enormous impact on processing systems.

### 2.5.5 COMPANY IDENTIFIERS

Apart from instrument identifiers, having company identifiers in place is also crucial. It is important not only what you trade, but also whom you trade it with. Some countries have official identification numbers. In other countries company identifiers are in use that are issued either by a tax authority or by the chamber of commerce. Company registration numbers include the SIREN number in France, the Crefo (creditreform) number in Germany, the Employer Identifier Number in the United States, and the Registration number from the Companies House in the United Kingdom. Identifiers for the (offices of) banks are called the Bank Identification Code (BIC)[20] and are composed of the following:

- A four-character bank code (e.g., ABNA for ABN AMRO);
- A two-letter country code (e.g., NL for The Netherlands);
- A two-letter location code (e.g., AM for Amsterdam);
- Optionally, a three-character branch code. When none is given or when XXX is used, the primary office is meant.

SWIFT plans to extend the BIC universe to also include codes for funds. If that happens, the BIC code could be used more broadly. Meanwhile, an ISO standard for the unique identification of parties to financial transactions has been proposed: the International Business Entity Identifier (IBEI).[21] If that is in place, the work involved in cross-referencing the various legal entity databases will become less cumbersome given that there will be a common standard to work against which will, one hopes, be picked up by content vendors.

### 2.5.6 CREATION OF EXCHANGE-TRADED FUTURES AND OPTIONS

In these cases, the derivatives exchange maintains a set of contracts along the twin dimensions of time and strike price range. For equity options, contracts would expire within 1- or 3-month intervals and would typically go out around 2 years in time. Futures (stock index futures, commodity futures, bond futures) are also typically traded out 2 years and sometimes longer although liquidity will be concentrated in the near-term contracts.

The exchange needs to be predictable in what bands of instruments are live to remain an attractive venue. Besides, many investors will employ these derivatives instruments as hedging vessels and will want to roll over the contracts. In some countries, exchange-traded options and futures are given NSIN/ISIN codes; in other countries, they are not. In that case, automatic processing and identification become more difficult.

### 2.5.7 PRODUCT INNOVATION: NEW OTC DERIVATIVES

In the OTC derivatives space, there is a continuing trend of pricing new types of risk and finding novel ways to package various exposures together to fine-tune structures to investors' needs. As mentioned earlier, we have seen derivatives initially around commodities and then around equities, interest rates, and foreign exchange. Derivative product development has grown rapidly in credit and volatility and will continue to grow in weather/natural phenomena ("catastrophe bonds") and property. A lot of product innovation has taken place in structured finance in the area of CDOs and CMOs, as was discussed in the debt section earlier in this chapter.

Other structures include constant proportion portfolio insurance (CPPI) and constant proportion debt obligation (CPDO). The CPDO is a Special Purpose Vehicle that invests in an index of bonds and periodically rolls to keep exposure to the current composition of the index. Any new OTC derivative contract is basically a new custom financial product. When products become more commonplace, market conventions to identify and process them will fall into place. Sometimes it takes a few well-publicized cases of misunderstanding and trading losses to accomplish this.

### 2.5.8 OTHER NEW FINANCIAL PRODUCTS: POLITICAL REASONS AND MARKET MATURITY

The tradable universe also expands in other ways. Every now and then a new currency code appears, following a redenomination (e.g., a folding of, say, 1,000 old units into one new unit) or a dramatic regime change. Also, as economies mature, we will see a more diverse and longer term money market develop around these currencies. First, short-term deposits and currency forwards will be traded. Also some point perhaps, money market futures will develop. Also at some point of economic development and stability, countries can tap into the capital markets and issue bonds, after which a credit market will develop, e.g., swaps and perhaps other interest rate derivatives. The quality and the length of the yield curve will increase. Currencies can also disappear, for example, because of dollarization[22] or because currencies merge into the euro.[23] New tax rules and new international banking (solvency) requirements also lead to tax and regulatory arbitrage and also foster product innovation.

## 2.6 Describing a Financial Instrument

We have discussed the large variety of different product types and terms and conditions that come with them. Market participants need to be on the same page with regard to what they are buying and selling or when they are facilitating a trade as a broker or an exchange. In this section we will discuss standards in the realm of financial instrument processing and describe the most common ones.

In general, a standard is an agreement among a user community on naming, definitions, encoding, and descriptions. Standards can be either public or nonpublic. In the former case, they can be ISO standards (i.e., driven by the International Organization for Standardization) or non-ISO standards. In the latter case, they are typically driven by trade organizations such as ISDA on behalf of its members to lower the cost of doing business. The ISO process means a transparent public process with all countries represented. The downside is that it can take a long time and sometimes no longer be relevant when something is produced. As with any ISO standard, there is a registration authority, whose function it is to be the guardian that has responsibility of maintaining the standard and keeping it up-to-date. In the case of ISO 15022, the registration authority is SWIFT.

Standards can be proprietary, either within a product company where multiple products share a data standard or within an organization where different internally developed applications share a data standard. This will especially be the case in larger financial services institutions that do a lot of their own development given their unique needs and scale.

Many standards committees have attempted to crack the problem of standardizing the terminology and encodings used in the financial industry. Some of the difficulties are as follows:

■ The very large number of jurisdictions that give rise to products or that tax financial products and the international nature of the financial markets.

■ The pace of product development, which means that every standard is always behind.

■ In some cases standards threaten incumbents who benefit from disparity or their own proprietary "standard."

Notwithstanding these difficulties, some progress has been made. Many data standards have sprung up based on XML as a method of encoding information. Some of these are in direct competition; others focus on a specific domain. The surprising thing is, of course, that there are multiple standards. The plural term *standards* is, of course, a contradiction in terms for standards that focus on the same domain. We will first discuss the non-ISO standards and then the ISO standards.

### 2.6.1 FpML

FpML stands for Financial product Markup Language. It was initiated in 1997 by JP Morgan and PricewaterhouseCoopers. The standard is freely licensed and is intended to automate the flow of information between derivative participants, independent of the underlying software or hardware infrastructure, supporting activities related to these transactions. In 2001, ISDA and FpML.org announced their intention to integrate the development process of the FpML standard into the ISDA organizational structure. FpML is currently[24] at release 4.2/4.3 in draft. The standard includes messages and business processes such as the following:

■ Pre-trade
■ Trade execution/confirmation

- Post-trade
- Reporting
- Pricing and risk
- Validation, i.e., business rules to validate if the content of a document is *semantically valid*—for example, whether the start date is before the end date

FpML aims to streamline all business interactions surrounding the trading process of OTC derivatives such as negotiating terms, doing the deal, confirming it, and exchanging settlement information. It should ease the exchange of financial information and reduce processing costs. The flexibility of OTC products has challenged technology because legacy systems were often designed and used to dealing with more standard securities and financial products. Hence, OTC derivatives processing has often been manual and therefore an error-prone process. FpML coverage includes the products[25] listed in Table 2.12.

**Table 2.12** FpML Product Type Coverage

| Asset Class | Product | Variants | FpML Version |
|---|---|---|---|
| IRD | Swap | break clauses (cancelable, extendible, early termination), asset swap (since 4.2), inflation swap (since 4.2) | 1.0 |
| | Fra | | 1.0 |
| | bulletPayment | | 2.0 |
| | capFloor | | 2.0 |
| | Swaption | (American, European, Bermuda, Cash/Physical) | 2.0 |
| FOREIGN EXCHANGE | fxSingleLeg | (Forwards, Non-Deliverable Forwards) | 3.0 |
| | fxSwap | | 3.0 |
| | fxSimpleOption | Knock-in and knock-out options | 3.0 |

**Table 2.12**  (*Continued*)

| Asset Class | Product | Variants | FpML Version |
|---|---|---|---|
| | fxAverage RateOption | | 3.0 |
| | fxBarrierOption | dual and window barrier options | 3.0 |
| | fxDigitalOption | dual digital option | 3.0 |
| | termDeposit | | 3.0 |
| CD | creditDefault Swap | CDS index (since 4.1), CDS basket (since 4.2) | 4.0 |
| Equities – EQD | equityOption | various option features/exercise types | 3.0* |
| | brokerEquity Option | | 4.1 |
| | equityOption Transaction Supplement | | 4.1 |
| Equities – EQS | equitySwap | variance swap (since 4.1), total return swap (since 4.2) | 4.0** |
| | equitySwap Transaction Supplement | | 4.1 |
| Equities – EQF | equityForward | | 4.1 |

## 2.6.2 FIX(ML)[26]

Whereas FpML is focused on OTC derivatives, FIX focuses on exchange-traded products. The original FIX protocol goes back to the early 1990s (just prior to the XML boom) as a bilateral agreement on the way of information exchange between Fidelity and Salomon Brothers. It has become a standard for pre-trade and trade information around exchange-traded products. FIX 5.0 supports the following financial product types:

- Equities
- Futures and options (not OTC)
- Fixed income
- Foreign exchange

The standard includes messages for almost all processes from pre-trade, trade, and post-trade for all product categories mentioned here, including basic order flow, market data, trade reporting, and regulatory reporting.

There are currently three variations of FIX:

- The "classic" variant of FIX. In this case the message is made up of a number of expressions of the form "tag = value." A tag is used to represent a piece of information, the value of the information follows the = sign.
- FIXML, which is a 1:1 translation FIX classic in FIXML.
- FAST, FIX adapted for streaming, to handle volumes on exchanges, which could not be handled by FIX classic.

Sample messages are as follows:

- *Market Data Snapshot:* Real-time price information (stream) from the trading party, such as an exchange, e.g., orderbook.
- *Trade Capture Report:* Trade capture reporting allows sell-side firms (broker, exchange, ECN, central counterparties) to provide timely reporting of completed trades to parties involved in a trade as well as to external entities not involved in the execution of the trade, such as for regulatory reporting.
- *A Range of Security Definition Messages:* This includes static information needed for all phases of the trade cycle from pre- to post-trade. These messages can carry information useful in the construction and maintenance of a security master file.

## 2.6.3 MDDL[27]

Market Data Definition Language (MDDL) is an initiative from the Financial Information Services Division (FISD) from the Software & Information Industry Association (SIIA). FISD provides a roundtable where exchanges, other data providers, vendors, and users come together to discuss issues. The agenda covers market data business and commercial issues, reference data, industry participation, regulatory issues, and MDDL. MDDL is primarily a market and reference data descriptive standard, not so much a transactional standard like FIX and FpML. Version 1.0 covering equities, indices, and mutual funds was released in November 2001. Version 2.0 covering fixed income was released in July 2002. Release 3.0 completes the coverage to the originally intended point.

## 2.6.4 ISO **15022**

The ISO 15022 standard focuses on post-trade and settlement messages. It is a non-XML standard which has succeeded ISO 7775. ISO 15022 messages are typically relayed over the SWIFT network and include messages on trade confirms, corporate actions, collateral management, and status reporting. The securities processing messages are included in the SWIFT 5XX message category, which consists of the groups of general messages, trade orders and confirmations, securities lending and borrowing, settlement instructions and confirmations, corporate actions, capital and income, inter-depository and clearing institutions, and statements. Whereas FIX is mostly in the realm of the exchanges, FpML is in the hands of OTC derivatives transactions partners; in the case of ISO 15022, there has also been some adoption of this standard by data content providers, especially where corporate action announcements are concerned.

ISO 20022, or the UNIversal Financial Industry (UNIFI) message scheme, is the sequel to ISO 15022. Compared to ISO 15022, the ISO 20022 standard is more of a prescription of a process that lays down a platform for the development of financial message standards. Industry bodies such as the Securities Markets Practice Group (SMPG) lay down best practices as to how to code against the standard.

## 2.6.5 ISO **19312**

Whereas the ISO 20022 standard defines the process to get to messages, ISO 19312 aims to lay down the data model for financial instruments. The final (3.0) release of MDDL could well find its way into this standard.

## 2.6.6 OTHER STANDARDS

There have been other standards aimed at a particular functional domain. They include the following:

- RIXML (rixml.org) is aimed at research information. This message standard could be used for investment and financial research.

- XBRL (xbrl.org) is a financial reporting standard used by governments, regulators, and tax authorities to collect financial information and to replace paper-based filings.

- VRXML is a market data billing standard. Vendor Reporting eXtensible Markup Language (VRXML) was developed by Gemini systems for the NYSE for exchanges, vendors, and subscribers.

- TWIST is a treasury standard used in the financial supply chain, e.g., on sourcing foreign exchange.

- The ISO 16372 standard aims to define an International Business Entity Identifier (IBEI), which is a single global system to identify the parties around financial instruments.

The focal points of some of the common models are shown in Figure 2.5.

Any standard that has been in use for some time will always imply vested interests. If a standard works, it can become incredibly sticky. Therefore, standards have to have a clear governance structure and have to be in the public domain. Any attempt at commercialization by charging license fees or any expectation that this is the hidden agenda of a standards body will at best cause enormous irritation among users and at worst kill the entire standard.

Having said that, there have been companies which have made it their business to create a comprehensive logical data model of the entire range of financial products and processes. They have either done this as a common layer for their applications or to sell it in its own right or as part of data modeling consultancy. One approach to these data models is a purely descriptive one in the

| General instrument descriptive | Research/News/ Pretrade | Trade execution | Post-trade | Corporate reporting |
|---|---|---|---|---|
| FIDM MDDL ISO 19312 | RIXML NewsML | FIX(ML)/FAST for exchange traded products, focus on trading workflow FpML for OTC derivatives, focus on instrument definition | ISO 15022 ISO 20022 | XBRL |

**Figure 2.5** Focal points of usage of different models and standards

sense of defining a table structure with a data dictionary explaining all terms and conditions for product types. The drawback is that such a model can age quickly due to new financial product development. Therefore, conceptual data models abstract from merely listing known terms and conditions and represent, for example, cash flows. Through these basic building blocks, it is in principle possible to create any financial instrument by stacking different cash flow (profiles) together. As any financial product will lead to cash flows going one way or another, this would be a more future-proof approach.

## 2.7 Active Life of Financial Instruments

### 2.7.1 INTRODUCTION

Responsibility for the various product types described in Section 2.3 is often spread out over multiple trading desks and departments within a financial institution, even though one client may need most of them. In this section we will describe the various kinds of market participants and various roles in which they interact with financial products. There are two sides to every transaction (and often one or two players in the middle brokering the deal as well), and parties engage in transactions for different reasons. In this section, we will explore some of the common roles including the selling, trading, market making, asset managing, hedging, and also policing of the financial markets. Using such a conceptual standard in a financial institution can insulate it from aging models and dependencies on external products but would require substantial initial investments in terms of mapping of all terms and conditions.

### 2.7.2 SELLING SECURITIES

Investment banks play a role in being the intermediary between investors and companies that need funding (issuers). Their activities include creating and pricing the securities (pricing in such a way that both parties are happy) based on their market knowledge, being involved in *book-building* (i.e., creating demand so that all issued securities can be sold), and also taking the role of *underwriter* (i.e., giving the issuer the guarantee that securities are sold at a certain [minimum] price and picking them up themselves if there is insufficient demand). When an issue is undersubscribed, the entire issue may be called off. When it is oversubscribed, there are various ways to allocate securities over prospective buyers. When a new security such as an equity is sold for a fixed price, often an allotment formula is used to distribute the securities over the investor. Alternatively, new securities can be auctioned off, whereby prospective buyers can bid for bonds, for example, by indicating a minimum yield at which they are willing to buy. Bids will be filled from the lowest yield up until the funds to be raised are complete. The clearance level is at the yield level by which the last funds are raised, so everybody who receives securities pays the same price. This is the way in which the U.S. government raises funds through the Federal Reserve Bank of New York.

Apart from this selling process in the primary market, banks also try to create demand for products in the secondary market or for derivatives. A bank may have created a new product which it is marketing to its clients by actively pushing it. Alternatively, it can just promote its capabilities in a certain market, e.g., foreign exchange options. One way to do this is through active advertising, through publishing research in this field or to create an index for a certain market.

### 2.7.3 MARKET MAKING

Making a market in a certain financial product means being willing to take either side of the transaction, i.e., buy or sell. Normally, there will be a spread between the price at which a market maker is willing to buy and the price at which a market maker is willing to sell. This bid-offer spread is the price that the investor pays in exchange for the liquidity. It will be made up partly of a transaction cost part (the market maker needs to earn a living) and partly to cover the uncertainty and risk of knowing less about the future movement of the instrument than the counterparty. The spread can be tiny (e.g., for very liquid markets such as the EUR USD exchange rate) or can be very large (e.g., for illiquid bonds with deviating features, unusual maturities, and currencies, etc.). Often there are a number of market makers in a particular product such as UK Gilts (government bonds), e.g., Barclays Capital; or Danish Crowns, e.g., Nordea; and so on, which reflect on certain specialties or backgrounds of these banks.

Market makers have to adjust their quotes—the level, the spread, the order size for which they quote—to manage their instrument inventories. Market makers want to refrain from large directional bets and thus have to limit the inventory of the instruments they trade.

### 2.7.4 TRADING SECURITIES

Generally, money can be made when there are discrepancies in information (slow dissemination of news) or financial understanding (different valuation models) and, consequently, different opinions as to the likely direction of a price.

A mismatch in a pricing model and an understanding of the intrinsic nature of the product and a mismatch in access to most accurate and up-to-date information and a mismatch in understanding consequences between one price movement and another of a (related) product can lead to a wrong perception of the value of a product. When new information has almost instantaneously become common knowledge, prices can change on little or no volume. When only a few market participants know about new price-sensitive information, price changes are correlated with larger volume.

There are many strategies in trading financial products. Market behavior itself is not static and there is a place for quantitative models as well as psychology in modeling market movements. Typical strategies involve making directional bets on the move of a price-driving factor, or can involve arbitrage, basically skimming off smaller discrepancies between pricing of inherently similar products. Time has always been important in trading, but the critical time unit has decreased from days to hours to microseconds. The information advantage measured in time was more or less equal to how much faster you could travel than the next man (steamship over sail, telegraph over horses). And it was also, of course, a function as to what extent information could be encoded. Whereas in the 19th century it was possible to gain an information advantage of hours, this steadily eroded to microseconds during the late 20th and early 21st centuries.

The extent to which this is critical depends on the trading strategy. In case of algorithmic trading and arbitrage strategies where small differences in various elements of related products (the hedge portfolio) are watched, investment in speed is required. For the traditional long-only buy side and for hedge funds that employ long-term event-driven strategies, this will not be justified. Also note that speed will always be more relative, than absolute speed; you merely need to be faster than the competition.

## 2.7.5 HEDGING

Hedging means the elimination as far as possible of exposure to a certain risk factor. Hedging can be undertaken both by financial institutions and by corporations. In the case of a financial institution, consider, for example, the credit trading desks. They would be interested in taking directional bets on the credit spread, i.e., the difference between the yield on a corporate bond and the government bond curve. They could isolate this credit spread by taking a position in the corporate bonds and offsetting the interest rate risk (government bond part) by buying or selling treasury bond futures. This would be hedging the interest rate risk. For corporations, hedging would come down to the same thing: making a decision in the corporate treasury department as to which risks will be kept and which risks will be hedged. A company may report in EUR and receive large payments in GBP. It could hedge the EUR GBP exchange rate risks by buying EUR forwards, in effect already selling the to-be-received GBP. Generally, companies would hedge away those risk factors that are not part of their core competence and retain or seek those for which they have special management and valuation skills.

### 2.7.6 INVESTMENT MANAGEMENT

Investing is just like trading—only for the long term. Investors will tend to look more at fundamentals and will not be concerned so much with market timing. Investment management is normally called the *buy-side* as opposed to the *sell-side* (banks, brokers), whose products and services they purchase. They would select securities on behalf of investors who buy units in an investment fund. The fund has a certain mandate, an agreement as to which products the fund will invest in and a general understanding of the level of risk. The investment manager charges a percentage of assets under management and/or a performance fee, typically a percentage of the returns. Sometimes a high water mark is used; in this case the performance fee kicks in only for performance over and above a certain level, such as the performance of the relevant benchmark.

### 2.7.7 SERVICING ASSETS

Apart from taking a position in financial instruments, parts of many financial institutions make a business in *asset servicing*. This basically means looking after the assets and can include activities that include the following:

- *Custody.* Keeping the securities and making sure the owner is kept up-to-date with regard to corporate actions (see also Section 2.9) and receives the capital that is distributed, such as dividends and interest payments. Custody is a very concentrated business. The top five global custodians (billions of dollars under administration) are listed in Table 2.13.[28]
- *Proxy Voting.* Representing the owner at shareholder meetings and voting on his or her behalf.
- *Securities Lending.* This involves short-term lending of products to a party that needs it, for example, because it has sold the product short. Industry bodies such as the International Securities Lending Association provide best practices in this area.[29]

**Table 2.13**  Example Major Global Custodians

| Company | Assets Under Administration (B$) |
|---|---|
| Citigroup | 4,529 |
| JPMorgan Chase & Co. | 3,006 |
| Bank of New York | 2,761 |
| BNP Paribas | 2,416 |
| State Street Corp. | 2,250 |

These kinds of activities are typically priced in the same way as investment services, i.e., a percentage of total assets serviced or managed. For investment management, the term *Assets under Management* is used; for asset servicing, the term *Assets under Administration* is used to denote the size of the portfolios looked after. *Transfer agents* are to transfer ownership, i.e., the (re)registering of (physical) securities. They maintain books of the registered holders of the securities for which they are a transfer agent, e.g., for corporate actions handling. The *registrar* monitors and audits the transfer agents. *Paying agents* are used for payment distributions, e.g., dividends, interest payments, and redistributions.

Different services at different points of the securities value chain are often unbundled as service providers specialize and financial institutions want to outsource part of the post-trade activities.[30]

### 2.7.8 POLICING THE MARKET

Public trust in the financial sector is vital: After all, this is the sector that people entrust with their money and which holds their (retirement) savings. Hence, regulation to establish and maintain a fair and orderly market is crucial. The reason that a significant portion of banking regulation originates at a supranational level is that banks are active internationally and that it is important to create a level playing field and to avoid regulatory arbitrage. Regulation comes in different types:

- *Prudential.* This regulation oversees the behavior of institutions. For example, is their marketing not misleading? Are they not involved in insider trading?
- *Solvency.* This is often the role of the central banks. Is the financial institution adequately capitalized to weather financial turmoil? Risk management on trading positions and the banking book falls in this category of oversight.

- *Transactional.* This includes investigations into insider trading based on unusual transactions, the checking of market conformity of transaction prices to see that the clients have received a good price, and investigation into frontrunning by looking at the institution's own trades compared to the timing of those trades executed on behalf of customers. It also asks banks to perform checks on the behavior of their clients—for example, that they are not involved in money-laundering activities.

- *Safeguarding Client Interest.* Are investors being given a fair deal? What execution quality did they get of their trades? Are they sold products adequate for their specific (financial) situation?

- *Overall Transparency* of the financial marketplace. This also applies to exchanges and other market infrastructure, not just to banks!

The financial markets and financial institutions are regulated by a large number of institutions, at a national and to some extent at a supranational level. This can include global regulatory organizations such as the Bank for International Settlements (BIS). The BIS is the international organization of central banks which regulates capital adequacy. Within the European Union, regulation of the financial markets originates at the European Commission level and ultimately needs to be enshrined in national laws.

A major recent piece of legislation in the European Union is Markets in Financial Instruments Directive (MiFID). This succeeds the original Investor Services Directive (ISD)[31] from 1993 which defined the legislative framework for investment firms and securities markets within the European Union. MiFID includes a number of pre-trade transparency requirements according to the venue type:

- Continuous order book trading systems shall make public the five best bid and offer levels including the number of shares and orders at each price level.

- Periodic auction trading systems shall publish the indicative auction price and volume.

- Quote-driven trading systems shall make public the quotes of each market maker.[32]

MiFID is the result of a so-called Lamfalussy process named after Baron Alexandre Lamfalussy who chaired the Committee of Wise Men. This committee was established by the EU Finance Ministers who had to review the European securities markets' regulation. This legislative process goes through four stages. Level one is adoption by the European Parliament of a core piece of legislation. Progression to level two includes advice from industry specialists on technical details. Level three means that national member states' regulators collaborate on the new regulation. Level four is compliance and enforcement.

Sometimes regulatory responsibilities are also split between different agencies that cover prudential oversight and solvency checks or by market. In the United States, the commodities markets and securities markets are regulated by different organizations: the Commodity Futures Trading Commission (CFTC) and the Securities and Exchange Commission (SEC), respectively. An example of a national regulator is the Financial Services Authority in the United Kingdom, which regulates around 29,000 firms. This regulation varies from a continuous relationship (less than 1% of the firms) to a reliance on thematic studies and general statistics. Over 90% fall in this category.[33]

A distinction often made as to type of regulation is that between principles-based regulation or rules-based regulation. Rules-based regulation aims to set out the rules in detail, meaning you cannot go wrong if you follow the letter of the (often very lengthy) law. Principles-based regulation aims to embody the "spirit" of a desired result and is often very succinct. The FSA has 11 principles[34] in the following areas:

1. Integrity
2. Skill, care, and diligence
3. Management and control
4. Financial prudence
5. Market conduct
6. Customers' interests
7. Communications with customers
8. Conflicts of interest
9. Customers: relationships of trust
10. Customers' assets
11. Relations with regulators

The key points on rules-based versus principles-based regulation are summarized in Table 2.14. In reality, regulation is not a case of one or the other, but often a mix.

The legal powers of regulatory bodies vary by jurisdiction. Some of them can bring criminal cases and have the authority to set their own fines. The reality for large geographically diversified banks is that they have to deal with dozens and potentially hundreds of regulatory agencies and central banks.

**Table 2.14** Rules Based and Principles Based Regulation

|  | Rules Based | Principles Based |
|---|---|---|
| **Pros** | Clarity | "Spirit" rather than "letter" of the law |
| **Cons** | Lots of paperwork<br>Loopholes likely to remain | Can remain vague, interpretation issues |

The information disclosure effort on risk statistics, pricing models, and processes to satisfy all these requirements is enormous. We will discuss this issue in more detail in Chapter 4.

## 2.8 Dependencies Between Instruments

### 2.8.1 INTRODUCTION

If we look at the behavior of the financial markets (i.e., including all financial instruments) in its totality, we see that there are many factors at work to drive prices. The financial market can be seen as a very complex ecosystem, where every element influences everything else to a greater or smaller extent. Apart from the valuation of assets through discounting expected future cash flows, both the expectation on cash flows as well as the discount rate will vary through time and by investor perspective. Often, however, there are pools of instruments that react to the same price drivers. Factors that drive prices include the following:

■ *Changes in Fundamentals.* This means price changes on resources on which a company's profitability ultimately depends. This includes changes in commodity prices due to new finds (new mines, new oil reserves), weather (more demand for natural gas in cold winter, good/bad crops), and natural phenomena such as earthquakes (can hit reinsurance business, benefit construction industry).

■ *Macroeconomic Outlook.* A general weakening or improvement can change credit spread levels or multiples applied to profit when valuing stocks. This sentiment will be determined by fundamental economic figures such as interest rates, macroeconomic data, and overall investor confidence.

■ *Political Events.* For example, such events include a change in regime to more or less business friendly; change in openness of a particular economy, for example, open to foreign ownership, currency controls. This can also include central bank decisions on the interest rate, which affects a company's funding costs and will impact all outstanding debt in that currency or currencies linked to that currency.

■ *Laws of Supply and Demand.* Apart from intrinsic valuation criteria based on assessing an asset's future cash flows, the pricing level also comes down to supply and demand. In this case, the effects can be very long term or very short term. For the long term, we have to look at demographics and at how a country's pension system is funded. For the short term, often emotion is at work. Why do people make buy or sell decisions? They change their cash position (move out of cash into a product or out of a product into cash) or swap one financial product for another. In the latter case, they typically react to news. Positive news can mean high demand for a product leading to temporary overpricing.

■ *Change of the Composition of Stock Indices.* This is another, more mundane price driver. Instruments can move in and out of a stock market index, e.g., based on market capitalization. Because of the rise in index trackers, this can result in a lot of order flow. Buy when a stock joins an index, sell when it leaves it. Similarly, news that a certain well-known fund has taken a stake in a company can also trigger a lot of order flow. Also the initial inclusion in an index may guarantee a certain level of liquidity.

Apart from that, instruments can depend directly on other instruments, as is the case for all derivatives. Here, the underlying influences the price; the extent by which this happens is called the *delta*. We discussed this earlier in Section 2.3.

As we saw in the discussion on derivatives, in those cases instruments directly depend on another instrument. For example, the price of a call stock option depends on the price of the underlying equity and on the interest rate. Other direct dependencies are prevalent wherever there are common price drivers. Thousands of bonds dance to the tune of the EUR and USD government curve, all driven by interest rate fluctuations. Often instruments seem to move in parallel. By definition of the index, large cap stocks move together with it. Oil prices will move together with natural gas prices because one is to some extent a substitute product of the other. Price changes in an underlying can be magnified in derivates that leverage the risk driver. Often the relations are more subtle. Price drivers for equities require a solid understanding of the business and what business risks that particular company is exposed to. For example, what are the resources it needs in terms of, for example, commodities such as energy, precious metals (semiconductor industry), soft commodities (FMCG companies), and so on.

Often effects can ripple through from one asset class to another and the sphere of a price driver's influence can be huge (such as a government bond benchmark) or tiny (such as something that affects only a local Smallcap). (See Figure 2.6.)

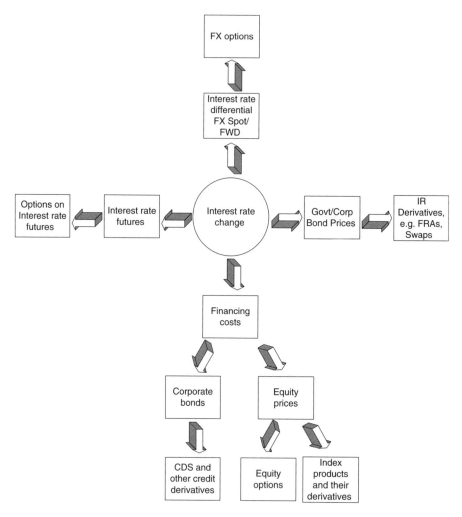

Effects ripple through. Every arrow can mean that the effect of the change is magnified.

**Figure 2.6** Sphere of influence of risk drivers, interconnections between instruments

### 2.8.2 MAKING SENSE OF PRICE DATA

There is a whole army of chartists looking at price histories and drawing conclusions from them. This can range from studying long histories of close prices to looking for fundamental trends. It is perhaps very human to look for structure and to regard the financial markets as natural phenomena from which fundamental laws can be observed. In the case of time series of financial instruments, there will be spikes and movement due to supply/demand imbalances. In the case of commodities, these spikes can also be introduced due to underlying physical constraints. Examples would include constraints in storage or distribution (pipeline capacity) and generation capacity. The specific type of time series on which you are looking for or flagging exceptions has to be taken into account.

Numerous indicators are used in technical analysis. Some examples are the following:

- *Moving Average.* This is the price movement smoothed out over a number of observations. Trading rules are triggered from different moving averages that display crossover—for example, if the 5-day moving average crosses the 30-day moving average. Implied behind these kinds of rules is the belief of a "true" fundamental market trend around which shorter term noise can lead to temporary mispricings.

- *Momentum.* The analysis looks at price difference over time and how long it took. The idea behind it is to uncover trend lines.

- *Charting.* From studying graphical charts of prices, many patterns can be seen. These include trend lines, "resistance levels" with the idea behind them that once they have been penetrated, price movement can be accelerated (in any case until the next resistance level). Other patterns are more complex. The idea behind all this is that history is a guide to the future.[35]

One aspect of technical analysis that is perhaps less controversial is that of more micromarket studies that look at overreactions to specific news items, for example, and how quickly an earnings announcement is absorbed in the price. Therefore, chartism and technical analysis range from the extremely esoteric to the very practical. Practical cases include algorithmic trading, using market impact data to slice up orders and to distribute them intelligently to various venues to hide the buyer's or seller's intent.

## 2.8.3 SUMMARY STATISTICS

To make more sense of the market, we need to summarize the bewildering array of price histories. For this, indicators have been defined which give summary information and which are a proxy of the true state of the market.[36]

One approach to summarize (part of) the market or a portfolio is to isolate and define the key drivers of change; these are called *risk factors*. For example, the price/yield movement of tens of thousands of U.S. corporate bonds can be summarized into the movement of the USD government bond curve, plus the change in the spread of a few dozen combinations of industry sector (utility, telecom, energy, FMCG, industry) and rating class (AA, A, BBB). Inevitably, some information is lost, but the bulk is preserved, which is the job of any summary statistic. Indices also provide quick "dashboard" information on the behavior of a market.

The risk of a portfolio can be summarized into one dollar amount, the *Value at Risk* (VaR) number. This defines the maximum dollar amount that can be lost within a given time frame under a certain confidence level setting (e.g., 99% or 97.5% confidence). We will discuss this in more detail in the risk management section in Chapter 4. Note that measurements such as correlation matrices tell you nothing about cause and effect. To get a quick overview of the market, you can analyze information such as volume and open interest (the total number of contracts with identical terms that have been opened and not yet closed because of exercise, expiry, or through a closing transaction) to get an idea of liquidity and what trade sizes the market will bear without significant distortion.

Another summary statistic in the case of options is *risk reversal*. Risk reversal is the difference between implied volatility of the call option and implied volatility of the put option. If this number is positive, the implied volatility of the call is larger; this in turn indicates higher demand for the call option, indicating in turn a distribution of expected returns skewed to the upside.

Note that all summary statistics are snapshots as market behavior itself is dynamic. A correlation matrix gives you a snapshot of the situation right now; correlations can change over time and indeed do so often in quite dramatic ways. A correlation matrix also tells you nothing about cause and effect. Two factors may be correlated but may be due to seasonality, may be due to a third underlying driving factor, or may be pure coincidence. This snapshot is a mechanical way of condensing information and should not replace logical reasoning on cause and effect of price change.

# ▌ 2.9 Ups and Downs Throughout an Instrument's Life

Throughout the life of a security, many events initiated by the company that issued it may affect it. These *corporate actions* are the topic of this section. The bulk of these events will be expected, such as dividend payments (although the amount may be a surprise), annual general meeting announcements, and interest payments. Other common events include changes to the number of outstanding shares through share buybacks, stock splits, or the issuing of new shares. The calling or early retirement of bonds may be more of a surprise, and tender offers can come out of the blue. Other events which do not relate to the security but to the company include announcements of key hires or news on patents and so on. On the negative side, class action lawsuits can be initiated. It is the custodian's job to inform the owners of the securities about these matters.

Dealing with corporate actions comes down to good data management, communications, and processing, which we describe next:

■ *Data Management.* There are different corporate action content providers with different categorizations of event types (similar to the financial instrument type classification problem). There may be a cumulative total of 250 types which need to be standardized into the set of ISO 15022 event types, for example, also keeping track of key dates/rates, client positions, and narrative. This is a major mapping and cross-referencing task.

■ *Communication.* Events are held against an Asset Master system, typically a legacy system, in which the accounts affected by a corporate action are held. Note that this does not mean an immediate effect; e.g., the dividend declaration date can be today, but as long as the equity is bought before the ex-date and held, its owner will be affected. The institution has to send notices to its clients (custodians, agents) as a result of these matches and track responses depending on the type of event, e.g., voluntary, mandatory, or mandatory with options, while observing the response deadlines. There can be longer dialogues, for example, in the case of tender offers for only part of the shares (e.g., a controlling stake). The owner of the security may sign up to the tender offer yet not be able to participate if the response was received too late.

■ *Processing.* This includes the calculation of *entitlements* (who gets what), processing of the responses, other asset services such as securities lending, collateral, class actions, proxy voting, and so on. It also includes tax handling and actual payment of capital distributions into the securities owners' account.

### 2.9.1 DIFFERENT PERSPECTIVES ON CORPORATE ACTIONS

With regard to a corporate event, there are different stakeholders within a financial institution. The focus can be the event itself or its effect on the value of financial instruments. The answer depends on the role somebody has within a firm. If you own a stock or manage a portfolio on behalf of clients, that includes the stock you want to receive your dividend and maybe also want the fiscal aspects to be taken care of. If you are trading the instrument, you want to know what is happening to it (e.g., splits, dividend yield). If you are developing a new product which incorporates exposure to the instrument on which a corporate event takes place (let's say you are creating a warrant on a basket of stocks), you have yet another interest.

For traders, a corporate event is in the same category as general news around a company, so anything that affects the price is important. For research purposes, history of dividends may be kept, and forecasts are also important—for example, to price options or when doing index arbitrage. Compliance officers have yet another interest in corporate actions. They need to report on shareholdings above a certain threshold. A share buyback could put a company over the threshold, and holding reports may need to be filed.

### 2.9.2 CORPORATE ACTIONS DATA MANAGEMENT

Both financial institutions and data vendors spend large sums to staff departments whose primary function is to gather, verify, and correct corporate action information. The data problem starts with the initial capture—often poor information coming from the issuer (company) of the action itself through meetings, press releases, or local newspapers. This means that sourcing this data is to some extent always a catch-up game. It is surprising that while there are increasingly rigorous accounting standards for filing of financial statements, yet nothing remotely similar for the filing of corporate actions, this also directly impacts the owners of securities of public companies. The task is left to the agents/custodians, which causes a lot of redundant work. Industry groups such as the Association of Global Custodians[37] have stressed the need for standardized messaging in corporate actions.

The burden could be shifted to either the issuers or the primary exchange. One idea could be to file it via a controlled entry point into the market via a registrar, e.g., the national numbering agency (who can then also issue a unique identifier for a corporate action associated with the identifier of the underlying security, date, and type) or the exchange of primary listing.[38] Unique identifiers are also relevant for storage and for future reference. The question of a central facility is difficult. Candidates include exchanges and issuers. Exchanges are including corporate actions in their content feeds. Issuers start the whole process but have no local tax knowledge; this would argue for exchanges and central securities depositaries.

Just as institutions have to authenticate their own settlement instructions (e.g., in the settlements directory for CLS), something similar could be imposed as part of the requirements of a listing on an exchange. Companies or their agents or registrars would have to authenticate their corporate actions, i.e., through standard forms. SWIFT could play a big role in the distribution of this content. We will discuss these kinds of information supply chain issues at length in the next chapter.

### 2.9.3 TYPES OF CORPORATE EVENTS

Corporate actions can be said to fall into a broader category of *business-critical events*, which would be anything that can materially affect the valuation of the company and/or its securities and hence derivatives on those financial products. This is not limited to events that originate at the company; other examples include departure of key staff, lawsuits initiated by third parties, macroeconomic numbers, major commodity price changes (oil, metals, soft commodities that are needed to run the business or make the product/service), political events, and natural phenomena.

Within the ISO 15022 classification, the field 22F is used to indicate the event type. The ISO 15022 standard includes around 70 different event types, which are summarized in Table 2.15.

Most corporate actions are scheduled interest payments on bonds and dividends. They also include announcements on general meetings and mergers, tender offers, and spin-offs. Other announcements include extraordinary events on securities (early call) and changes to the company (place of incorporation, court meetings). The total number of corporate actions comes to around a million events per year; this does not count the 3 million plus scheduled fixed-rate interest payments and scheduled maturities. Between 10% and 15% of corporate actions represent voluntary events; this means that there are between 100,000 and 150,000 complex events annually. Table 2.16 presents a percentage breakdown of types. Note the large regional variety in breakdown.[39]

Corporate actions remain one of the more tenacious areas in automating. Even though there is a fairly broadly used standard (ISO 15022), this is not heavily used at key parts in the information supply and event processing chain. The length of the supply chain, including many different players such as

**Table 2.15** Corporate Action Event Types

| ACTV | Trading Status: Active | Name | Name Change (Frozen) |
|------|------------------------|------|----------------------|
| ATTI | Attachment | ODLS | Odd Lot Sale (Frozen) |
| BIDS | Repurchase Offer/ Issuer Bids/Reverse Rights | ODLT | Odd Lot Sale/Purchase |
| BONU | Bonus Issue/ Capitalization Issue | OMET | Ordinary General Meeting |
| BPUT | Put Redemption | OTHE | Other Event |
| BRUP | Bankruptcy | PARI | Pari Passu |
| BSPL | Bonus Share Plan (Frozen) | PCAL | Partial Call |
| CAPG | Capital Gains Distribution | PDEF | Partial Defeasance/ Pre-Funding |
| CHAN | Change | PINK | Pay in Kind |
| CLSA | Class Action/ Proposed Settlement | PLAC | Place of Incorporation |
| CONS | Consent | PPMT | Installment Call |
| CONV | Conversion | PRII | Interest Payment with Principal |
| CPNR | Adjustment of Interest Rate (Frozen) | PRIO | Priority Issue |
| CPST | Coupon Stripping | REDM | Final Maturity |
| DECR | Decrease in Value | REDO | Redenomination |
| DETI | Detachment | REMK | Remarketing Agreement |
| DFLT | Bond Default | RESU | General Meeting Results (Frozen) |
| DLST | Trading Status: Delisted | RHDI | Intermediate Securities Distribution |
| DRAW | Drawing | RHTS | Rights Issue/Subscription Rights/Rights Offer |
| DRIP | Dividend Reinvestment | SCOP | Suspension of Corporate Action Privilege |
| DTCH | Dutch Auction | SMAL | Smallest Negotiable Unit |

**Table 2.15** (*Continued*)

| ACTV | Trading Status: Active | Name | Name Change (Frozen) |
|------|------------------------|------|----------------------|
| DVCA | Cash Dividend | SOFF | Spin-Off |
| DVOP | Dividend Option | SPLF | Stock Split/Change in Nominal Value/ Subdivision |
| DVSC | Scrip Dividend/ Payment | SPLR | Reverse Stock Split/Change in Nominal Value |
| DVSE | Stock Dividend | SUSP | Trading Status: Suspended |
| EXOF | Exchange | TEND | Tender/Acquisition/ Takeover/Purchase Offer/ Buyback |
| EXOP | Exchange Option | TREC | Tax Reclaim |
| EXTM | Maturity Extension | VOTE | Proxy or Voting Preferences (Frozen) |
| EXWA | Warrant Exercise/ Warrant Conversion | XMET | Extraordinary General Meeting |
| INCR | Increase in Value | COOP | Company Option |
| INDE | Installment Default | EXRI | Call on Intermediate Securities |
| INTR | Interest Payment | SHPR | Shares Premium Dividend |
| LIQU | Liquidation Dividend/ Liquidation Payment | WRTH | Trading Status: Worthless |
| MCAL | Full Call/Early Redemption | CMET | Court Meeting |
| MEET | Annual General Meeting | DSCL | Disclosure |
| MRGR | Merger | | |

issuers, exchanges, custodians, CSDs, broker/dealers, fund managers, and investors, complicates matters. A more fundamental factor inhibiting automation is that issuers are under no obligation to adhere to a certain finite set of event types' terms and conditions and can create whatever they like.

**Table 2.16** Percentage Breakdown of Corporate Action Event Types

| Type | Worldwide | North America | Europe | Asia Pacific |
|------|-----------|---------------|--------|--------------|
| Cash dividend | 26.9 | 27.7 | 23.0 | 33.1 |
| Income distribution | 16.4 | 23.8 | 2.6 | 0.0 |
| Partial call redemption | 14.6 | 17.7 | 12.6 | 0.1 |
| Full call | 12.5 | 18.1 | 1.7 | 0.3 |
| Meeting | 7.1 | 0.6 | 18.7 | 18.4 |
| Dividend omitted | 2.7 | 0.8 | 3.5 | 18.7 |
| Return of capital | 2.0 | 1.6 | 3.7 | 0.5 |
| Name change | 1.8 | 0.8 | 5.2 | 1.3 |
| Other | 16.0 | 8.9 | 29.0 | 27.6 |

## 2.10 The Demise of a Financial Instrument

The tale of the instrument lifecycle is coming to an end. We saw why they are conceived, how they are created and named, where they live, and what kinds of interest different players in the market take in them. We explored what can befall them during their life. Now we must talk about how they come to an end.

### 2.10.1 SCHEDULED TERMINATION

Fortunately, in most cases the end of an instrument life is business as usual and has been planned in advance. This is the case for the great majority of exchange-traded derivatives and also of most fixed-income instruments. Options and futures have a predetermined end of life—sometimes a few weeks or months away, sometimes a few years. Exceptions would be in the case of call options if something extraordinary happens to the underlying stock during the life of the option. For example, it can split or merge. In that case, the exchange has to determine what to do with the outstanding options. Either the contracts that are already active are changed (e.g., modify number of shares on which the contract works after a split), or the exchange can choose to terminate the options early.

Normally, fixed-income instruments also have a predetermined end of life, from overnight money up to 50 years.[40] Equities, on the other hand, represent ownership in a business that is a going concern and have no end-of-life unless something happens to the company, either a buy-out, merger, or bankruptcy. If an instrument matures, e.g., a debt instrument, the principal is repaid and ends up in the hands of the owner of the instrument. The identifiers assigned to instruments that are expired are often reused[41] after a while, which can lead to problems in record keeping. For example, in a time series of prices identified by such an identifier, the following patterns could occur: first, normal movement followed by a flat line (when the instrument is expired and the identification code not yet reused); then a sudden shock occurs to the time series as the identifier is reused for a new instrument that trades at a very different price point.

### 2.10.2 UNSCHEDULED TERMINATION

Apart from normal expiry or maturity, instruments can also end prematurely in other ways. Sometimes this was foreseen under the terms of the instruments. An example of this occurs when a bond is called by an investor because more attractive financing can be found. This call event will happen under the provision of the call schedule of the bond.

However, instruments can also default or be delisted. What happens in those cases?

In the case of equities, an equity instrument can go off exchange due to a tender offer that has become mandatory. The conditions on which an offer becomes mandatory depend on the proportion of the company already under control by the prospective acquirer and will vary by jurisdiction. Derivative products that depend on the underlying that disappears will be governed by the exchange's rule book. If an exchange-traded option or future comes to the end of its predetermined life, it is settled. Parties that wrote call options can be called upon to deliver stock if the options end in the money. Parties that wrote put options can be called upon to purchase stock if the options end in the money.

In the case of bonds, issuers can default on their payments. Sometimes this means they temporarily stop paying interest; sometimes it means they will repay nothing of the principal. Corporate bond holders will depend on the outcome of bankruptcy court proceedings. In the case of sovereign debt denominated in a foreign currency, there are often more complicated salvage operations. Bond holders come before equity holders in the queue for the spoils of liquidation, but the *recovery rate* will vary dramatically from practically zero to nearly 100%.

Custody systems are often a veritable archive of inactive instruments. Sometimes instruments live on like ghosts that continue to roam around and haunt the custody systems. A famous example is the old Tsarist Russia bonds.

# 2.11 Conclusions

In this chapter we examined steps in the instrument lifecycle. We looked at the reasons behind instrument creation and at the various product types available to investors. We noted the different data elements and different levels of unique identification and propensity for automation of instruments. We also presented the habitat of instruments in the form of trading venues, their different market models, and the birth of instruments and data standards. We also discussed price drivers and the linkages between instruments. No instrument is like an island. We looked at various events that could befall instruments during their lifetime. The discussion on corporate actions gave us a brief preview of the potential difficulties in the information supply chain. In the next chapter we will look in much more detail at the content markets around financial instruments. We will discuss who is who and who does what, and where everybody fits in with regard to the information supply chain around financial products.

# Endnotes

[1] Whether to call financial engineering an art or a science can be an open-ended discussion.

[2] The CFI classification is ISO standard 10962.

[3] The yellow keys are Equity, M-Mkt (money market); Crncy (currency); Client, Pfd (preferred); Muni (municipals); Corp (corporate bonds); Cmdty (commodities); Mtge (mortgage securities); Index; and Govt (government bonds).

[4] See http://www.anna-web.com/ISO_10962/iso10962.htm for an overview.

[5] There are also mutual funds that invest in other financial products such as futures. There are also mutual funds that invest in commodities and even some funds that invest in fine wines.

[6] Roughly speaking, venture capital invests in companies that consume cash, and private equity invests in companies that already generate cash.

[7] For example marketing specific funds for men or women, or funds that seek to appeal to specific regions within a country.

[8] Source: www.morningstar.com, copyright Morningstar.

[9]This last tranche gets hit the worst and is called the "equity part" or less affectionately "the toxic waste." These "dregs of the deal" are often regarded as part of the cost of doing business.

[10]See http://www.optionsclearing.com/initiatives/symbology/default.jsp.

[11]See, for example, http://www.lme.co.uk/linear_low.asp.

[12]They also became the focus of the first derivative scandals in the early 1990s, for example, those of Procter & Gamble and Hallmark Cards.

[13]For example, through the VDAX index calculated by Deutsche Boerse.

[14]On the other hand, new types of exchanges that are more inherently local have sprung up in the wake of the liberalization of the electricity markets. Because electricity grids are predominantly national and there are not a lot of interconnectors, these exchanges can, at least for the moment, cater to regional markets.

[15]itraxx is owned by Markit; CDX indices are owned by Dow Jones.

[16]See http://derivserv.dtcc.com/.

[17]The average OTC deal is $4 million USD; the average exchange deal is $200,000 USD. Eighty-three percent of all transactions are OTC. Total notional in OTC derivatives outstanding was $446 trillion USD in mid-2006. *Source:* Bank for International Settlements, www.bis.org.

[18]ISO standard 6166.

[19]*Source:* http://www.iso15022.org/MIC/homepageMIC.htm.

[20]ISO Standard 9362.

[21]ISO standard 16372.

[22]For example, Ecuador adopting the U.S. dollar.

[23]For example, the recent disappearance of the Slovenian tolar.

[24]Mid-2007.

[25]*Source:*http://www.fpml.org/spec/index.html.

[26]Material from this section was based upon information on www.fixprotocol.org.

[27]For more information, see www.mddl.org.

[28]As of 2005, at www.institutionalinvestor.com.

[29]See www.isla.co.uk.

[30]We could also say that pre-trade processes such as price discovery are outsourced to the stock exchange or other execution venues. The alternative is doing it yourself through calling many brokers or prospective counterparties directly.

[31]Note the difference in European Union terminology between a *directive* and *regulation*. A directive has to be followed directly; regulation has to be transcribed into national law.

[32]Quoted from http://www.exchange-handbook.co.uk/index.cfm?section = articles &action = detail &id = 60608.

[33]Callum McCarthy, FSA Chairman, Speech, Financial Services Skills Council 2nd Annual Conference, October 31, 2006.

[34]See http://www.fsa.gov.uk/Pages/Library/Communication/PR/1999/099.shtml.

[35]Working with charts implies a disbelief in the efficient market hypothesis. Charting can become quite esoteric, with alleged regularities found in *Elliot Wave Theory* and *Fibonacci patterns*.

[36]This is analogous to the world of accounting where ratios, such as quick ratios, can be used as rules of thumb to provide quick information ("acid tests") on the state of the overall business.

[37]Composed of the Bank of New York Mellon Corporation, Brown Brothers Harriman, Citibank, HSBC Securities Services, JPMorgan Chase Bank, RBC Dexia Investor Services, and State Street Bank and Trust Company. See also www.theagc.com.

[38]Such as the London Stock Exchange, which publishes corporate actions in the LSE SedolMasterfile product; see http://www.londonstockexchange.com/en-gb/products/informationproducts/sedol/.

[39]Source on overall numbers and type breakdown: Oxera report, "Corporate Actions Processing: What Are the Risks?" sponsored by the Depository Trust & Clearing Corporation, May 2004.

[40]There are also some perpetual bonds still outstanding; one was issued by the Dutch city of Harlem in the 1700s.

[41]This can be after 3 months or after 10 years depending on the code and the product type. Codes for options, for example, will be reused more quickly.

# Chapter 3

# The Information Supply Chain: Overview of the Financial Content Market

## 3.1 Introduction

Fresh content has been compared to the oxygen supply of the financial markets, and it is indeed critical in ensuring a smooth process flow. It is a boundary condition to any decision making, whether it means doing a trade, informing an investor, selling a product, or complying with regulations around the instrument and transaction lifecycles. Between creators of data (e.g., market makers, research agencies, exchanges, and issuing parties) and end users, there is an often complex and lengthy information supply chain. The transaction lifecycle depends on internally and externally sourced information; the instrument lifecycle, often on external data. The external part of this chain includes the ultimate sources and content intermediaries such as information aggregators, validators, enrichers, and distributors. An institution often sources content from many different providers and has to do substantial internal integration and quality assessment work. After purchasing, integrating, and cross-comparing, the information supply chain continues internally until it reaches users or applications where the information can be acted on. Effective content management is about getting the right content to the right place at the right time—for the lowest possible cost. The more intermediaries in the supply chain, the larger the time delay and the higher the potential for error. In this discussion we will take a bird's-eye view of content and divide it into four main categories, depending on where it is sourced from. These categories are the Internet and public sources, vendors or commercial sources, proprietary information, and information obtained through clients or other business relationships.

We will dissect the different chinks in the data supply chain and discuss different sourcing and distribution strategies. We will also cover the different roles in the content market and discuss who creates, who distributes, who redistributes, and who aggregates. We will also cover intellectual property issues, comparing the different content licensing models in operation. Apart from an in-depth discussion of each type of content and its quality aspects, we will also discuss shifts in the content sourcing landscape through sections on alternative sourcing strategies, including cooperative data sharing, commingling of commercial and communal data, data exchanges, and "data clearinghouses."

This chapter is organized as follows: In Section 3.2, we will discuss the four main categories of data providers. This section is followed by a discussion as to who the actual players are. We will address who is selling data, and whether it is their core business or an integral part of another product or service. We also will discuss the size and evolution of the financial content market. Section 3.4 dissects the information supply chain and devotes attention to each stage. In the following section, we will take an in-depth look at the different content types from the perspective of how the content is sourced and delivered, but above all from a functional perspective. What is the role of each main content type within the financial institution? This section can be seen as a companion section to Section 2.3 in the preceding chapter, where we discussed the main financial instrument categories. In this chapter we'll take the approach of grouping it into functional areas such as research information, pricing information, trade support information, and so on. Each category of information we will discuss in Section 3.5 has a pivotal role to play in decision making throughout the steps in the core financial processes discussed in the next section. We will discuss what role the information types take in pre-trade, trading, and post-trade processes and assess the effects of industry developments such as an increasing move to real-time processes and proliferation of content interdependencies through more "hybrid" innovative products. In Sections 3.6 and 3.7, we will discuss various sourcing strategies, plus licensing and contract issues. We will end the chapter with a discussion around technical distribution within an organization, completing our discussion of the financial information supply chain with the last step: putting information in the hands of end users who can act on it.

## 3.2 Overview of the Content Market and Its Changing Dynamics

If we look at the overall financial content industry, we can distinguish four main sources of information. A summary and examples of data categories of each of these four types of sources are provided in Figure 3.1.[1] This breakdown covers the following four main types of information, categorized in information supply chain terms, i.e., how the information is obtained.

Each of these four categories plays a large role in providing the information that is needed to run the instrument and transaction lifecycle processes in a financial institution. Technological changes have increased the distribution

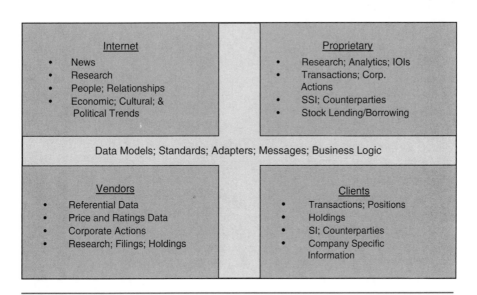

**Figure 3.1** Different channels of sourcing financial information

options and have made it easier to create and distribute new content products. The Internet has caused some information categories to become more commoditized during the last decade and has eased access to them. On the other hand, new financial market and product development has led to many highly specialized data services. In the following subsections, we will discuss the main characteristics of each of these four source types.

### 3.2.1 PUBLIC SOURCES OF INFORMATION

Public information includes all content freely available either because of regulatory disclosure requirements (e.g., filing, prospectuses) or because it concerns government-published information (e.g., macroeconomic numbers). It includes chamber of commerce information and public filings on financials (cash flow statement, income statement, balance sheet). The Internet and online databases has greatly facilitated the ease and speed of access to these materials; yet in some cases vendors can still add sufficient value collating and reformatting public information to make a marketable product out of it. This includes press releases, patent office information, information published by government or central organizations such as macroeconomic statistics (from the statistics office of the government), or interest rate changes from the relevant central bank. It can also include information on which derivative products are priced, e.g., macroeconomic data such as GDP numbers for macroeconomic derivatives, weather data from government meteorological offices for weather derivatives. Other relevant information includes rulings from courts or competent authorities, policies from regulators, verdicts in lawsuits, and information on bankruptcy cases. Apart from this highly structured information where the exact coverage is often dictated by regulation or procedures, there is another set of less reliable public information; a lot of this includes gossip—hearsay from forums, blogs, and so on.

### 3.2.2 COMMERCIAL DATA VENDORS

Commercial vendors include all players who are selling information to whatever financial services firm is willing to pay for it. We can make a distinction here between *data providers* (that actually *create* content) and *data vendors* (that specialize in *aggregating and distributing* that data). The first category ranges from niche vendors that specialize in, for example, price evaluations of a certain esoteric class of derivatives to rating agencies that rate instrument issues only in a lesser developed country. The second category ranges from specialized players that collate and reformat highly focused information (e.g., MBS pool information from public sources such as the U.S. government-associated agencies) to the handful of large-scale, globally active aggregators that have hundreds of sources, including rating agencies, brokers, exchanges, governments, and banks. We will discuss the types of data vendors and types of information sold commercially in Section 3.5.

### 3.2.3 PROPRIETARY DATA

Every financial institution generates enormous amounts of proprietary information. This constitutes the "edge" on which business decisions are based. It includes the body of specific and private knowledge on customers (such as specific credit information), knowledge on the pricing of specific instruments, the institution's strategic planning, the current state (the current portfolio), and its own research through proprietary financial mathematical models from macro-economic developments to specific internal credit ratings. Apart from elements that provide the institution its competitive edge, proprietary information also typically comprises information that is needed to run business processes such as standing settlement instructions, unique identification of counterparties, cross-references between different instrument identifications, and identifiers for OTC instruments outside the ISIN scope, and so on. These kinds of data, although proprietary, are generally not competitive and could potentially be shared with peers to improve operational efficiency.

### 3.2.4 CLIENT- AND COUNTERPARTY-SOURCED CONTENT

The last major category is that of content sources through the business relationships an institution has. First, this category includes data that define the relationship, such as what products a client can trade, what the composition of its portfolio is, what the benchmark is against which investment returns are assessed, and what execution strategy has been agreed. In addition, and in particular for the professional trading counterparties, this information includes "master" agreements or legal frameworks that provide for, for example, the netting of transactions (see Section 3.5) and other settlement-related information, such as standing settlement instructions. An interesting development in content sourcing has been the *pooling* of information between peer groups to arrive at a higher data quality and more comprehensive picture together at lower cost. Pooling can work for data categories that each institution would typically gather itself on a piece-meal basis and for which no off-the-shelf commercial content products exist and which constitute data sets that are not the basis of competition. Examples include the following:

- Nonsensitive information on legal entities (such as location, legal structure, address details, identification, country of incorporation, and full legal name from the articles of incorporation).
- Settlement instructions such as location and account information, payment instructions, and perhaps standing instructions on corporate action handling (which helps smooth the transaction processing, so it is immediately mutually beneficial).
- Information on operational risk such as losses. Loss data are required for all banks that want to do their own modeling on operational risk; these data are hard to get. On the other hand, a large data set is needed to arrive at statistically meaningful estimates.

In the last case, as long as the data set is made anonymous, pooling can help. For the customer data as well, pooling can reinforce quality and lead to a more comprehensive view. Note that competitive information on customers such as credit assessment (internal ratings) would be less suitable to share because this is closer to the core business of a bank and would represent the value add of the business. Advantages of peer-to-peer sourcing are that it is cheaper because it can often be done with a closed wallet, and it will be reliable because it comes from people who are using it on a daily basis.

## 3.3 Who Are the Data Sellers?

Many companies have made it their core business either to create content or to package and distribute it. In the first category, we find many research institutions such as the rating agencies that provide information on instrument and company level, plus research groups that look at the outlook for certain industry sectors or regions, for example. The second category contains many well-known names in the financial industry, such as IDC, Reuters, Telekurs, and Bloomberg. In this category we find both companies that derive the great majority of their revenues from data sales as well as companies that have a more diversified revenue base with a data business that complements their other activities.

Examples in this category include trading venues such as exchanges and brokers. The proportion of revenue due to information products is rising. Other examples include content offered around securities services (prime brokers); content offered free as part of a marketing strategy (custom indices provided by some of the banks to signal market leadership in a certain product set); or data offerings combined with technology offerings, e.g., integration of content with a trading, risk, or portfolio system. The bundling of applications with a data offering can provide for a powerful vertical integration case because it simplifies the data supply chain.

Many of the larger information vendors, including IDC, Reuters, Thomson, Dun & Bradstreet, Standard & Poor's (part of McGraw-Hill), are publicly traded companies. Other companies such as Bloomberg are privately owned. New players such as Markit Group are privately held by (predominantly) the larger banks. Telekurs Financial is part of the Telekurs Group, which is owned by the Swiss banks.

The total number of information sellers runs in the hundreds or even thousands and includes many sellers of local data (exchanges) and specialized product data (brokers). The number of large aggregators that provide comprehensive content solutions is very small. There are large barriers to entry, and to become a major all-round packager and distributor of data requires economies of scale. The likes of Reuters have large data collection departments to gather data from hundreds of different trading venues, exchanges, brokers, and so on. Newer content players can set themselves apart by becoming market leaders in certain subsegments.

More parties are starting to sell data. Whereas there were the classic aggregators and research institutions such as the rating agencies, now more players are entering the market. First, there are institutions that already had large amounts of data as a byproduct of other activities such as clearing and trading but want to realize some or more of its value. This includes many exchanges that, after demutualization, strive to make their own information business. It also includes former government-linked entities that try to commercialize their content, for example, weather bureaus. New players are also entering the market—for example, companies that grew up in the wake of demand for information on newly developed financial product categories; last but not least, this includes the financial institutions. Since they originate a lot of the content on, for example, prices and quotes anyway and are allowed to run their own execution venues as a result of new regulation (e.g., MiFID in the EU), they can also start selling their own content directly. Some pooling consortia to create a central platform for the aggregation and distribution of pre- and post-trade information have sprung up—for example, BOAT in the EU.[2]

Interestingly enough, in the case of financial institutions, this holds not only for information, but also for some of the tooling/analytics that have been developed on top of it. Interestingly, banks have also started to sell not just data, but also more value-added services on top of it. This can be derived data sets such as risk factors or evaluated prices coming out of their own quantitative models, but it can also include tailored risk advisory services based on specific portfolios. On the other hand, pure information providers also move to downstream vertical integration, for example, by expanding into data display/manipulation terminals and applications.

The content market will continue to grow for various reasons including the following:

- Technology advances so more data can stream into an application or pricing model within a certain time frame;
- Pricing model and computing power advances making models more data hungry;
- New financial product development requiring more prices;
- More basic asset classes such as $CO_2$ emissions and forward electricity prices;
- More emphasis on accurate and timely reporting from both regulators and customers;
- A proliferation of execution venues due to new venues and internalization by banks leading to new data sources (e.g., due to MiFID in the EU as of November 2007);
- More users due to a boom in hedge fund and alternative investment categories.

As information is sold more and more globally and financial services firms are consolidating, the structure of the content industry is also changing. One example of this is a smaller number of country-specific products but a move to more and more global information products, both functionally in terms of content, but also in information providers' sales and marketing strategies. However, the basis for competition among content providers will likely remain largely unchanged and includes factors such as:

- *Coverage.* What financial products, what markets, and what other data types are made available through one channel and one data format? To what extent is a one-stop shop—commercially and technically—provided?
- *Accessibility.* How easy is it to integrate the data into processing? Can one or more steps of the often cumbersome supply chain sketched here be skipped? Are data made available in standards? What access options are available, e.g., APIs, services to retrieve content dynamically? Can data retrieval be tailored to the institutions' needs, e.g., on a portfolio basis? Can subselections of attributes be made to limit unnecessary data flow and spending?

■ *Value Add.* Is sufficient value added in cross-referencing and linking between different data elements offered? Often insights and value can be created by providing cross-references and structure over multiple types of data. See also the discussion in Section 3.5.

■ *Latency.* How timely are products delivered? *Timely* can refer to timely batch delivery so that information is in time to be used in a daily batch process, and it can also refer to low latency for streaming data and the time lag in relaying price-moving information such as press releases, earnings, and corporate actions.

■ *Quality, Pricing, and Service.* How reliable is the vendor? What is the quality of the information? Quality is a hazy concept that means different things to different people. We will explore the various quality dimensions in Chapter 5. Do the quality dimensions meet the institution's needs? What is the overall pricing and service (this also includes training and support) around the product?

## 3.4 The Information Supply Chain

Information becomes useful only when it is acted on or needed to create new information. However, before it ends up in a decision maker's hands, information can go through an often lengthy supply chain. Knowledge about the information supply chain, about changes and additions to information at each step, is a condition of success for any activity that critically depends on this information. Unfortunately, all too often information arrives too late, incomplete, or degraded at the place where it is needed. Information even can get lost on the way and get stuck at a certain stage in the supply chain—for example, when incomplete records are passed through or when incorrect assumptions are made. Sometimes it is a bit like a game of Chinese whispers. Furthermore, transparency as to *data lineage* (i.e., the origin of data elements used in pricing and reporting) is increasingly important for audit and regulatory reasons. In this section, we will explore the stages and players in that supply chain. The supply chain extends on both sides of the actual entry point of the information into the organization. Costs for the information paid to a third party are thus only a part of the costs of getting it to where it is needed. The external part of the information supply chain includes the ultimate sources, aggregators, validators, enrichers, and distributors. As an institution often sources content from many different providers, it has to do substantial integration and quality assessment work. These steps of integrating, cross-comparing, staging, and enriching the original information purchased normally take place within the

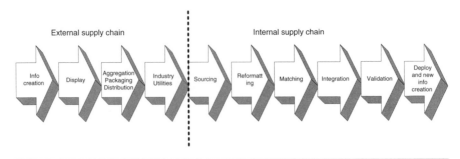

**Figure 3.2**   Information supply chain and information creation process

financial institution, although some have taken tentative steps to outsource some of this process.

A complicating factor is that distribution models differ. They vary from a *terminal model*, where the information supplied is directly linked to end user's desktops, often bundled with an application such as a trading system or research system, and where the information supplier exercises tight control over who was using it, to a very open electronic delivery through files or messages. We will discuss the relative merits of these models in Section 3.7.

In the following subsections, we will discuss the main stages and players in the supply chain, including original creators, display, aggregators, utilities, and the internal supply chain up to and including deployment to decision-making places. The main stages and players in the information supply chain are shown in Figure 3.2.

### 3.4.1 CREATORS OF DATA

The creating of data can cover information as ephemeral as an indication of interest (IOI) or a quote, or more solid information such as an audited income statement. Why is a piece of financial information created, and what happens to it?

- It can be created because it is legally required for investor disclosure, e.g., annual reports or prospectuses.
- It can be created because of a government research mandate, e.g., national statistics agencies that produce macroeconomic indicators.
- It can be created as a means to do business directly, such as a quote or an IOI.
- It can be a contract definition from an exchange that launches new products.

- It can be created to support doing business: e.g., Standing Settlement Instructions (SSI).

- It can be part of the core business of the company to create information that can be sold, such as ratings and industry research reports.

After creation, content can be sold directly; it can be posted on an order book or bulletin board, for example, in case of quote data; and in many cases, it is sold indirectly and bundled, aggregated, and packaged with information created by other institutions to create a content product.

### 3.4.2 DISPLAY VENUES

Trading venues want business conducted, so they will try to attract liquidity. They pool the quotes and orders from the market makers and dealers active on their trading system to present a full view of the market. The level of detail of data made available depends a bit on the market model that is used by the venue. Market models were discussed in Section 2.4 in the preceding chapter.

### 3.4.3 AGGREGATORS

The function of aggregators is to bundle and pool information together on, for example, a large amount of financial products, often standardizing the format and presentation of the content. Aggregators pool information from a wide variety of sources, including corporations, agencies, courts, brokers, newspapers, exchanges, and the financial institutions themselves.[3] Aggregators offer their products to financial institutions via an increasingly wide palette of options. Often these are standard "one size fits all" file products, but increasingly they present more interactive ways of getting content, such as working through shopping lists whereby an institution can choose what pieces of information about which financial instruments it wants to receive. Aggregators of content have to keep close track of what they aggregate for whom (i.e., the entitlements to information and attribution of revenues) so that the original owners of the data can verify where their content has been distributed to and are compensated according to the redistribution agreements. The extent to which aggregators have to *interpret* information supplied to them in different formats and encoding conventions determines the level of potential value added, but also of subjectivity. It can be important to pass on the basis of these interpretations within the overall aggregated content product.

One particular category of aggregators is companies that offer *tickerplant technology*,[4] which aggregate multiple real-time direct exchange feeds. The basis of competition with traditional aggregators is low latency; getting streaming data to trading systems faster will give their users an edge.

Typically, financial institutions source most information from the large integrators, but several trends have changed this picture somewhat. First of these is the latency trend. To reduce latency, there has been a trend toward *Direct Market Access* (DMA) and to source price data directly from the exchanges or via ticker plants rather than through the aggregators. The second trend is that of *disintermediation* from some of the original content providers, especially the rating exchanges which sell their own products directly and want to retain or extend the direct relationships with the larger financial institutions.

### 3.4.4 INDUSTRY UTILITIES

Utilities constitute an intermediate step between aggregators and user firms, acting as "super" aggregators, making one format and bundling content with data validation services. This standardization and validation of aggregated data may eliminate a lot of the work in the internal part of the supply chain and could be offered as a managed service. Arguably, many organizations do the same thing in-house, possibly together with other Business Process Outsourcing services, such as cleansing of data according to client-defined business rules. These cleansing rules could vary from client to client, making the scalability of these kinds of offerings somewhat difficult as we move closer to the area where the core business of financial institution starts: the value-added proprietary business rules and models. Examples include the following:

- A simple example would be which data vendor to use. Not every client will take the same sources, and different clients may have different perspectives on the relative quality merits of vendors for various market segments.

- Another simple example would be which market makers to use to get a snapshot price. In a risk management process, an organization would normally exclude itself as a source, so the set of eligible market makers to contribute a quote differs necessarily from client to client.

- More complex cleansing rules can have to do with how to fill gaps in time series (e.g., replace by fair-value price based on bond cash flows and proxy spread, expectation maximization algorithm, some kind of interpolation, taking proxy return versus a benchmark time series, etc.; in this case there can be a large diversity in rules).

The number, type, and configuration of cleansing rules would depend on the data type and downstream usage. The efficiency of the cleansing rules could be periodically reviewed by the number of errors missed, but equally as important, the number of false positives they have generated: If many false alerts are raised, the results of the rules will quickly lose credibility.

As we enter the financial institution, the information supply chain is far from over. It typically continues for at least as many steps within the financial institutions.

### 3.4.5 INTERNAL SUPPLY CHAIN

Most institutions have multiple content providers. There are several reasons for this. First, especially for larger financial institutions, there is not one content provider—even the larger aggregators—which can satisfy all the information needs. Second, for business continuity purposes and so as not to depend on one vendor both operationally as well as commercially, institutions often opt to have multiple sources for the same information. Third, when content from multiple information providers is compared and commingled, discrepancies and errors can be caught and corrected.[5] An example of this in the case of mingling various price sources to produce an approved revaluation price is provided in Figure 3.3. The ability to trace the process back upstream is typically a critical requirement.

Thus, data from multiple sources is combined for the purposes of business continuity, to plug the gaps in coverage, and for quality improvement. The internal information supply chain usually includes the following steps, which could be distributed over multiple applications and departments:

- *Sourcing* of the data from the provider. This step can be performed through a variety of technical ways, as discussed in Section 3.7, but more mundane ways of sourcing still abound. For example, manual capture/ entry of data through copying from faxes, emails, web pages, and newspapers and the scrubbing, scraping, or shredding of web or broker pages are also part of the information supply chain. This step includes retrieving the information from the web, pulling it from an ftp server, calling a vendor's API, invoking a web service or just reading a hard-copy report or newspaper, making a phone call, scanning a prospectus, parsing an email, and so on.

- *Reformatting* it into a common format. Often an organization has standardized on a certain naming convention, has defined its own XML structure,

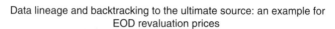

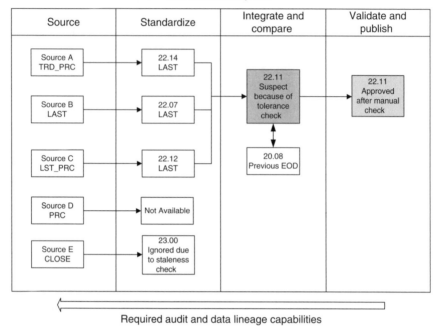

Data lineage and backtracking to the ultimate source: an example for EOD revaluation prices

| Source | Standardize | Integrate and compare | Validate and publish |
|---|---|---|---|
| Source A TRD_PRC | 22.14 LAST | 22.11 Suspect because of tolerance check | 22.11 Approved after manual check |
| Source B LAST | 22.07 LAST | | |
| Source C LST_PRC | 22.12 LAST | 20.08 Previous EOD | |
| Source D PRC | Not Available | | |
| Source E CLOSE | 23.00 Ignored due to staleness check | | |

Required audit and data lineage capabilities

**Figure 3.3**   Price consolidation with lineage

or relies on a standard from a vendor of one from the public domain. This step can also include *staging systems*, holding data in intermediate containers, e.g., to bridge different incompatible technologies. Reformatting the data can involve extract, transform, and load (ETL) tools, a set of products that specialize in manipulating and reformatting data, XSLT tools that can transform one XML standard into another. A whole cottage industry around Enterprise Application Integration has sprung up. Often a lot of proprietary and local information needs to be part of the configuration of these tools, so although they help solve the problem, they are just part of the answer. The common format to which data is mapped can be an internal proprietary standard or an open (ISO) standard. Section 2.6 in the preceding chapter provided an overview.

■ *Matching* different sources for the same instrument, corporate action, and legal entity. This can vary from exact matching on common identifiers such as ISIN code and place of trade for listed instruments to more "fuzzy" matching for legal entities where you have to check on the same company name. This comparing of company names often includes text comparison and text manipulation, including expanding abbreviations and stripping away legal form markers such as "Ltd," "SA," or "Inc." In the case of corporate actions, on the other hand, matching is more straightforward and typically takes place on a combination of fields that define the event type, effective date, or identifier of underlying security. Note that the use of ISO 15022 helps here; otherwise, the event types need to be standardized to a common set first.

■ *Data integration and consolidation.* Combining the content from various providers becomes possible after they have been matched. Blanks can be filled in because vendors often provide complementary information, and at the same time discrepancies can be detected. For example, vendors can disagree about certain information, or one can be later than another in supplying a piece of information. Note that there are also commercial sources that act as aggregators of identifiers and provide this cross-reference information. The creation of these products is complicated, since there are many vendor proprietary identification schemes in use; hence, agreements need to be struck up with the owner of each code included in the cross-reference scheme.[6]

■ *Validation.* This step can include formatting checks (e.g., correct structure and check digit of the ISIN code), consistency checks (e.g., does the maturity date lie beyond the issue date?), and price validation checks (deviation against index). In the case of price data, for example, if a raw continuous quote stream is taken in or if frequent snapshots are taken, rogue prices can show up which do not represent true bids or offers. These have to be filtered out; the same holds for technical errors such as mistakes in the decimal point (a price of 1234 instead of 1.234) Data are thus molded into information. Going a step further, consolidating and comparing prices from various market makers and execution venues transforms it into actionable intelligence. Validation often takes place with a "four-eyes" methodology employed; this methodology is required for certain data types in some jurisdictions. In this case, one pair of eyes does the actual correction or validation action, and a second pair of eyes signs off on the work. For validation, workflow tooling is frequently used to group together related issues for easier routing and processing; it also distributes data issues over staff members, also for load balancing among staff. Issues can be organized by priority, by portfolio, by (internal) client, by owner, and so on. The approved data are often called *master data* or *golden copy data* and still need to be delivered to end users and applications.

Note that when we're talking about sources of data, this can mean something fundamentally different for time series and reference data. The word *source* for reference data often refers to the distributor or carrier of the information. There is normally only *one* ultimate source: the company that created the financial product. In the case of time series data, the source is normally the quoting party or trading venue; in this case, multiple sources are *expected*. Also note that when there are multiple "sources" for reference data, the expectation is that they are the same; if they are not, at least one source is wrong. In the case of time series, the sources can be the same but will generally give different values reflecting different quoting times, different trading strategies, and product inventories of market makers. This means that consolidation over multiple sources of reference data is a matter of comparison and, for time series, much more of statistics, taking a mean, taking an average, or taking other factors such as quote time, quoted volume, and bid/ask spread into account. An exception in the case of reference data is ratings, where the various agencies' ratings all constitute potentially different *credit opinions*, so in this sense they are more like time series.

### 3.4.6 DATA DEPLOYMENT

After the data have been approved, the data set has to be brought to a place where it can be acted on. This can mean loading the information into the application where it plays a role or that it can be seen, queried, inspected, or changed by an end user. This we call *data deployment*.

Traditionally, a key difference between client and proprietary information on the one hand and vendor and public data on the other hand is how it is stored. Data that are sourced from public and/or commercial sources are often stored in a separate data store decoupled from applications that may need these data. Such data are often abstracted out of applications and are common to a variety of business functions. Proprietary and client data, on the other hand, are usually stored at the application level itself, such as with a risk management, portfolio management, or banking system, which implies a far lower degree of standardization in terms of data model, taxonomy, semantics of client, and counterparty data. These are either typically legacy-built applications or commercial systems. We will explore the various types of applications alongside a discussion on business processes surrounding the instrument lifecycle in Chapter 4.

There are different ways in which the approved data can be brought to the attention of the user. They include the following:

■ The approved data can be put onto a distribution layer such as middleware which routes it to, for example, a portfolio management, trading, settlement, or risk system. This can be done on a publish-subscribe model, where updates to a certain data universe such as a particular group of clients, set of EUR corporate bonds, or cash dividends are pushed through to the using system. Or, it can be done on a request-reply type basis. In a publish-subscribe model, there is normally a need to also store the golden copy data at the application level; in request-reply, the data-consuming application requests data whenever information is needed and will go to a central store to obtain it. We will discuss distribution methods at more length in Section 3.8.

■ The approved data can also be put into a downstream master or golden copy database where it is available for online access. Typically, you would want to separate the processing (loading, reformatting, validation) storage system from an online store where data are accessible to end users. The reason is that you want to control what you make available (only approved data) and you also do not want ad hoc queries to interfere with a scheduled process of loading, reformatting, and cleansing to arrive at updated golden copy sets in time. Simultaneously, at the place where the data are processed prior to publication, you want to keep audit information on who changed what and when, and you want to store the *lineage* of the golden copy data, i.e., which sources contributed what. Downstream data stores are called *datamarts*, *datawarehouses* (DWHs), or *operational data stores*. To some extent, the meanings of these terms overlap. In general, datawarehouses are larger data stores with broader coverage; they also often contain statistics on updates, which data are most used, or control access in case there is some kind of (internal) cost allocation in place. Datawarehouses are normally open to the whole organization. Operational data stores (ODSs) would contain more focused sets of data and would typically be used by a certain department or certain business function. There would potentially be more of these, e.g., one for retail client information, one for equity derivatives prices. Datamarts could be positioned somewhere in the middle as far as scale and complexity are concerned. Whatever name we give them, these data stores are consulted by different applications, either through regular standard reports or through ad hoc online queries.[7]

Any financial services institution should carefully measure and control where information is distributed to and how heavily it is used. This is not just to satisfy business requirements and to conclude the appropriate content licensing agreements, but also to be able to attribute the cost of the information and its processing in an equitable way to the business owners. Cost attributed is cost controlled, and treating information as overhead will lead to overstated requirements.

### 3.4.7 FULL CIRCLE

Within the application, the requested data lead to actions and decisions (e.g., cash transfers, financial instrument orders, dividend processing, client portfolio revaluation, withholding tax calculations, regulatory reporting, etc.). For whatever business function the application or end user is using the data, at this point new information is created, and we have come full circle. This new information can, in turn, become the starting point of the next information supply chain because it is published externally to business relationships or regulators or internally to fuel other processes. The effectiveness with which an institution can produce new content determines its success. In Chapter 5 we will discuss metrics that can be used to measure this.

Generally, this supply chain holds for all commercially and publicly sourced data. Sometimes, some of the steps are skipped or combined in one. In the case of information retrieved from peers or clients and for proprietary data, it can differ a bit. Client or peer-to-peer retrieved data are that which are sourced on a piece-by-piece basis through a business relationship. Proprietary data are created as a result of internal business processes and can include internal ratings, client profiles, pricing models, and the institution's own trading portfolios. In this case the overall picture still holds, but there is less automation and standardization. Often, information is keyed in manually. These sources will not have the creation of information products as their core business, so it will come in through emails, faxes, spreadsheets, and so on and can be more difficult to process automatically. Also, as we saw previously, this kind of information is also typically more often stored at the application level. It is also often entered directly through this application, in which case we arrive at a very much condensed supply chain.

### 3.4.8 THE LATENCY QUESTION

The time delays that can occur as a result of a lengthy supply chain can be considerable. The delays incurred in each of the steps are becoming smaller as the process itself becomes more integrated. The steps we see internally (cross-reference, identification, error correcting) also occur to some extent at each of the steps in the external part of the supply chain. The difference is that in the external part multiple companies are involved. Time delays can also have a technological nature (because of manually rekeying data), sourcing information from printed material (such as newspapers, faxes) instead of electronically. The trade-off between speed and quality will be different depending on the business function serviced. To take two extremes: For real-time data, speed is of the essence. The trader will know the market level and not be too bothered or distracted by the odd, rogue quote. For regulatory reporting, speed is less important, and quality of information is critical because penalties and reputational damage can be immense.

In this section, we discussed the various steps in the external and internal financial information supply chain. In the next section, we will take a closer look at the various types of content that pass through these stages and will cover the various categories of information that can be *externally* sourced.

## 3.5 Different Types of Content

### 3.5.1 INTRODUCTION

In this section, we will look at the types of content that play a role in the transaction lifecycle. If we split up the trade cycle in three parts, we arrive at the rough breakdown illustrated in Table 3.1.

This table shows that different types of content will be required in the pre-trade (idea generation, price discovery process), trade (execution), and post-trade (settlement, asset servicing, revaluation, risk reporting) steps.

Note that this is yet another way to look at the multifaceted world of information. Figure 3.1 (see Section 3.2) divides information according to source; in Table 3.1, we have divided it up along the part of the trade cycle. In the following discussion, we will divide the world of commercially sourced information into the following four categories:

- *Reference Data.* With this, we mean all descriptive information on instruments, clients, issuers, corporate actions, and so on. This category includes terms and conditions, dividends, legal structures, cross-reference information, names, addresses, and so on.

- *Time Series Data.* With this, we mean all intrinsically dynamic information. This category includes all frequencies of pricing, whether streaming data, evaluated prices, historical prices, snapshots, or macroeconomic data. Apart from pricing, other dynamic information such as order books, volumes, and open interest is also included.

- *Trade Support Data.* With this, we mean information needed to facilitate the trading and settlement process. This includes standing settlement instructions,[8] master agreement information, holiday calendars, and company/person directories. Without such services, the institution has to contact maybe 8 or 10 brokers if something changes. Standing instructions

**Table 3.1** High Level View of Trade Cycle, Activities and Data Requirements

|  | Function | Data Requirements |
|---|---|---|
| **Pre-Trade** | ■ Quantitative Modeling<br>■ Broker/Trader Discussions<br>■ Management Approval | ■ Research; Time Series; Reference Data<br>■ Counterparties; Costs<br>■ Limits; P&L Histories |
| **Trade** | ■ Account Management<br>■ Execution<br>Order Management<br>Order Routing<br>■ Margin & Securities Lending<br>■ Account Management | ■ Accounts; Counterparties<br>■ Execution<br>Algo Parameters; Brokers; EMS Model<br>Reference;<br>Counterparties<br>■ Inventory; Availability; Margins<br>■ Accounts; Counterparties |
| **Post-Trade** | ■ Clearing and Settlement<br>■ Corporate Action Processing<br>■ Risk Management<br>■ Compliance Management<br>■ Account Management<br>■ Fund Management | ■ Transactions; Standing Settlement Instructions; Accounts<br>■ Positions; Corporate Actions Accounts<br>■ Counterparties<br>■ Positions; Prices; Risk Parameters<br>■ Positions; Regulations<br>■ Accounts; Counterparties; Positions; Prices |

refer to a client's instructions not only where to settle (account information), but also what to do with dividends and other distributions, how to handle excess cash (e.g., put it into a money market fund) and the proceeds of sales and disposition of securities, proxy voting at shareholder meetings, and default choices if there is the option to choose between a cash and stock dividend.

**Table 3.2**  Main Data Type

| Reference data | Research/Price discovery data |
| --- | --- |
| ■ Instrument information | ■ News |
| ■ Company information | ■ Financial information/research |
| ■ Corporate actions | ■ Ratings |
| Time series data | Trade support data |
| ■ Basic price data | ■ Contract data |
| ■ Derived/risk factor data | ■ Holiday calendars |
| | ■ SSI data |
| | ■ Who's who/CRM |

■ *Research/Price Discovery Information.* With this, we mean all news; financial statements (balance sheet, cash flow, earnings); prospectuses; research such as credit ratings, projected earnings and dividends; and industry/macroeconomic research.

In Table 3.2, we summarize the classification we will use throughout Section 3.5.

After discussing these four categories of content, we will devote short subsections to discussing emerging content products, the combination of these types of information into more comprehensive content packages, and the result of information—decisions, which, in many cases, means transactions. In Chapter 4, we will explore more fully the role this content plays in various business processes and the business applications that the vendor community has come up with to support them.

### 3.5.2 REFERENCE DATA

Reference data are also often referred to as *master data* or *static data*. Ironically, the fact that this information is not *static* causes all the data gathering and data processing issues. We will segment these categories into company reference data, instrument reference data, and corporate actions data.

#### Company Information

Reference data can include basic information such as the full legal name, country of incorporation, and address. These data often also include identifiers, should they exist,[9] and information on the company's business, shareholders, and management. Some entity data products specialize on the cross-referencing between various identifiers and showing the linkage between issuers and issued instruments. This can help the client identification within a bank and is needed for credit risk to link issuers to issues.

A separate set of content products is that around corporate structure which shows a holding company with all its wholly-owned or majority-owned subsidiaries. Good quality information on who owns who, who owns what, and who is ultimately responsible for any obligation incurred somewhere in the legal hierarchical tree is very important. Whereas many suppliers provide some basic roll-up information so that you can find the name of the ultimate (domestic or global) parent, other suppliers specialize in the provision of the full structure, which allows you to track down all subsidiaries of a holding. As many larger companies can have well over 1,000 subsidiaries which often have similar names in a structure perhaps six or seven levels deep, this can be quite a complex picture. Additional information around the structure is that around legal guarantees, ownership percentage, names of board members, and names of the major shareholders of the holding. The users for such products would be corporate finance departments on the one hand who need to know the ins and outs of clients they advise, and credit risk departments on the other hand who need to know how certain credits roll up into one exposure.

Sample products include BankersAlmanac from Reed Business, which provides specific financial and organizational information on banks, and Mergent Online and various products from Bureau van Dijk Electronic Publishing. This company provides different company databases including Amadeus (covering 9 million public and private European companies), Bankscope (providing information on over 25,000 banks worldwide), ISIS (focusing on insurance companies), Oriana (focusing on the Asia-Pacific region), and ORBIS (the global product, 33 million companies).[10]

Company data also normally include the identification of the industry sector in which the company is active. Different coding systems in use present classifications of business segments. The U.S. government created the Standard Industrial Classification (SIC) standard, which has been succeeded by the North American Industry Classification Scheme (NAICS) standard. Widely used commercial classifications include the Global Industry Classification Standard (GICS), which is owned by Standard & Poor's and MSCI Barra, and the Industry Classification Benchmark (ICB) from FTSE and Dow Jones Indexes. Generally, these standards offer a directory structure with various levels to designate major industry groups with various levels of subsections to more precisely identify company types. This information can help group exposure to companies into different industry buckets to monitor, for example, concentration risk, to create industry segment indices and also to create a peer group to assess performance of, for example, a stock relative to similar companies.

In recent years, the demands on client data management have increased. This is partially due to consumer protection legislation and increased screening of clients' behavior to detect illegal activities. Measures include Know Your Customer (KYC), which refers to due diligence a bank has to do on a client's background before the client is taken on, and Anti-Money Laundering (AML), which refers to the monitoring of a client's money transfer behavior. KYC includes checking the client's name against a watch list of known money launderers or criminals. There are even data providers that specialize in the provision of such lists;[11] more often such lists are kept by governments and law enforcement agencies such as the *Specially Designated Nationals* list from the U.S. Office of Foreign Assets Control.[12] AML includes checking the behavior of clients against their anticipated or recorded profile. Specialized software that detects suspicious patterns in payment behavior can flag clients for investigation.

### Security Master

*Security master* describes the terms and conditions of securities. Typical terms and conditions were presented in the preceding chapter for the top-level CFI product categories. Information products on mutual funds contain, for example, information on the main holdings (if disclosed), on the mandate, pricing and trading information, and the fund manager. The number of terms potentially needed to describe securities is enormous. Many data vendors that offer larger aggregated products around security master have data dictionaries that contain many thousands of different fields. Especially in structured products, large numbers of parameters can be needed to fully and accurately describe the structure. Whereas a simple MBS may be described by a similar number of fields as a corporate bond (a few dozen), in a CMO this can expand into hundreds of fields. When an extra layer is added, such as in a CDO^2 or a CMO of CMOs or *reremic*,[13] the number of terms in the total structure explodes, and the number of parameters needed to completely describe the structure (including every ultimately underlying bond) runs into the many thousands or tens of thousands. Some content vendors specialize in providing this information; some of the larger aggregators provide only summary information. This is due to the variety of financial products and terms that arise mostly due to different profiles of investors and structures and different regulations and fiscal regimes to which products are tuned.

Note that reference data can mean different things for different instruments. For securities and exchange traded derivatives, reference data means a common objective set of terms and conditions of the instrument, the unambiguous golden copy, a single version of the truth. It is independent of the transaction. For OTC derivatives, there is a blur between instruments and transactions—here reference data can refer to the actual terms of the transaction.

## Corporate Actions

Within reference data, corporate action data play a special role. Corporate actions are initiated—as the name indicates—by a corporation. The different perspectives depending on the role that financial institutions and departments have on corporate actions are also reflected in the content products. There are pure corporate action feeds, as well as larger content products that contain corporate action information as an ancillary to maintain the security master. A special category of content products is that of the integrated corporate action product that aims to help out in this difficult data space. Here, some custodians or very large investors have been able to offer product in this space that competes with the pure aggregators. This is possible because they are in a unique position and can leverage or capitalize on the information they already need to run their own business. Examples of these products are Global Corporate Actions (GCAs) from DTCC and ActionsXchange from Fidelity.[14]

Although in the case of corporate actions, there are common message formats such as ISO 15022, there is still a need for data scrubbing, data comparison, and a second source. As there is a trend to clusters of custodians, the number of independent sources will diminish; hence, it may make sense to include, for example, a data vendor feed to have an independent opinion to cross-compare with. The increase in volumes and complexity of events has meant a requirement for specialist labor, for "people with data in their blood." The special thing about corporate actions is that in choice events (tenders, choice dividends) there is a dialogue between the bank, custodian, and owner of the securities; therefore, the information supply chain gets much more lengthy and complex. The total number of corporate actions is around 4 million, 3 million of which are scheduled interest payments and maturations. Of the remaining 1 million, the bulk are dividend announcements. What is left are the tricky cases such as the approximately 500 rights issues a year which require normally manual intervention. The more intermediaries, the greater the risk of information loss on the way. The corporate actions market is a harsh and unforgiving marketplace. Doing it right is hard; then nobody notices. But one missed action affects a large number of positions, so the consequences can be dire. Especially voluntary actions are not to be missed and can have very costly ramifications.

## Reworking the Corporate Actions Supply Chain

The trigger for securities operations is often a SWIFT message from a central securities depository (CSD) or an institution's own custodian department. Effectiveness could be improved by adopting a more *proactive approach*, e.g., creating an alert if you do not receive information when you expect it. Given the lengthy supply chain, sourcing data closer to the source would make a lot of sense. The burden could be put to the issuer, requiring the company to publish its announcement in a standard format to data aggregators or through the SWIFT network. Corporate actions often have an especially lengthy supply chain and the process is sketched in Figure 3.4. An alternative would be the exchanges or central securities depositories[15] because they would have more knowledge of different fiscal regimes. Indeed, the DTCC in the United States already has a corporate actions product. As it is, corporate action processing still leads to lots of operational losses. The main risks as defined in a report written by Oxera and sponsored by DTCC[16] are as follows:

- Direct risk of processing failures such as choice dividends and rights;
- Direct costs of late payments via interest accrued on late dividend payments, potential cash flow problems;
- Risk of suboptimal trading decisions by the front office if information is not quickly disseminated;
- Indirect cost of ineffective corporate governance through faulty proxy voting processes;
- Costs to reputation and costs of reconciliation through systems and staff.

## Information Issues in Corporate Actions Handling

Corporate actions have long defied automation because, just as in the case of OTC derivatives, everything is possible in principle. As an example, we list a few common data problems found in the area of corporate actions:

- Corporate actions that are discretionary such as tender offers. In this case there is a need for follow-up, and the custodian needs to secure a response from the owner of the securities. The information supply chain is an interactive process that needs to come up with a response before a certain deadline.

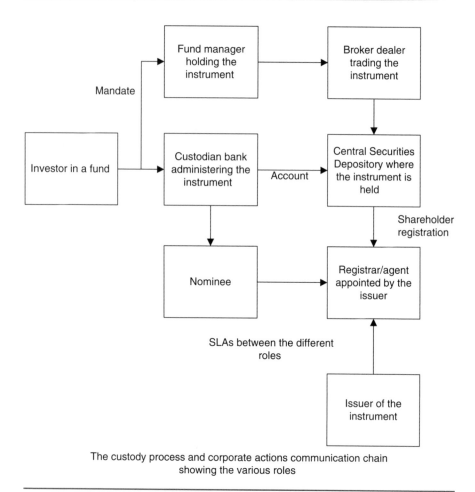

The custody process and corporate actions communication chain
showing the various roles

**Figure 3.4** Corporate actions communication flow

■ Embedded instruments where a corporate action takes place on an instrument that is underlying something else that is traded. This could be a warrant, an index, or something else. A separate internal announcement on the derivative that is affected by the event on the underlying (e.g., option, stock split) would be needed. In any case the structure of the derivative product needs to be clearly defined and linked to the corporate events on the underlying.

■ A need to *identify and track security family trees*, i.e., what happened over time to a security as a result of name changes, capital events, mergers, spin-offs, renaming, and new identifiers. This can mean integrating the corporate actions data with a legal entity data product.

■ If a company trades IBM shares in Germany and in the United States, for example, there will be delivery on two places. Stock will reside at different depositaries, e.g., DTCC and Mellon, or for depository receipts and common stock. Instruments that are fiscally treated differently have different ISINs, and often you will want to aggregate per ISIN code.

■ A choice has to be made on the granularity of the data and the processing model—for example, whether processing is based on an instrument or on a listing level. Representing events on an instrument level means a requirement to have some more depth to support, for example, multiple ex dates. (Some exchanges may have a bank holiday on the ex day.) Eighty-five percent of all corporate actions are plain vanilla and can be represented in a flatter model, e.g., not based on the listing but based on the instrument. The tricky cases that remain include multiple spin-offs; an entity that spins off something can also be subject to an identifier change.

■ The existence of multiple "fraction dispositions." Let's consider a 2-for-3 split and a current position of 5; this can be mapped to a new position, which will be 7.5; then the question is how to treat the 0.5.[17] Alternatively, we transform 4 old shares into 6 new shares, and the question is how to deal with the remaining 1 of the old position. Table 3.3 summarizes this discussion. The issue is that most vendors look only at the fraction post-split and not any fraction pre-split. Similarly, some information of layouts can be region or country specific, e.g., how to express ratios of splits. In the European Union versus the United States, a 2-for-1 split could be expressed either as a *swap 1 for 2* or *have 1 get 1*, 1:1 or 2:1, respectively.

■ Events can change or be filled in over time; e.g., a provisional dividend is followed by an exact dividend amount, or an additional option can sometimes be added. This means tracking the history of an event.

**Table 3.3**  Different Fraction Dispositions

| Current Position | New Position | Question |
|---|---|---|
| 5 | 7.5 | Treatment of fractional new share |
| 5 | 6 | Treatment of remaining old share |

### 3.5.3 TIME SERIES DATA

We will break the discussion on time series data into two parts. First, we will discuss basic pricing information. With this, we mean market-observed information. After this, we will discuss derived data such as risk factors which can be said to be price data that have gone through analytics.

### Basic Price Data

Time series and pricing data come in various categories, which we can distinguish by their frequency and latency. We distinguish between real-time, snapshots, historical, and end-of-day (EOD) data.

The term *real-time*, also called *streaming*, data refers to a direct quote and price stream from a broker or execution venue. It will typically include not only prices, but also time and sales information (level 2) detailing time and volume of transactions and order book information. The depth of the order book that is disclosed depends on the exchange.

Regulation on both sides of the Atlantic (REG NSM in the United States and MiFID in the European Union) aims to make this pre-trade information more transparent. The driver behind this is investor protection: to make sure the investor gets the best available price and can potentially shop around for execution venues. This means that if an instrument trades on various execution venues, an institution may need to consolidate different quote streams and order books internally to get the full liquidity picture. Other dynamic pieces of information closely related to pricing are volume and open interest. *Open interest* refers to the total number of open options or futures contracts. The speed and quality of streaming data depend on the exchange's trading system. In floor-based systems, the data on quotes and trades must be manually entered, whereas in automated systems the data are already there, so they will be reported in a faster and more reliable way. Streaming data are often made available in real-time at a premium price and distributed free or at a greatly reduced price in a delayed mode. The delay varies by exchange but ran range from 15 minutes to several hours.

*Snapshots.* For OTC markets there is no official close price; therefore, the institution that has to revalue a position has to take a snapshot at a certain cut-off point. Consistency in time for all instruments in the portfolio is important. Sometimes an institution takes streaming data from an interval around the desired cut-off point and takes, for example, the median or the average price to prevent a freak outlier or rogue price at the snap time from distorting the picture. Sometimes an institution takes, for example, the $16.00 price from a respected market maker in that particular instrument. Sometimes a combination of both is used, e.g., taking the median price of a set of trusted market makers approved by the risk control function.

*Historical data.* These can be historical end-of-day (official close or consistent snapshot) data or historical tick data. Historical end-of-day data can be used for risk management purposes and also to calculate the historical volatility needed to price derivatives. The 1996 Market Risk amendment of the Basel I accord proscribes a minimum of 1 year's worth of time series data to be refreshed at least once a quarter. Some banks use upwards of 5 years' worth of data for risk management (VaR, historical simulation). Historical data are also used for stress testing on top of normal risk measurement. Specific historical episodes that often play a role in stress-testing scenarios include the 1987 crash, 1998 downfall of Long Term Capital Management, 1997 Asian Crisis, 2000 dot.com meltdown, and 2003 slump. Apart from using these data to see the effect of shocks on the portfolio, historical price data can also be used to backtest portfolio and trading strategies.

Historical intraday and tick data can be used also for the backtesting of strategies that rely more on the microstructure of the market and can be used to study market impact and to measure liquidity. Market impact can arise both from a large volume entering the market, but also when the identity of the buyer and/or seller is known, this can have a signaling effect. In addition to this, historical data are used in the pre-trade area for research and for technical analysis.[18]

Price histories of some of the major exchanges go back a long time. In the case of the Dow Jones Industrial Average, the available history of stock indices goes back to the 1890s.[19] The history of credit ratings goes back to the early 20th century when John Moody realized there was a market for independent company evaluation and started rating railway bonds in the United States. This can be seen as early outsourcing of financial statement and credit risk analysis.[20]

*End-of-day (EOD) prices.* This can have two meanings:

- It can simply be the price that is used in the end-of-day process of a financial institution at whatever point the cut-off is.
- It can be the price that came about at the end of a trading interval/session, e.g., an official EOD of an exchange.

There are many different methodologies in place that various exchanges use to arrive at a close price. A close price could be defined, for example, as the volume weighted average price (VWAP) of the last 5 minutes of the trading session. Sometimes a close price is simply defined as the price of the last trade or best available price at the time of the last trade, e.g., in the case of NASDAQ.

When a portfolio needs to be revalued, some assets are easier to value than others. In the case of illiquid instruments, "mark to model" is sometimes the only option. Normally, banks employ one of two approaches. The quotes can come from an independent middle office function that collects them from trustworthy sources and signs off on any models that may be used. Alternatively, the quotes to revalue them come from the traders, and the middle office compares those against, for example, a neutral source from the market. Altogether, at least five different approaches are used to value the assets on a portfolio:

- ■ *Evaluated Prices*. Evaluated prices represent an opinion as to the accurate price which can be based on the instrument characteristics, market conditions, and price of comparable products at the time the evaluation is made. Evaluated pricing services have been started by data providers as well as by some banks such as Bear Stearns.[21]

- ■ *Contributed Prices*. A set of contributors provides input to arrive at a composite price. A pool of contributors can lead to an average price, a median price, or the calculation of the average after the highest and lowest price points have been discarded.

- ■ *Trade Prices*. Prices from transactions that the dealer has done are used; the trader reprices his or her own portfolio.

- ■ *Theoretical Price* or *Fair Value*. This refers to an "objective" valuation of the cash flows. In the case of government bonds of an OECD country denominated in its own currency, this is relatively easy. The bond is risk free and comes down to calculating the net present value of the cash flows using the bond curve.

- ■ *Exchange Data*. This refers to the use of official close data from a regulated trading venue.

In the pricing process, the breadth of coverage, timeliness, and accuracy are important criteria to evaluate vendor products. When a portfolio is revalued or when the NAV of a fund is recalculated, the prices also need to be consistent. Consistency refers both to timing and to taking the same side of the quote. Picking the ASK quote when you are long and BID when you are short would misrepresent the value and be too aggressive. Also the time of the quotes needs to be roughly the same; if not, events and market developments can be represented in part of the portfolio and not in another part. We will discuss these quality issues at more length in Chapter 5.

Time series data that are not available on a daily basis include macroeconomic data. Numbers such as unemployment, inflation, and GDP are typically released on a monthly, quarterly, or yearly basis. Financial statements can also be considered as time series data and are typically made available on a quarterly, semi-annual, or annual basis. These, we discuss in the research section.

The concept of time series is spreading beyond prices, order books, and volumes. As we will see later when discussing ratings, banks also have to keep histories of internal credit ratings and operational losses as part of new regulatory requirements under the Basel II accord. This allows for a more detailed quantification of credit and operational risk.

### Derived and Risk Factor Data

To make sense of the often very large sets of time series data, numerous statistics and indicators have been developed. Services such as RiskMetrics[22] provide market summary information which can already directly enter an application. RiskMetrics provides correlations and curves which can directly be used by a risk and pricing engine; several steps in the information supply chain, such as sourcing of the basic prices, comparing and validating them, and doing the calculations, are skipped. In a way, this is a data service provider, a service bureau that takes care of the data collection, scrubbing, and risk factor calculation.

Risk factor data from providers such as RiskMetrics are part of the group of derived data, i.e., calculated prices based on market data and the terms and conditions of the instruments. This category also includes yield curves, spread curves, implied volatilities (for example, from companies such as Option-Metrics), trade volume data, and other analytical measures such as the following:

■ *VWAP.* This is the volume weighted average price for a certain time interval. From all the transactions in this time interval, the price and volume are multiplied and then summed. The VWAP is the ratio of this sum to the total volume traded within the time period. It is a key benchmark to measure the level of execution of a trade, i.e., to see how good the achieved price is.

■ *Convexity Adjustment.* A correction factor used in the context of interest rate futures.

■ *Option-Adjusted Spread.* The part of the yield spread of a fixed-income security that is a result of the embedded optionality, for example, in convertible or puttable bonds.

These kinds of data will be used in pricing and risk systems and for portfolio analytics.

Another category of data is that of factor models which are often used in statistical arbitrage. Factor models are statistical models that represent instrument returns by a weighted set of common factors plus an instrument-specific factor. The weights are called *factor loadings*, and the factors can include macroeconomic variables, interest rate, inflation, credit spreads, stock index level, and volatility.

Derived data services are offered by many data vendors; it is in this space that there is more room for new entrants who can offer a superior valuation or modeling service. More importantly, the appetite for these products is large because they can directly drive revenue growth.

### 3.5.4 TRADE SUPPORT DATA

Under trade support data, we include all information needed to facilitate the transaction process. This includes contract data, data for the settlement of transactions, general lookup information such as "who's who" lists, and business holiday calendars.

### *Contract Data*

Contract information refers to the legal framework trading parties put in place and includes agreements on settlement terms. The settlement risk can be reduced by agreement between two parties to have all their dealings in a certain product type (e.g., credit derivatives) governed by the relevant ISDA master agreement. The first ISDA master agreement came out in 1992, and an amended one was published in 2002. The master agreement covers different product categories and for different geographical areas, and determines the basic framework within which two parties trade.

Under a master agreement, confirmations of specific trades fall under the provisions of the master agreement. This will, for example, imply a *netting agreement*; the cash transfers between two parties will involve only the balance of all the sums due for all the trades under the master agreement. *Transactional netting* means parties can net out amounts payable on the same day and in the same currency. The scope of *close-out netting* is broader. In this case, when a master agreement is canceled, all the transactions under it are valued to determine settlement amount. These settlement amounts are converted into a termination currency and added up; the result is one net payment from one party to the other.

Contract data also include the administration of which products can be sold to which customers. This includes both exposure limits to cap the risk of the institution and the set of "eligible" products for retail clients, high net worth individuals, professional counterparties, and so on. Increasingly, financial institutions have to take proper care that they offer only appropriate products to commensurate with a client's risk appetite and investment objectives. In the case of professional counterparties, contract information can also include details on "best execution" agreements that stipulate, for instance, the eligible execution venues for a transaction plus other execution criteria.

## Holiday Calendar Data

Holiday calendar data contain the business day conventions of a country or region—for example, listing the typical working days, Monday to Friday, or Sunday to Thursday and the bank holidays when trades cannot be settled—and can also include trading hours of exchanges. Holiday calendars can be organized by a geographical indication such as country, region, or city (normally country) or by trading center such as the exchange. Holiday information is often more complicated than thought at first because

- Holidays can be dependent on the occurrence of other holidays during the week or on the weekend.
- Holidays are sometimes announced at short notice, for example, to coincide with an election or other political event.
- Some countries have a mix of holidays from various religious calendars.
- The authority that determines the holiday varies. Sometimes it is enshrined in law; sometimes it is the central bank, a religious authority, or the government.

Holiday information is needed not only to know when to settle, but also for interest rate calculations, for example, to calculate the number of business days.[23]

## Settlement and Payment Instructions

This category of trade support information indicates how to route payments or where to settle certain products for certain counterparties. This category of information is typically pooled from the market players; after all, they have to specify where and how they want their trades settled, so the content again originates with the users. Settlement data include the following subcategories:

- Commercial payment data—this includes the SWIFT bank identification codes (BIC) directory and includes the CLS bank directory for settlement of foreign exchange trades.[24]
- On securities' settlement instructions, there are several "poolers" of account information; examples include Omgeo.[25]

Many institutions are only now starting to consolidate their settlement information. Historically, changes in settlement instructions were communicated over the phone or via fax or email. The purpose of electronically sourcing settlement instructions through aggregators is to increase STP, transactions processed without any manual intervention, and rates to cut costs. Any failed transaction will lead to costs for staff who have to investigate and possibly claims from the counterparty such as interest rate charges.

## Who's Who Directories

Who's who directories typically contain the names and contact details of dealers in various products. These directories can be divided into product types (e.g., overview of currency houses) or company types such as hedge fund directories. They are used as reference books and can also be used for sales and marketing purposes and for customer relationship management. Publishers of this kind of information include Euromoney.[26]

## 3.5.5 RESEARCH DATA

Within the category of research data, we include all information used to form an opinion on the value of a certain product. This includes the categories of fundamentals, estimates, and macroeconomic data, but it also includes credit ratings and news.

## Fundamentals, Estimates, and Macroeconomic Data

Earnings estimates and fundamentals are important data categories. Public companies have to periodically file their financial statements such as income statements, cash flow statements, and balance sheets. Information on past performance is therefore in the public domain and is disclosed in different ways. In the United States, there is the Electronic Data-Gathering, Analysis, and Retrieval (EDGAR) database, and SEDAR is the Canadian equivalent.[27] In some other countries the chamber of commerce keeps registers of companies and financial statements.

More interesting, of course, is the future. Many analysts around the world occupy themselves with forecasting earnings and dividends. This research is collected by large content providers such as Reuters (e.g., through the Reuters Estimates product) and Thomson (e.g., through the Institutional Brokers Estimates System, or IBES, product). Forecast information on different financial measures such as revenue, cash flow, dividend, earnings per share, and many accounting terms such as EBITDA is collected, and a standardization onto a common accounting standard such as US GAAP or IFRS is done.[28] Companies such as Factset[29] offer access to multiple underlying databases for financial information and analytics through one front end. This also includes information on ownership of equities. Many large U.S. institutions have to report their portfolio holdings quarterly to the SEC via the 13F holding reports. This information is assembled by data vendors such as Factset (Lionshares database).

Other research information is supplied by media companies that provide, for example, industry sector reports looking at the state and future of the oil industry, steel industry, and so on. This type of research is done both by departments within buy- and sell-side firms and specialist research companies.

## *News*

News is provided by agencies which can be commercial wire services, corporations (e.g., Reuters), and cooperatives such as newspapers that pool their content. Financial news on macroeconomic data, key hires, financial results, patents, client wins, lawsuits, and so on is actionable information and a major driver of prices. Companies such as Factiva provide add-on services to make the classification, processing, and distribution of news content easier.

The International Press Telecommunications Council (IPTC)[30] has created a standard for the formatting of news called NewsML. NewsML aims to facilitate the formatting and smooth the supply chain within news which is composed of agencies, editorial systems, news aggregators, and users. The standard includes meta information such as status information (e.g., a press release could be embargoed) and copyright information. Other than this, the standard allows for the identification of various multimedia types of content such as images and video. When used in archiving news, it should make querying and retrieving information easier.

Standards such as NewsML help to feed scanning software that analyzes news. This can be simple—for example, to scan for keywords such as company tickers to put a news item in the right bucket or to make personalized web pages—but also, more interestingly, to actually parse a piece of news, to be able to understand that it is an earnings statement, to filter out the key numbers of a company press release, and to then compare it to an analyst's forecast or to detect the positive or negative in a news statement. The automatic interpretation of news and also the ability to trigger orders/decisions from it is a next step. Protocols such as RSS help in filtering public sources on the Internet to create a custom news feed to a desktop.

Apart from the formatting of news to facilitate interpretation, vendors of news could also *flag* news stories to indicate interesting content, possibly based on clients' instructions. Apart from this, they can also offer *news archives*, which clients could analyze if they research, for instance, price behavior following certain types of news stories. Special news services collect, for example, information on mergers and acquisitions, such as Zephyr from Bureau van Dijk.[31] These kinds of services provide up-to-date information on M&A activity, venture capital deals, IPOs, joint ventures, and private equity deals.

## Rating Information

Ratings are assessments of creditworthiness of a retail or corporate client, of an issuer, of a financial instrument such as a bond or structured product, or of a country. They are either provided by research agencies through research on behavior, financial analysis, or statistical analysis, or created within a financial institution (internal rating). In this section, we will distinguish between the following types of ratings:

■ Credit ratings
■ Mutual fund ratings
■ Commercial ratings
■ Retail credit scores
■ Internal ratings

Each of these four categories is discussed in the following subsections.

## Credit Ratings

Several large rating agencies such as Moody's, Standard & Poor's, and Fitch dominate this market. These three agencies all have NRSRO[32] status in the United States, which means that their ratings can be used under SEC regulations. Smaller agencies include start-ups or specialists in certain product sets or geographies through deep knowledge of the local market (e.g., agencies specific to Japan such as Mikuni and JCR, Indian agencies, Canadian Bond ratings from Dominion). Credit ratings are normally based on accounting and macroeconomic models and are positioned as "through the cycle"; i.e., they are not a mark-to-market snapshot of creditworthiness, but a relatively stable and consistent assessment of credit which should last through a business cycle.

Credit ratings are assigned to issuers, issues, and countries (sovereign ratings). Typically, the issuer will pay to receive a rating because a rating will help investors to assess the product and will make it easier to sell securities. The rating scales go from AAA (or Aaa depending on the agency) down to D (default). Several other scales are in use to rate specific company types or products, for example, the Financial Strength Indicator for banks. Rating agencies also keep watch lists that indicate whether an issuer or an issue is likely to be downgraded or upgraded in the near future. The agencies have made their ratings products more granular, often providing both long-term and short-term ratings, for the local currency and for the foreign currency. *Composite ratings* present an average of various ratings, similar to a consensus estimate for financial results forecasts.

Credit ratings are used in product pricing, in credit risk management to assess the credit of an exposure, but also as a selection criterion on which to invest. Certain funds are allowed to invest only in products above a minimal rating, typically **BBB** on the rating scale, which is the boundary between *investment-grade* products and *high-yield* products.

Ratings agencies provide various add-on content products to help banks in their credit risk process. These products include the provision of a history of each rated issue or issuer and *transition matrices*. Transition matrices show the probability of an issue or issuer moving from one rating class to another within a certain time frame. The approach of assessing credit risk in such a way is also called an *actuarial approach* because it rests on compiled historical data. Alternatives would be to create an analytical model to simulate migration between credit bands.

Following criticism about ratings severely lagging market development in the early 2000s, new product development has taken place within the rating agencies to present more market-driven ratings. These developments include the Market Implied Ratings from Moody's that also incorporate signals from the credit and equity markets and financial statement analysis, as well as information used in the "traditional" ratings.[33] Other measures of credit that are directly priced in the market are through instruments such as corporate bonds and credit default swaps. Apart from these measures, the *expected default frequencies* (EDFs) of MoodysKMV[34] compute the credit risk for public companies through valuing the equity as an option on the firm using the Merton model. These developments have led to a continuum in credit assessment between research through macroeconomic and financial statement analysis and dynamic market information.

### *Mutual Fund Ratings*

Mutual fund ratings aim to guide investors through the enormous number of mutual funds available both by providing a classification of funds into styles (for example, Morningstar through its Style Box[35]) and by rating mutual funds within a certain peer group on their past performance. This can, for instance, be done by handing out a number of stars as a result of a statistical analysis on past performance.

## Commercial Ratings

Commercial ratings are also company ratings but are aimed not so much on solvency, but rather as an indication of supplier risk. They provide an indication of the time companies take to pay their bills. Therefore, they can be used by a treasury department or to predict working capital needs. They are not just used by financial services institutions, but more typically by companies with a very large number of (corporate) clients. The major provider of commercial ratings is Dun & Bradstreet.[36] Dun & Bradstreet also provides other information on companies and has the largest company database in the world. Its company identification number, the Data Universal Numbering System (DUNS) is one of the de facto standards in company identification and is, for example, required for any company that does business with the U.S. federal government. The rating from Dun & Bradstreet is called the Paydex score.

## Retail Credit Scores

Apart from ratings of corporate clients, banks also require an indication of creditworthiness for their retail customers. There are companies that compile credit reports on private individuals and companies that provide credit scoring models that can be used within banks to rate private individuals. Major suppliers include Experian and FairIsaac.[37] Many countries also keep national registers of credit exposure through loans and credit cards that can be consulted by banks and other lenders prior to granting new credits. Privacy laws have to be carefully watched in all these cases. The most commonly used credit score is the FICO score developed by FairIsaac.

## Internal Ratings

As the pricing of credit is the core business of a bank, one could ask why it is left to an agency. First, an agency rating is an independent assessment and therefore valuable as a second opinion. An analogy is in revaluing an investment portfolio where a company will normally not use the trader's own price, but an independent price instead. Second, agencies fulfill other roles as well. Their credit stamp on an instrument or structured-product SPV often has regulatory implications. For example, it can make the difference between an instrument or structure being eligible for investment by many pension funds and mutual funds.

Recently, internal ratings that banks used to assess credit and price loans have been more formally recognized by regulators as sound risk measures. Under the Basel II solvency rules, banks can calculate capital requirements on their banking book doing their own assessment of credit factors. The Basel II rules allow for different approaches to measure credit exposure. The first approach, the *Standardized Approach,* relies on external ratings only. With the second approach, the *Internal Ratings Based* (IRB) approach, the bank can use its own credit ratings to measure credit risk. This approach comes in two flavors, called the *foundation* and *advanced* approaches. Credit factors include the probability of default (PD), which a bank has to estimate itself when using the Internal Ratings Based foundation, and the Earnings at Default (EAD) and Loss Given Default (LGD), which a bank has to estimate itself when using the IRB advanced approach. For the IRB advanced approach, 7 years' worth of historical loss data is required to estimate LGD; 7 years' worth of historical exposure data is needed to estimate EAD. Five years' worth of historical data is needed to estimate PD already in the Foundation Approach of IRB. The approach under Basel II of allowing internal data to quantify credit risk is mirrored in the Advanced Measurement Approach (AMA) to operational risk measurement. Here, internal data on historical losses per business line and event type can be used.

Rating information can be extremely static, e.g., in the case of an AAA rated sovereign, but can also change repeatedly within weeks. Given the nature of "through the cycle," they will, on average, not change very often.

## 3.5.6 NEW CONTENT FEEDS

The market for content is developing rapidly. New vendors occur in established content types, but as financial product development and changes in new execution venues take place, we also see new types of content products. Speculating on areas where we could see more automation and product development, the following comes to mind:

- *Legal Feeds.* Content products which, for example, cover all court decisions in a certain jurisdiction. This can be on a retail basis to give information that affects a personal credit scoring (bankruptcy, divorce) or company rulings on, for example, new concessions, licenses, or anything else that can materially affect a share price or company credit assessment. Currently, this information could be constructed to some extent by filtering news feeds, but it could perhaps be obtained more directly. A data model to categorize court rulings would be needed to categorize information quickly so as not to be overwhelmed and to route information easily and speedily to users.

- *Property Feed.* A content product that provides all the property deals in the land registry. This can include a change of ownership, partitioning of a lot, new allotments, and information on transactions. Again, if this information can be filtered on, for example, certain cities, certain planning permissions such as commercial real estate versus residential, it would increase the value of the offering. This kind of information could be used in the nascent market in property derivatives.

- *Weather Data.* More and more information on temperatures, rainfall, and wind speeds is made available, both by the traditional national weather bureaus as well as by commercial meteorology companies. This information can be used not only for the current weather derivatives such as the CDD and HDD futures discussed in Chapter 2, but also as part of a commodity trading strategy. Temperatures determine, for example, natural gas consumption. This kind of information could be part of a total data strategy for commodity trading, including emissions. Because many investment managers have added commodities to diversify their holdings, the proportion of fund holdings in commodities has increased. Many hedge funds have been extending their trading platforms to energy commodities, seeking higher returns, as spreads in many regions and products have been attractive. Banks are offering power-based or emission-based risk products; and more hybrid products, products linked to indices such as the GSCI,[38] can be expected from the banks for institutional investors and retail individuals. These developments have caused commodities to be no longer fundamentally different from other products in trading. The main system providers in risk and portfolio management now have commodities integrated in their product lines, which means that the data supply to these systems should keep pace, too.

- *Mortality Tables.* This information is available but not easily disclosed. Longevity information is needed for life insurers and for longevity derivatives such as longevity swaps. Recently, indices have been defined in this space, for example, the LifeMetrics index.[39]

In all the preceding cases, the information is already there, but the content products are not yet fully up to speed to allow for electronic processing and easy integration with other data categories. New product development and processing demands for maturing markets will drive content product development for the foreseeable future.

### 3.5.7 COMBINING THE PIECES OF THE PUZZLE

The preceding sections covered content that is either publicly available or is obtained from vendors. In the case of proprietary data, such as transactions and holdings, there are other considerations in the supply chain. Whereas in commercially sourced data, users have to abide under the content licensing agreement; in proprietary data, there may be confidentiality agreements with clients, "Chinese walls" between different departments imposed by regulators, and privacy laws that restrict access to the information. This implies other restrictions on the use of the information.

All the various data categories discussed in the preceding sections are often serviced by separate content providers through separate information products. This has had its effect on the information architecture of financial institutions, which typically display a similar siloed implementation. Yet the value lies in combining these data sources and showing interdependencies between different content types. For example, consider the case of a CDO: When you are structuring a CDO, you need to pick names—e.g., preferences for individual company names, rating constraints, industry sector dispersion to stick to concentration limits, etc.—to accommodate the investors and to create an optimal portfolio. You need to piece together security master, rating, legal, and company information, as well as pricing information to get the full picture.

Other examples of the need for cross-silo information can be found in risk and credit assessment. To calculate an enterprise risk figure, you need market data and correlations on all held instruments, plus the aggregated holdings. In the case of credit assessment, you need to bring together nearly all these data types. For any company to which there is exposure, you want to know the different ratings, you want to know how its common stock is trading at several listings, and you want to know its corporate bond spread and the price of its CDS. For your internal assessment, you want your own interactions with that company, you want to know the legal structure, and you want to have the financial statements and the projections/estimates from the analysts. In addition, you want to be kept abreast of relevant news about the company, its executives, and its industry peer group. Bringing all this together and combining it with loan exposure is an enormous task which can be abetted by integrated content products. (See Table 3.4.)

### 3.5.8 THE RESULT OF INFORMATION: DECISIONS

In many cases the end of the supply chain is a decision—typically, a transaction. Transactions can be on behalf of clients or on behalf of the institution itself.

**Table 3.4** Different Activities that all Create Exposure to the Same Entity, in this Example Alliance Boots

| Treasury sales | Credit trading |
|---|---|
| ■ Foreign exchange/money market sales | ■ Alliance Boots GBP, JPY bonds or FRNs |
| ■ Cash management services | ■ CDSs on Alliance Boots |
| ■ Transaction processing | Equity |
| M&A | ■ Cash equity trading on Alliance Boots shares |
| ■ Bank loans | ■ Arbitrage against index |
| ■ Advisory services to holding or subsidiaries | ■ Equity derivatives |

A separation between these two order flows needs to be secured to prevent the bank abusing the client. When the order is large, the initiator will do well to hide it from the market, lest it is distorted through sheer volume or because the identity of the initiator and purpose of the trade are revealed. *Algorithmic trading* entails the chopping up of an order to possibly spread it out over a number of different venues so as to limit market impact. Order management systems have connectivity to a large set of different execution venues and help play the market infrastructure. Execution management systems (EMSs) aim to limit transaction costs. We will discuss this issue in more detail in Chapter 4.

Transaction cost analysis (TCA) is a metric of the operational effectiveness of the trading process. It measures the total cost of the trade and aggregates information on the following:

■ Direct costs, including tax, settlement charges, and fees and commissions;

■ Indirect costs, including market impact, timing gains or losses, and spreads;

■ Opportunity costs, including the cost of trades lost due to mispricings or wrong limit orders.

*Best execution* refers to an optimal execution in terms of a lowest TCA given a certain scoring of these factors. Methods to measure operational trading performance include the comparing of actual trade prices to other prices available during the day. This can be done in a simplistic way by simply looking at the price range during the day or in a more advanced way by taking the size of trades into account, such as through a VWAP measure or other benchmark. Other methods look at, for example, the total proportion of volume taken up by a certain trade and take into account price trends and market capitalization. A simple way to look at transaction costs is through the measure of *implementation shortfall*. In this case, you simply look at the difference between the value of an actual and a corresponding paper portfolio. For the paper portfolio, you use the prices prevalent at the time the transaction was decided: the difference between these decision prices and the actual prices at which the trades executed is called *slippage*. These methods can be used to score and compare an investment manager's brokers. Fund managers need to watch their costs; costs per trade add to the management fee for a portfolio.[40]

## 3.6 Licensing and Contract Management

The market for content is very large and growing. The length and complexity of the supply chain mean that content can enter an organization at different points in the processing. Some content will be directly distributed to a desktop, but other content will be processed automatically and can be distributed enterprise-wide. In Section 3.3 we gave some indication of the size of the content market; obviously, appropriate licensing is hugely important. In this section we will discuss licensing issues around content and various pricing models. We will end with some observations on the branding of data.

### 3.6.1 ENTITLEMENTS AND CONTRACT DATABASES

The term *entitlements* refers to the administering of rights on content and the reporting on data usage. Many data owners such as exchanges have started to appreciate the value of the content. Consequently, they have become more assertive about monetizing the value of their information products and are demanding more reports on data usage by user or by application. Therefore, it is important that users properly control and report on the usage levels of the data. Products such as Reuters DACS[41] can keep track of data use by different applications. The advent of digital rights management will secure a more prominent place for such applications in the future.

Vendors do not always have control on the downstream distribution of their content products because users can copy and paste information and route it throughout the institution or even outside. Apart from a true "black market for data," contracts are not always clear and unambiguous, and there tend to be shades of gray. Roughly, as far as the unauthorized use of data is concerned, we can distinguish between different types of "revenue leakage" for content providers:[42]

- There can be uncontrolled internal redistribution of data. Data may be passed on to users and applications outside the contractually stated use.
- There can be unreported external redistribution. For example, an institution can use price data in balance and portfolio reports to external clients.
- Data can be scraped or shredded from display products such as web pages, terminals, or broker pages. This practice, when not authorized, is also called *data snooping*. Although this process is far from robust—it tends to break down around Christmas when season's greetings appear on broker pages—it is nevertheless widely used.

Apart from this, there is also a fine line between commercially sourced information and any derivative content created by a financial institution's own proprietary models and content for which the vendor's content served as one of the inputs. When price data are used as part of the input to create something else—for example, an index or to price a derivative based on proprietary models—it is not always clear at what point a vendor's intellectual property claim ends. Vendors could claim that their content is critical whenever the result would have been different without their input. In any case, market data use is more and more carefully audited.

Licensing issues also occur between different trading venues. An example is the dispute around the ownership of prices used for settlement of trades in a *crossing network*. A crossing network is a type of ATS where buyers and sellers submit orders which are crossed periodically. The price used to settle successful crosses is typically derived from a regular exchange, for example, the average execution price during a time interval preceding the cross or an execution price picked at random from a time interval. In these cases, the exchanges may feel taken advantage of, the more so since the crossing networks also take order flow away from them.

Just as sometimes institutions may have overused certain data, they have also frequently paid for data they did not use. With procurement and sourcing becoming more and more centralized, these mismatches have become more obvious. Another reason that has brought these contractually permitted and real usage discrepancies to light has been the decrease in the number of processing centers of an institution as IT departments are consolidated and redundancies in processing addressed. Content licensing contracts and the invoices to which they lead can be very complex. To help institutions and their data users better match the usage needs of a department to available services in the market, contract and spend management for the content industry has become a niche industry in its own right. Contract management application providers and consultants in this space offer consulting services on (market) data needs and can offer packages such as contract databases, which include information on many commercial data products and in which a financial institution can keep track of its own purchased data inventories.[43]

## 3.6.2 PRICING MODELS

All pricing models are essentially about striking a balance between serving the customer properly and getting value out of an account for the supplier. They also serve to preserve potential upside for the party that is selling something; vendors normally do not want to sign up to an enterprise-wide, unrestricted, perpetual license to all the content they can offer because that effectively takes away an account from the market for the future. However attractive such a deal may look short term, invariably it is a bad idea long term.

Content is licensed and priced in different ways. Roughly, we can distinguish between the following pricing models around content:

- *Itemized Pricing.* This refers to pricing commensurate with the number of items and how often they are accessed. Often this is the case in "portfolio" type content products, i.e., products that deliver information against a customer's particular universe (e.g., a certain list of CUSIP, ISIN, or SEDOL codes of instruments). Pricing often is a dollar amount per item per time window, e.g., a month. A variation on this model is a pay per use or view report. This category is found at vendors that used to supply hard-copy reports, for example, on credit scores or on the legal structure of a company.

- *File-Based Pricing.* A less granular approach compared to itemized pricing is pricing on a per file basis, which can be done when a data product is partitioned into different categories. A product can, for example, be broken up into chunks representing different markets, geographical areas, or asset classes.

- *Usage Restrictions.* In the case of usage restrictions, pricing is not so much done on content basis, but on a usership basis. This will normally be done whenever an information product is offered in bulk. For example, the content may be offered to be used within certain business processes, within certain departments, by a certain number of either named users or concurrent users, within certain sites, geographical areas, and so on. In a user-count model, the unit of measurement has to be clearly defined. It could be a generic user account, a natural person, and there could be cases of persons sharing the same password/user ID. To what extent a vendor restricts this depends on the product. It does not make a lot of sense for a targeted niche product but does make sense for the larger aggregators.

There can sometimes be multiple intermediaries between the ultimate source of the data and the end user. Responsibility for the unit of count of content usage and for reporting it back to the source needs to be clearly defined. Typically, the final intermediary/user reports back to the originator.

A vendor's flexibility in pricing schemes increases with the size of the account; the largest accounts will be able to negotiate package deals which often go beyond just content delivery to include services such as training, support, or customized content products. Some of the key characteristics of main approaches to pricing are listed here (see also Figure 3.5):

■ The pricing model should first distinguish between systematic consumption of market data (through applications) versus individual consumption (through terminals) and will also be related to the way the content is made accessible. When content is made available through a file, the vendor can quickly lose control over where it ends up because it can be endlessly copied and sent throughout an organization. Enterprise-wide agreements can be struck to prevent this problem. A result of enterprise agreements could be that consuming companies still need to count usage to allocate costs internally; it is to some extent passing on the problem. If content is made available through a password-controlled display facility, a vendor can exercise more control. In *browser-based access*, instead of physically delivering

| Itemized Pricing | Bulk Pricing | User Based |
|---|---|---|
| Physical delivery, e.g. reports. Pricing per instrument or on a portfolio basis. Tied to a service model. Smaller usage. | Pricing per category, per market, per asset class or on a geographical or site basis (enterprise wide is the extreme case) | Physically tied to a desk, e.g. terminal products. User id/password controlled, e.g. via logons, sealed media. Concurrent user numbers. Department/generic id's. |

**Figure 3.5** Characteristics of different content pricing models

the content through a file or through messages, the content is made available for looking up through a web browser. This way, users can look up information when they need it. This approach can be useful to look up reference information. A related way of *user-oriented pricing* is providing information via *terminals*. In this case, access to data is tied to specific desks. Vendors do not always want to police their users, so controls need to be in place to prevent underreporting on data usage in terms of number of terminals.

■ Terminal products typically combine content with applications, e.g., for portfolio management, research, or trading. Advantages of these distribution methods are the extensive customization of querying that is possible and the potential combination with analytics and other applications. Information is directly brought to the end user but cannot be easily used in an automated process. The pricing chosen for file-based products will typically reflect anticipated wider usage.

■ Some vendors publish different versions of the same content, typically in different quality grades. A common example is that of immediate versus delayed streaming exchange data, but content products can also be offered in a full detail or summary version.

### 3.6.3 CHOOSING THE VENDOR: THE BRANDING OF DATA

When selecting vendors to fulfill the content needs of an organization, institutions will look at coverage, price, and service. But another element which plays a role in sourcing of information is that of branding of data. Although there is pure competition on cost in some data distributors, such as real-time exchange data, in other cases the influence of data branding is underestimated.

Sometimes the vendor that is first to market with a certain concept can retain a dominant incumbent position. In other cases, a vendor has become established as market leader, and users will want to use that—for example, Bloomberg in the fixed-income space. Data branding has to be worked in as a factor in the overall data quality discussion. From a sourcing perspective, to get around branding, an institution could use a double blind test, giving control groups of users access to at least two anonymous sources. Alternatively, to get around the branding, an institution could keep close scores on where two sources (the premium brand and a "B" label) differ and, if so, where and how. The relationship with a vendor's support team and other support can help position an information product more as a service and cement user loyalty.

## 3.7 Sourcing and Disseminating Information Internally: Technical Perspective

Vendor content can be made available and distributed internally in different ways. In this section we will explore some of them. First, however, it typically needs to be commingled or consolidated with internally sourced information. We discussed how that happens in Section 3.4 on the information supply chain. In Table 3.5, we just recap the main types of internal information.

### Data Delivery Methods

The technical delivery methods of content are closely related to the pricing and data usage control options a vendor has. They include the following:

- *Synchronous Versus Asynchronous Dissemination.* Whereas synchronous distribution occurs at regular intervals, asynchronous distribution can occur at any time and with irregular intervals, which makes it less predictable.

- *File-Based Methods.* Here, a vendor has split up its product over one or more files which the user can retrieve, typically through ftp. Normally, the files have clearly defined structures, and sometimes files are specially cut for clients. In that case there is flexibility in selecting which information fields are included and which objects (instruments, companies, etc.) are included. This selection can take place through a web browser, for example, or through supplying a shopping list file to the vendor. These are also

**Table 3.5** Classification of Internal Data

| Client Data | Market Data |
|---|---|
| ■ Limits for clients | ■ Internal holdings |
| ■ Internal ratings | ■ Trading limits |
| ■ Exposure | ■ P&L |
| ■ Management accounting information | Logistics |
| Management Data | ■ Contract management |
| ■ Market VaR | ■ HR, who's who, organization chart |
| ■ Credit VaR | ■ Compensation committee |
| ■ Operational losses | ■ IT architecture |
| ■ KPIs, e.g., costs per transaction | |

called *portfolio type* products. A disadvantage of files for vendors is that they can be easily copied and redistributed without the vendor's knowing.

■ *Reports.* This is a special case of a portfolio type product in which information is requested on a piecemeal basis, e.g., a particular credit report, a particular analysis of a certain industry sector.

■ *Streaming Data.* Here, a client retrieves a continuous price stream, either direct from exchanges via a direct market access (DMA) feed, through ticker-plant software, or indirectly through aggregators and software products.[44]

■ *APIs.* In this case, applications at the user site can directly access vendor content through using the vendor's application programming interface (API). The API will provide a number of function calls in which information can be retrieved. As data have to be requested and directly end up in applications, data usage can be more easily measured and controlled.

■ *Services.* The case of services is conceptually similar but makes use of a more standard architecture using XML and HTTP. Client applications can invoke a vendor service to request data. For the vendor, this has the same advantage as far as keeping tabs on data usage is concerned.

■ *Hard Copy.* The provision of paper reports or books, e.g., credit reports or handbooks containing listings of persons or companies.

The main characteristics of the different media providing data are summarized in Figure 3.6.

For a long time, there has been a trend for information to go electronic and to become more amenable to electronic processing through common data models. This process started with the ticker tape, which Edison patented in 1869,[45] through the rise of the telegraph and telex, through the Reuters IDN feed, through the move from reports first to CD-ROMs and then to file- or

| File based | Streaming data | Access via APIs | Access through services | Standard reports |
|---|---|---|---|---|
| Usability strongly depends on quality and consistency of data dictionary and the format of the files. (XML, csv, fixed width, etc.) | Speed, speed, speed. For direct action often raw data required which can lead to interpretation issues. | Direct integration with consuming application. | More loosely coupled integration. Typically addresses data requirements at a higher level. Meant for broad usage. | Aimed at end-user, ready-made. Collection and presentation of material effectively outsourced to the content vendor. |

**Figure 3.6** Different data sourcing characteristics

message-based electronic feeds with the rise of the Internet. Company reports and credit ratings have both gone this path. A more recent trend is to make data products more tunable to client needs through the provision of portfolio-flavored products and to make content accessible via APIs and services so that the customer can call for the data whenever it is needed. This last approach also has the benefit for the vendor that it is easier to control usage. For the customer, it may be beneficial that applications can directly use content so that part of the supply chain is skipped. This can be done only when the quality and coverage of the content offered this way are sufficient for the specific application; the fact that the application is then essentially "locked in" to that specific vendor is not an overriding concern.

## Data Dissemination Methods

Once the information is in-house, there are several ways of distributing it. It can be made directly available to end users by pushing through certain events or by having applications directly interface with vendors, or it can go through an internal quality assurance process such as discussed in Section 3.4. We distinguish between *direct* and *indirect* access to vendor data. Direct vendor access methods include the following:

■ Streaming data can be pushed through to users to keep them abreast of changes and to make sure fresh information is displayed. This pushing can be done to users' desktops, their email, their PDA, mobile phone, and so on.

■ It can be requested directly by the application by having the application call the vendor's API or by invoking a vendor's service. The application could also store it and periodically refresh the data by calling the vendor; however, this means redundancy and potentially stale data.

■ Browsers can be used to directly consult a vendor's database, and terminal products can be purchased to make use of vendor data.

These direct access methods are also commonly referred to as *point-to-point solutions*. Because they imply a separate connection for each vendor/application combination, they tend to give rise to convoluted architectures with many different data streams.

Indirect vendor access methods include the aggregation of files through an internal quality assurance process before making available the content to users and applications. If files are designed to be database ready—i.e., set up for automatic processing by clear structuring, and being self-describing through column headers or tags—this will facilitate processing. Information can pass through the internal information supply chain stages of normalization, matching, and validation. After this, the resulting golden copy information can be stored into data warehouses or operational data stores (see Section 3.4.6). On top of these databases, browsers or reporting applications can query the data, or extracts can be made to be fed into applications. An alternative would be to define a set of web services which would be made available to any application that has a need to consult information. This presupposes a common data dictionary or central registry of services using Universal Description Discovery and Integration (UDDI) across the organization. Updates on golden copy information could also be posted onto a messaging layer which routes them through to applications.

Apart from centralized data management solutions, an approach that is more evolutionary and that aims to leverage existing data stores is to make *mash-ups* using web services. In this case, content from third parties is sourced through services or APIs and combined with internally sourced content onto a web portal. The question would be whether data quality can be guaranteed when using such a disparate collection. There seems to be a Catch-22 element here: To be able to do this comfortably and confidently, you need a well-defined set of web services and a common data dictionary, in which case you probably would not have had data discrepancy issues in the first place.

Direct access methods can be used for content which affects only local decisions or where every microsecond counts. Indirect access methods will slow down the process of making content available but can improve quality and add value by providing an integrated overview of information.

## 3.8 Conclusions

In this chapter we looked closely at the various stages in the information supply chain from data origination to processing within a financial institution. We also looked at dynamics in the content market and at the different types of content financial institutions typically sourced externally. New players and products come up and generally—because of the lengthy and costly information supply chain—there will be more demand for products that can be more easily deployed.

■ From a content perspective, the products need to become more accessible in terms of using industry standard identifiers or providing cross-references between the most commonly used keys of instruments and issuers.

■ From a technical perspective, the products need to become more accessible in the sense that they should become easier to integrate either directly with applications (potential for vertical integration for software and content vendors) or with an organization's distribution infrastructure such as middleware.

■ From a user perspective, the products need to become more tailored to the actual data requirements. This means a tuning capability, both in terms of what information fields are received, but also offering a more granular selection on instrument types, markets, and so on. Products have become much more "pay as you go" rather than one-size-fits-all solutions. We see this trend already with more and more portfolio type content products launched where a client submits an instrument universe to the vendor, which then keeps the information on those selected instruments up-to-date. The success of this approach ties in with easier technical accessibility in the previous point.

The content industry has struggled to address the information jungle. On the one hand, selling directly into desk-level applications may be in the vendors' commercial interest short term. On the other hand, vendors have made their content products more flexible, both technically in the sense of more retrieval and processing options (files, XML, APIs, portfolio-style products allowing selection on specific instruments and attributes), as well as commercially (per use pricing).

The quality in terms of well-formedness of commercial data products varies enormously. The ultimate test for a data vendor's product quality is often to see how easily it can be integrated and automatically processed. Typical information management issues in content products are

■ A need for complete separation between content and processing markers; clarity on special values and spaces, nonavailable markers, markets such as "9999," and so on;

■ Unique identification of financial objects and their linkages.

Vendor products can range from well-structured XML feeds but also—still quite often—complete data jungles with pointers and in directions left, right, and center. When things such as special values and identification are not clear, making interpretations or assumptions at the moment of storing the data can be lethal and is never a solution.

In this chapter, we discussed some of the main players, main content types, and licensing and data distribution issues. In Chapter 4 we will discuss the transaction lifecycle: the research, trading, settling, and servicing of the financial products discussed in Chapter 2.

# Endnotes

[1]This idea of high-level source classification and presentation is due to Dave Hirschfeld.

[2]BOAT is owned by Markit, see http://www.markit.com/information/boat.html.

[3]These institutions thus pay to some extent for the privilege of getting their own content back.

[4]This includes vendors such as Wombat, Infodyne, Hyperfeed, and Logiscope.

[5]Some companies, through partnerships with data providers, also attempt to do this, e.g., Valuelink (http://www.valuelink.co.uk).

[6]Examples of these products include Security to Entity Crosswalk from Standard & Poor's, Telekurs, and Dun & Bradstreet, which includes a cross-reference between DUNS codes and Telekurs GK (Gesellschaftskey) codes.

[7]There are various data access techniques such as OLTP, which is transactional and means many short queries and updates, and OLAP, which stands for much more complex queries that impact a larger data set. Different downstream process needs impact data modeling choices because these two techniques do not go together.

[8]Various services, including Alert from Omgeo, pool this information from the institutions to make it available to brokers/dealers, thus simplifying this data-collection task; see www.omgeo.com.

[9]For example, supplied by tax offices or issued by vendors and numbering agencies. Some agencies start to assign International Business Entity Identifiers (IBEIs).

[10]*Source:* www.bvdep.com.

[11]See, for example, http://www.world-check.com/overview/.

[12]See, for example, http://www.treas.gov/offices/enforcement/ofac/sdn/t11sdn.pdf.

[13]A CDO squared is a CDO which is backed by tranches of other CDOs. *Reremic* stands for "Resecuritization of Real Estate Mortgage Investment Conduit" and is a transaction secured by a pool of MBSs.

[14]See http://www.dtcc.com/products/gca/index.php and https://www.actionsxchange.com/.

[15]Euroclear as an ICSD has asked ISO (June 2006) to create standards for issuers announcing corporate action information to CSDs.

[16]See http://www.dtcc.com/downloads/leadership/whitepapers/2004_oxera.pdf.

[17]These fractional shares are also sometimes called *script*.

[18]To what extent the past is relevant is almost a philosophical question and also a matter of taste. It is about data versus a judgmental-based valuation.

[19]Only General Electric is left of the original 30 constituents of the index; stock baskets of other major exchanges have seen a similar attrition rate.

[20]Longer time series than that of the DJIA exist in economics as well as in meteorology. A graph charting Dutch government bond yields has been compiled by Rabobank and goes back to the 1580s. Time series in weather data started in the early 1700s

when accurate temperature observations started to be recorded daily in both the Netherlands and in Potsdam at the Prussian court.

[21]See, for example, http://www.pricing-direct.com/benefits.htm.

[22]See http://www.riskmetrics.com/index.jsp.

[23]Major providers of holiday information include Swaps Monitor (http://www.financialcalendar.com/) and CoppClark (http://www.coppclark.com/).

[24]There is a need for more cross-references between national clearing codes in the absence of standards. Within the European Union, firms can use clearing and settlement systems that are located anywhere within the European Union. To quote from MiFID article 34: "Firms from one member state have the right of access to counterparty clearing and settlement systems in another member state."

[25]See, for example, http://www.omgeo.com/solutions/product.php?s=22&p=HJROUEAUGZ_1_0.

[26]See http://www.euromoney.com/.

[27]See http://www.sec.gov/edgar.shtml and http://www.sedar.com/.

[28]In accounting at least, data standards such as US GAAP and IFRS are enforced.

[29]See http://www.factset.com/.

[30]See http://www.iptc.org/pages/index.php.

[31]See www.bvdep.com.

[32]Nationally Recognized Statistical Rating Organization; see also http://www.sec.gov/answers/nrsro.htm.

[33]*Source:* www.moodys.com.

[34]See http://www.moodyskmv.com/products/files/RiskCalc_v3_1_Model.pdf.

[35]See http://news.morningstar.com/pdfs/FactSheet_StyleBox_Final.pdf.

[36]See http://www.dnb.com/us/.

[37]See http://www.experiangroup.com/ and http://www.fairisaac.com/fic/en.

[38]Weather data is traditionally used in the (re)insurance industry through products such as AirWeather, see http://www.air-worldwide.com/_public/html/air_worldwide_weather.asp and Climetrix, see http://www.climetrix.com/

[39]See http://www.jpmorgan.com/pages/jpmorgan/investbk/solutions/lifemetrics/calc.

[40]See also http://www.itg.com/offerings/tca.php for an example of a comprehensive methodology using manager timing, trader timing, market impacts, and missed trading opportunity costs, all as elements in TCA.

[41]Data Access Control System; see https://customers.reuters.com/developer/rmdsandtools/dacs.aspx?

[42]*Source:* FISD; see http://www.fisd.net/presentations/20031205redistributionoutline.pdf.

[43]An example is Screen consulting; see http://www.screenconsultants.com/home.htm.

[44]For example, from Reuters Market Data System (RMDS); see http://about.reuters.com/productinfo/rmds/.

[45]See http://patentpending.blogs.com/patent_pending_blog/2004/10/thomas_edisons_.html for interesting background information.

# Chapter 4

# Information Needs in the Transaction Lifecycle

## 4.1 Introduction

In this chapter we will outline the transaction lifecycle, all the processes surrounding a financial product transaction. We will discuss what category of data is important where; at which stage it enters the transaction lifecycle; and present the most important criteria for success for data in different processes in terms of speed, accuracy, completeness, and control. The processes around the transaction are depicted with various levels of granularity so that we can easily see individual process steps in the perspective of the complete activities of a large financial institution. This way, it becomes clear how activities such as research, trading, settlement, risk, and reporting are closely interrelated in information flow terms.

The chapter makes the case that the evolution of financial product types from the classic dichotomy between debt and equity to a risk continuum has put enormous stress on the core processes of a financial institution. The chapter also shows how this evolution has led to a corresponding variety in technologies and both content and software application product offerings that seek to address specific niches and to provide institutions with a specific edge.

Application software in the financial industry represents an enormously fragmented market with many hundreds of participants. Competitive advantage in the financial industry is driven by the ability to process greater amounts of data faster than the competition into unique investment ideas and product strategies. We will therefore discuss this increasing specialization and describe the information management challenge of more and more product types on the one hand with a flowering of technologies and niches on the other hand.

In addition, we will discuss how the basic distinction in transaction processes between the high-volume/low(er) margin business of standardized products and tailor made low-volume higher margin products affects information management. The former typically follows a highly automated system with automatic means for price discovery, settlement, valuation, reporting, and so on. The second type of process relies much more on manual work by specialists and on smaller, niche applications that are often developed in-house.

In this chapter, we will start out revisiting content and discussing the *information manufacturing* that goes on *within* institutions. We will discuss the main types of derived data produced by the various business functions on the back of content sourced through the information supply chain. After this, we will discuss the transaction lifecycle in detail. We will do this both in sequential order—covering pre-trade, trade, and post-trade and reporting on risk and performance—as well as through a short description of application types found running these processes, listing the main functions and criteria for success.

The discussion on the overall *lifecycle* of a transaction is to some extent modeled on the lifecycle of a financial instrument. Of course, the latter makes possible the former. After this discussion, we will address the increasing focus on *sound process* and follow in Section 4.5 with a number of use cases taken from various points in the transaction lifecycle to show which information quality dimensions carry weight where and what the specific content challenges are in each case.

# 4.2 The Information Manufacturing Business: Basic Versus Derived Data

## 4.2.1 INTRODUCTION

We discussed the sourcing of information in the preceding chapter, but all the processes in financial institutions essentially manufacture new content. Information coming in through the information supply chain produces decisions which cause new information. It can be in the form of quotes and transactions, specific newsworthy events such as corporate or political events, research opinions, margin and collateral calls, corporate actions, and so on. On a continuous basis, data are processed and have to be transformed into meaningful summary information on the *positions*, *performance*, and *risks* that are taken.

Viewed abstractly, business logic and information cannot really be separated in financial services. All business processes are just the logical conclusion and continuation of the supply chain that started with the sourcing of data; the outcome of business processes is actions and results. Whatever the business process, it contains algorithms that spit out new information on, for example, the following:

■ A risk-adjusted performance number

■ A credit opinion

■ A loan price

■ A trading idea

This ends the information supply chain and simultaneously brings us full circle: We can start again. The content produced by one institution's business processes may well go into another institution's information supply chain as "raw" information, waiting to be processed in turn.

Information advantages lead to making money and a profitable business. A financial institution makes its money through essentially a handful of different activities:

■ *Asset and liability management.* This is the classic banking business of borrowing and lending money, of making money on the interest margin, and of managing the exposure to various time periods of interest. This would include many financing areas including mortgages, export finance, and trade finance.

■ *Portfolio management.* The business of investing someone's assets—usually against a fixed fee reflecting the size of the portfolio and investment complexity plus often a performance fee. This fee could kick in only after a high-water mark is reached.

■ *Asset services.* Various services offered on assets such as custody and securities lending. This could be included in prime brokerage activities. We will discuss these activities in Section 4.3.4.

■ *Sales and trading.* The selling and trading of financial products at the institution's own risk.

■ *Investment banking.* Typical services around origination of new financial products (bonds and equities) as well as advisory around mergers and acquisitions (M&A).

How data intensive are each of these revenue-generating activities? Where are the pain points in scaling, in being more effective in becoming more productive? In short, what are the core processes and the software plus data to run them as needed? We will discuss these questions in general terms in Section 4.3 and cover specific examples in Section 4.5.

To avoid drowning in information and to be able to make sense of it all, institutions have to summarize, to repair/complete, and to transform information continuously as part of the final stages of the internal information supply chain. We will discuss some examples of each of these three categories in the following subsections.

## 4.2.2 SUMMARIZING INFORMATION

Often organizations are at risk of drowning in the oceans of data unleashed by a global diversified business. To this end, summary information is needed in the transaction lifecycle we will discuss later. This includes the use of market summaries or indices, use of risk factors, and use of benchmarks and risk indicators. Following are examples of these categories:

■ Indices are used to provide a summary of the market, as a benchmark to gauge performance, and as a basis for product development. In their role as a *benchmark,* they provide a measuring rod against which a portfolio's return is gauged. They can be the reference portfolio whose returns need to be mimicked or beaten. Often an institution that offers funds makes its own benchmark as a weighted average of publicly available benchmarks. Other funds with a wider mandate will often have no benchmark. The correlation of an instrument with its benchmark is called the instrument's *beta.* The difference between the return of a fund and its benchmark is called the fund's *alpha.*

■ In risk measurement, to keep the process manageable, an institution needs to condense and summarize information from potentially millions of instruments to a much smaller number of risk and performance indicators. An automatic process to achieve this is that of Principal Component Analysis (PCA). In PCA, first, the price histories of all instruments are taken; from these a Variance CoVariance (VCV) matrix is created. Out of these, the largest eigenvalues are taken, called the *Principal Components*, to summarize a very large number of financial instruments into the most significant drivers. The portfolio is then summarized in terms of exposure to the principal risk drivers.

■ Spreads are often also used to isolate and to be able to refer to a certain price or risk factor. Common examples are different spread curves (the difference between the credit curve and risk-free rate curve) to measure credit risk by, for example, rating, currency, or industry sector. Spread curves can also provide information on the connection between different markets. Examples include the following:

- *The TED Spread.* This is the difference in interest rate between U.S. treasuries and the Libor rate for USD. It indicates credit risk as Eurodollar includes default risk.
- *Commodity Conversion Spreads.* For example, the *crack spread* represents the price of conversion of fuel to electricity. The *dark spread* can be the difference between the electricity price when produced from coal versus that when produced by another generating fuel.
- *Basis Spreads.* This is used to designate the price difference between two related commodities, also a risk factor when you use one commodity as a hedge against exposure to the price of another commodity.

■ Another example of summarizing information is through credit scores, also discussed in Chapter 3. For bank loan pricing, we need local knowledge on credit risk and the relationship. This is a huge data information funnel, which in the end results in a single score. For retail credit scores, an enormous amount of information on profession, past debt, financial outlook, behavior, demographics, and so on is condensed into one number.

■ Simple statistics such as the average price, or the minimum or maximum. Open, High, Low, Close (OHLC) charts are often used to summarize a trading session. Average price (often weighted by volume) is used to score the price achieved.

■ Through hierarchy and dependencies between instruments and companies, credit risk can be summarized into exposure to *ultimate obligor*. The ultimate obligor is the highest point in the pyramid of legal structure. Summing up exposure from low level to high level is called *rolling up* exposure. Here, we summarize all exposure to various members of a corporate family into one risk number.

## EXAMPLE: CONDENSING THE TERM STRUCTURE

A good example of summary information can be found in the case of a yield curve. Suppose the curve goes out to 30 years. A full picture of the curve taking a point for every day in a 30 year span would mean in excess of 10,000 numbers. Typically, the curve is expressed by picking a number of *tenor points*, reflecting different maturities from short (ON, TN, 1W, 1M), intermediate (1Y, 2Y), to long (10Y, 15Y, 30Y). Intermediate points when required will be obtained through interpolation. This narrows the information to a few dozen numbers. By taking a functional form to fit the curve, we can bring the information down to 4, in the case of the Nelson-Siegel model, or 6 points, in the case of the Bliss model.

If we want to express the changes to the term structure, we can look at the principal components. Heuristics for curves are to express the 3 principal components as "shift, twist, and curve," meaning the size of the parallel shift, size of the twist (tilting or change in slope of the curve), and change in curvature. These 3 factors catch the bulk of the information of the change in the whole curve.

### 4.2.3 SUMMARIZING A FUND

A portfolio or fund can consist of thousands of different holdings. We could summarize that portfolio in terms of *Net Asset Value* (NAV) to express the size or value or *Return* and *Value at Risk* (VaR) to express the riskiness. Summary information can also include the mandate, the portfolio's benchmark, its largest holdings, the trading style and degree of freedom, for example in borrowing money, for the portfolio manager. For rankings we can use ratings against its peer funds. Other summary information for portfolios is often expressed through various ratios, for example, the *Sharpe*, and *Treynor* ratios, which express different risk and return measures.

- The *Treynor* ratio is defined as:
  Excess_return/Portfolio beta, where Excess_return = Annualized_portfolio_return – risk_free_return
  This ratio measures returns earned over a riskless investment, scaled on unit of market risk (beta).

■ The *Sharpe* ratio scales the risk premium for the portfolio by its standard deviation and is defined as follows:
Excess_return/Annualized_standard_deviation_of_returns with Excess_ return = Annualized_portfolio_return – Risk_free_return

In both cases, the risk-free return is that of the risk-free interest rate. Note that this is not a constant and needs to be refreshed daily and kept in sync with the length of the reporting period, so take the right tenor point from the term structure.

### 4.2.4 TRANSFORMING AND EXTRACTING INFORMATION

The transformation of information means restating it into something else and includes many mappings that we discussed in the content of the information supply chain, such as standardizing on naming conventions. It is frequently used to automate information flows between applications with different (implicitly) embedded data structures. It includes transformations such as the following:

■ *Scaling* prices to express them in a common base. For example, a move from penny-based prices (e.g., for London Stock Exchange listed shares) to British pounds, to express prices in the same reporting currency, or to restate commodity prices into a common unit of measurement for financial reporting. (For example, conversion in the case of natural gas can be to change the price from US$ per mmBTU into CAD$ per gigajoule).

■ *Filtering* information through criteria such as AND/OR conditions, being in or not in a certain subset, equal or not equal. For all information that takes place in a certain time interval, we could note the earliest, latest, and average arrival time. This could, for instance, be used to measure response times for execution venues, but also to rank custodians in how fast they relay and correspond about corporate actions. Filtering information is often necessary to prevent flooding users and systems with irrelevant information. So filtering is also a special case of summarizing.

■ *Arithmetical operations* such as adding, subtracting, multiplying, or dividing information by a constant or by a dynamic element (e.g., a currency rate). These are the basic operations to, for example, create a spread curve or to do any transformation.

■ *Implied prices from related instruments.* Economically identical instruments should have identical prices. Through insight into price determinants and risk factors, we know that often pricing information is implied, for example, through related products which should move in tandem. Examples include the following:

- Extracting implied foreign exchange forwards and deposits. If the EUR 3M deposit, the EURUSD spot price and the EURUSD price in 3 months are all known, we can infer the USD 3M deposit price. Similarly, if the USD 3M deposit price was known, we could have inferred the EURUSD 3M forward price.[1]
- Foreign exchange triangulation. If the EURUSD and USDJPY spot price is known, the EURJPY spot price can be inferred.

  The process of implying prices can also be done when information is complete; in that case the implied prices can be used both in the post-trade process as a validation against the prices used in revaluing the portfolio as well as in pre-trade to find arbitrage opportunities.

■ *Implied additional pricing fields.* Often different price expressions exist for the same instrument, and conversions take place between the two or one is added to the other—for example, change from price to yield for fixed-income instruments or change from price to (implied) volatility in the case of options. If different pricing measures are used for different instruments, these conversions provide for a way of comparison. Note that clean reference data (for options strike, expiry date, option type, risk-free rate, underlying; for bonds coupon rate, maturity date, payment frequency, daycount convention, redemption price; and possibly optionality elements including call schedule and conversion price) are required to be able to do these calculations accurately.

Mappings also include many other types of operations such as table joins, filters on equality/inequality, null conditions of table values, creation of substrings (to find common elements in, for example, legal and security names), concatenation (to create, for example, an identification that is composed of several descriptive fields, e.g., in the case of options, one-to-one mappings, cross-references, and so on.

### 4.2.5 REPAIRING AND EXTENDING DATA

Another common data problem is that of filling in a missing value in a set of values. In the case of a time series, this can be a missing value which can be filled in by various ways with varying degrees of sophistication and use of context knowledge, such as

- Propagating the previous value;
- Interpolating through time between the previous and subsequent value;
- Using statistical estimation techniques such as the Expectation Maximization Algorithm;
- Using a proxy time series, either directly or by scaling the reference time series. For example, when missing a value for an equity, take the previous value of the equity and apply the return of the index times the beta to it. Alternatively, it could be proxied more specifically by taking the return of a peer group and applying that to the previous value.[2]

Other cases where a missing value has to be filled in can be found in completing, for example, a yield curve. Often, fresh data are available for part of the curve, but data for some intermediate points or the long end of the curve are missing. Tenor points can then be filled in using interpolation or extrapolation techniques such as

- A linear or loglinear interpolation or extrapolation;
- Interpolation via cubic splines or other polynomial methods;
- Finding a certain functional form/expression that characterizes or approximates the curve and then using that form to derive values for the required tenor points—e.g., using a model such as Nelson-Siegel, which is a four-parameter model to describe a government bond curve. The parameters of the Nelson-Siegel model would be estimated by the available data; this results in a function which can also be used to obtain values for the missing points.[3]

The specific interpolation method needs to be chosen in an intelligent fashion, i.e., reflecting knowledge of the product underneath. Cubic splines should, for example, not be used to extrapolate very far out; since the interpolation elements are polynomials, the values can become very large. Also, always check whether the results make intuitive sense: When a spread curve or credit spread becomes negative, something may be wrong with the benchmark.

To find errors in price data that need to be repaired or screened, we can run many validation functions. These could be functions in the following areas:

- *Source Comparison.* Compare two or more carriers of what should be the same information.

When calculations take place on raw data obtained directly from the markets, there are often thorny data repair and estimation problems. An example of a thorny-derived data problem is the difficulty in constructing an equity (index) volatility surface which is needed to value options positions. To construct it, we take observed option prices from the exchange. Issues include the following:

- *Stale Prices.* Quotes given by market makers may be outdated.
- *Low Liquidity.* There will not be many transactions and large open interest for many contracts, especially those far out or far in the money. Most of the value and trading activity will be around the at-the-money contracts.
- *Very Large Bid/Offer Spreads.* For example, in a quote of 0.05–0.15, it makes a big difference whether the bid or the offer side is taken. Also, in some cases a dealer may quote for only one side, and the bid or ask quote will not be available. Information on the open interest may also not be available.
- *Many Methods and Functional Forms to Fit a Surface.* This means that if, in the absence of out of the money data, points are fitted around the at-the-money point and near-term contracts, there can be wild swings at the extremes of the surface depending on the fitting method chosen.

Often a lot of assumptions and proxies need to be made, for example, taking the index on which there will be more liquid option contracts traded instead.

- *Semantic Validations.* In some content areas categories of filters with domain knowledge built in can be used: for example, for a retail CRM system, logic that knows the format of addresses, that has knowledge of postal code format and street name writing conventions in different countries. These validations could also include spelling and capitalization rules in languages and could expand on, for example, abbreviations of company legal forms.[4]

- *Reference Data Consistency and Presence of Information.* Check various fields in the terms and conditions for consistency. For example, if a bond is callable, a call schedule must exist and vice versa. In the case of an option, there must be a strike. When a maturity date and an issue date are present, the issue date must be smaller than the maturity date.

- *Market Data Consistency.* In case of a quote with a Bid, a Mid and an Ask consistency can be checked. Bid must be smaller than Mid, which must be smaller than Ask, and Mid must be the average of the Bid and the Ask. For a quote at the end of a trading session day which contains the Open, High, Low, and Close fields, the Low must be the smallest; and the High, the largest value. These sound like trivial checks, but they can help to uncover errors. More involved market data consistency checks can be done for economically similar or identical instruments, e.g., through foreign exchange rate triangulation and the forwards/deposits examples mentioned pre-viously.

- *Plausibility Checks.* In this case price movements can be checked against historical standard deviations or versus the change in a benchmark.

- *Tolerance Settings on Price Behavior.* Different data repair and data validation functions will be chosen with different parameters depending on the instrument type. A simple example is a threshold on return and marking everything that changes by more than a certain percentage or certain number of standard deviations. In the case of curves, we could use different percentage change tolerances for a curve, e.g., a different tolerance for the ON point versus that of the 10Y point. Stricter checks will be imposed on, for example, OECD currencies, and there will be a higher tolerance for instruments where bigger swings are expected, such as small caps, exotic currencies, and illiquid corporate bonds to prevent too many false positives.

The various types of derived data such as summarizing, transforming, and repairing discussed in this section overlap to some extent. Transformations are also used to summarize, and validations are one of the summary metrics when it comes to data quality.

## 4.3 The Transaction Lifecycle

In this section we will look at the main steps in the transaction lifecycle: How do transactions come about? How are they executed? And what happens afterward? We can think of the various business functions involved as the geographical areas on a map. How will we define our itinerary? Various routes are possible—for example, by organizing the discussion on the differences between over the counter and exchange-traded transactions, by client-initiated and proprietary transactions (buy versus sell side), or on the two fundamentally different process models of flow-traded products (commoditized asset classes such as foreign exchange and cash equity) versus that of tailored products such as exotic options and structured finance. Once again we will take the lifecycle approach and address a transaction from pre-birth and birth (two parties strike a deal and agree on terms) to death, when final cash flows are exchanged and both parties no longer have any liabilities arising from the original transaction. While doing this we will discuss the main types of applications found that serve every stage in the trade lifecycle. The main steps we will describe in this section are the following:

- *Pre-trade.* This includes the generation of trade ideas, the price discovery process, short-term and long-term research, and product control. On the applications side, this includes (pre)trade support systems such as analytics toolkits, quoting, and market-making systems and research applications.

- *Trade.* How are trades executed? Who is the counterparty? What are the various trading strategies' execution models and execution venues? We will discuss the information needs for different trading strategies, latency, order types, and liquidity. On the applications side, this includes algorithmic trading, execution, deal-capture, and order management systems.

- *Clearing and Settlement.* What is necessary to make sure that cash and financial product change hands safely and timely. We will discuss trade matching, various central counterparty services, and barriers to integrated clearing and settlement that still exist in the (EU) industry. From an applications perspective, we will cover post-trade systems including settlement systems, electronic trade confirmation, trade-matching systems, payment systems, and ownership transfer.

- *Asset Servicing.* What happens to products (securities) once you own them? They can cost you money (through, for example, custody fees), or they can make you additional money (e.g., through securities lending operations or other yield enhancement methods).

- *Risk, Reporting, and Performance Management.* This includes activities such as portfolio valuation and portfolio analysis, risk reporting, compliance, and financial reporting. From an application perspective, it includes portfolio management systems, Net Asset Value calculations, fund accounting, attribution, and performance measurement applications. On the risk side, it includes systems for liquidity and cash management, collateral management, market, credit, operational risk, internal rating systems, accounting, and general ledger system. We will discuss audits in Section 4.4.

Instead of this process breakdown, the market has also traditionally been split into front-, middle-, and back-office lines. Because functionality from one area to another has become more integrated, this division is not all that useful anymore. Outsourcing and offshoring have, on the one hand, led to a decoupling of functions, often across different entities. Similarly, many financial institutions offer services in one or more traditional back-office activities; they have, in fact, made back-office services such as revaluation, processing, matching, and custody into separate lines of business (and thus into new front offices). A schematic breakdown of activities is provided in Figure 4.1.

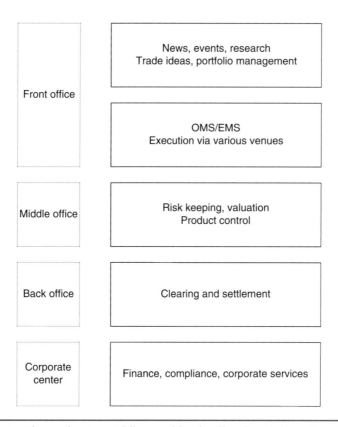

**Figure 4.1**   Classic front-, middle-, and back-office breakdown in a financial institution

Data are extremely important in the whole lifecycle—indeed, so much so that financial institutions can be said to be in the financial information data management business. This is also reflected by the IT budgets found in financial institutions.[5] Firm-wide consistent data dictionaries and standardization are often prerequisites to successful projects. All these application areas and business processes mentioned have their own unique data needs depending on the complexity of the product processed. Information needs vary in the following terms:

- *Frequency of Delivery*. Varying from streaming data for pre-trade to rubber-stamped end-of-day prices for NAV calculation and market risk control.
- *Granularity of the Data Sets*. From a reference data perspective, a trading system would need a few attributes to identify and price the security,

whereas the custody and portfolio system would need to know all the ins and outs of cash flows and potential corporate events. From a pricing data perspective, an order execution management system would need to have all the level 2 information (quotes from all the dealers or the order-book from the exchanges) to intelligently route the order; a collateral management system would just need the last prices to revalue the pledged securities.

■ *Size of the Universes Delivered.* Obviously, applications in different business lines seek information on different products, but within a business line different users will need different sets of securities. The settlement and portfolio system will need information on actually traded securities or products in which the institution has an open position. A trading or research system may track a much larger group of eligible financial products. A custody system will need detailed information on all instruments held in custody for every single customer.

■ *Preferred Sources.* Different end users could have different preferences as to the vendor they want. The branding element of content should not be underestimated; see also Chapter 3.

Note that this breakdown in steps in the transaction lifecycle is a gross simplification (see Figure 4.2). There are often many extra steps and complications that greatly depend on the specific product and market. Continuing specialization and competition foster new niche areas in which institutions can differentiate themselves from the competition. This in turn creates new niches for products.

The traditional silo nature of the organization charts of financial institutions is to some extent mirrored in product offerings. Products offered by content and software vendors compete for budgets held by product-line–oriented businesses. Hence, a silo budget structure leads to silo-like product offerings and silo-like licensing agreements. The task of putting in place lateral links is typically an afterthought and left to local implementations.

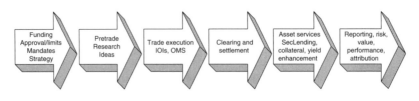

**Figure 4.2**   Transaction lifecycle

### 4.3.1 PRE-TRADE

Pre-trade is about coming to (tactical) trading ideas or trading strategies and getting the groundwork in place to be able to do trades. On the information-gathering and research side, this can be on a macro level to decide on a trading strategy that best reflects the company's resources in terms of human capital, clients, geographical presence, and other infrastructure. On a micro level, it can be about market timing, specific instrument selection, and so on. In terms of putting in place all the boundary conditions for trading to take place, this includes funding of trading activities, a mandate in terms of product, capital, counterparties, and risk limits. In the area of pre-trade, we can distinguish between the following activities:

- *Idea Generation and Research.* Research groups within banks and investment managers can cover macroeconomic and country-level research (sovereign ratings, business climate, default risk), which can be used, for example, for country allocation of funds. Apart from this more strategic research, the research function can also include more focused research groups that do, for example, cheap/dear or relative value analysis of certain parts of the bond market and that produce very specific and immediate trade ideas for their own front office or to pitch to clients to generate deal flow for the bank.

- *Product Control.* When an institution concocts a new structure (e.g., an exotic derivative) that it wants to sell to institutional clients or thinks up a new fund for the retail side, it has to go through an approval process. This is the role of product control, which is typically part of risk management. The job of product control is to check whether the risk factors in the product offered are properly understood and properly priced. It can also include determining eligible clients for this product as part of a marketing strategy.

- *Simulation of Returns.* To simulate returns, large historical data sets of prices can be required to run sample portfolios and to backtest trading strategies.[6]

- *Limits.* These limits are set by, for example, a credit committee or by trading operations management to guide the trading activities and to control exposure to a counterparty or category of counterparty (by country, by industry sector), or by risk driver (e.g., exposure to the U.S. stock market, the Japanese stock market, the Australian Dollar). A benefit of using a central counterparty (using central OTC clearing services) is that this works around limit constraints, and the credit risk of one counterparty will no longer be a constraint for business.

■ *Legal Trading Groundwork.* Part of the pre-trade process can also be the establishment of a legal framework with your counterparties. This includes completing documentation including master agreements, compliance documents such as Qualified Institutional Buyer (rule 144a) documents, clearing agreements, repurchase agreements (repos), and so on. Some organizations have a document control function that checks whether all the paperwork is in place. This can also include, for example, checking *corporate resolutions* which tell you which individuals are authorized to act on behalf of a company.

■ *Operational Groundwork.* This includes getting the administrative details right, including the sourcing of settlement instructions, basic data such as names and contact details, and creating a record in the counterparty database. This can all be done post-trade, but doing it ahead of commercial activities is more efficient.

■ *Working Capital.* To start a trading operation, an institution requires this capital to do the trades. In this case, there is often a link with an institution's treasury department. Treasury includes activities in cash management and short-term hedging and can also be deriving data to mark futures and swaps contracts and to monitor liquidity risk management and funding costs.[7]

■ *Price Discovery.* Here, the pre-trade process differs also by market. In OTC market, prices can be found on bulletin boards, by bilateral quote requests or IOIs through counterparties, or by using a broker who aggregates quotes and arranges trades. In some markets, the price discovery process is outsourced to central execution venues such as exchanges. In a quote-driven exchange market, there are roles such as market maker/dealer who have to continuously quote two-way prices and who are the counterparty to every trade. When there are enough buyers and sellers, an auction market model can function, and there is less need for someone to "make the market," since it already exists. In case of a large deal flow that comes to the institution, trades can also be *crossed*; they are arranged between the institution's clients.

Application types found in the pre-trade area include analytics providers and analysis tools[8] but also general reporting tools[9] typically used for longer term research. Excel and streaming data analysis[10] are used for shorter to ultra-short term research. When low latency matters, traditional databases no longer work where information first needs to be stored to disk before it can be exposed. Database technologies determine the query/information retrieval speed and thus latency. Low-latency requirements have driven innovation in this area. One complicating factor is the sheer volume of messages in the pre-trade area, which means that the relevant bits need to be filtered out.

In the whole trading process, there is a distinction between proprietary information (employing the institution's own capital and seeking revenue from market movements) or customer information when acting on behalf of clients (seeking revenue from client commissions). In both cases information on the trading counterparty is needed to facilitate the processing, including SSI data and basic data. In the latter case, information on these customers needs to be in place, including the following:

- *Regulatory Information.* This includes the initial screening of a client, as well as subsequent client behavior screening (AML); this can be online in real time, so before the transaction or payment goes through, or by retrospective analysis.

- *Policy Information.* This includes a set of products the client is allowed to trade, a set of eligible execution venues as per the client's instructions (more venues could mean better prices but will also mean higher trading costs), discretion in order execution, mandate when the institution is investing on the client's behalf, trading limits, and a list of trading-authorized persons from the client, possibly detailed by product and amount.

Many regulations have come into play to make the price discovery process more transparent, but especially to make sure that counterparties obtain the best price available in the market at that time. REG NMS in the United States and elements of MiFID in the European Union aim to provide for more transparent pricing information and price dissemination.

## 4.3.2 TRADE

### *Trading Styles and Data Needs*

This section covers *sales* and *trading*. We will discuss the implementation of trade ideas that are the result of pre-trade research (*trading*) or the result of client orders (*sales*). We will discuss various aspects associated with putting a trade into effect—for example, issues such as liquidity, costs of trading, volumes, and various different trading strategies.

The implementation of a trading strategy leads to orders. Orders are generally triggered because of conditions that occur that make implementing the trading strategy meaningful. The reason can be that (in the case of arbitrage) the price of certain instruments reaches a certain level or (in the case of event-driven strategies) certain events occur.

Data needs differ depending on the trading style. A plethora of trading strategies leads to very different data needs. Often a strategy will be about isolating a certain risk factor—for example, in equity index arbitrage, buying the index (future) and selling (the large-weighted) constituents; for credit trading, buying a corporate bond and selling the government bond future to isolate the credit spread. If you are doing a arbitrage strategy, the key activity is creating clusters of related instruments, baskets so as to isolate the risk drivers. Arbitrage or relative value trading involves instruments with similar risk factors/correlation.

In the case of a directional trading strategy, research and news, or general information about the direction in the risk factor to which you are seeking, exposure is critical so that you can fully form your view. With this type of trading, unlike relative value trading, big losses can be incurred if the factor moves against you and you cannot timely close out the position. From a regulatory capital (VaR) perspective, this is also much more expensive. You will seek exposure to those risk factors where you believe to have a competitive advantage.

In case of statistical arbitrage, very large histories of tick data are needed, e.g., to create liquidity/market impact models, simulation, tick, and real-time data. If, by contrast, you are a classic stock picker, you will study market fundamentals plus the financial statements of the company and will not require real-time data.

Statistical arbitrage is about the screening of quote streams. Event-based trading is about the scanning and interpreting of newsflow. Although these strategies have historically been less time-critical, tentative steps toward the automation of newsflow interpretation have been made. Parsing of news can be about scanning the news for keywords, or when the news story has been made up or tagged (see Chapter 3 regarding NewsML), financial statements could automatically be constructed out of the news story and be checked against consensus forecast. More complex newsflow interpretation is about looking for the sentiment in a story, picking up on words and counting them to see whether the prevailing tone is positive or negative. In Chapter 3 we referred to untreated news, made-up/formatted/flagged news, and archives. Mining of these news archives could lead to ideas to be used in trading strategies.

As the number of tradable products with reasonable market depth increases and as the timely access to market data on these products improves, more and more trading strategies become viable and cost effective. A lot of trading volume is driven by hedge funds. New arbitrage strategies around credit using the credit indices, around volatility, and correlation develop all the time. The number of players with (independent) trading operations has also increased dramatically.

A high-level distinction in process is that between a *flow* business where orders come to you from customers and where you are selling and trading low margin/high volume products such as foreign exchange and cash equity. This can be contrasted with the *bespoke* high margin game where you will uniquely tailor offerings to your clients who come to you for your expertise rather than for your low prices. The data requirements and internal processes will be fundamentally different. In the first case, you need to publish prices to *attract* orders; in the second case, you are continuously screening the market to find opportunities. It can be done together, e.g., screening the market to find trading ideas for your clients if you cannot commit your own capital to those trades.

Hedge funds can be seen as the spinning off of an investment bank's dealing room into a separate entity. Whereas they used to be a part of an overall bank with advisory, sales, and banking plus various support functions around them, hedge funds have raised capital independently and made independent trading operations. One result of this is that many services that banks provided for their own trading room—the research function, analytical tooling, data services—are now available as products and services for third parties and are serving hedge funds.[11] Hedge funds differ enormously in styles,[12] and the market data needs are determined by the trading style.

Some funds will change the portfolio within a day. Funds that engage in quantitative analysis and arbitrage will track real-time data on correlations; funds that engage in event-driven and macro strategies will have different needs.

At the end of June 2006, total hedge fund assets under management were over \$1.2 trillion according to Hedge Fund Research Inc.[13] According to Hedgefund.net, total assets grew toward \$1.9 trillion at EOY 2006.[14] The total number of hedge funds runs in the thousands and was over 6,700 at the end of 2005[15] and 9,000 at mid-2006.[16] Hedge funds started to take off for the same reason as derivatives: in the late 1970s and early 1980s when foreign exchange rates and interest rates began to fluctuate more wildly.

Not all hedge funds have technological sophistication; many rely on vendors and prime brokers for infrastructural services. Trading styles are also determined by the asset class, for example, fixed income and equity have very different price drivers. What are the characteristics of each game? Fixed income is more quantitatively oriented, as there is no getting around the mathematics and statistics. Credit instruments move in a much more homogeneous manner because the central bank controls the interest rates. In equity trading, there are many more risk drivers at play. Although fixed income may be more predictable, more mathematical, liquidity and credit effects in markets and "squeezes" that can occur if specifically needed bonds are in short supply can significantly distort the homogeneous picture.

## Types of Orders

Unless counterparties come to you with trade suggestions which help implement your trading strategy, you will have to implement the ideas yourself and find the right venues and prices. In the case of exchanges or other multilateral trading facilities, price discovery can be done automatically because the orderbook or dealer quotes are transparent. In OTC markets you can post interest in trading a product and post indication of interest and ask for a two-way quote so as not to show too much of your hand.

For exchanges there can be different types of orders; basically, they differ by the length of time that they are in effect and by conditions on the price sought. On the time dimension, orders can be day orders or "good till canceled" (GTC); sometimes there are more variations. On price conditions, orders can be limit orders or market orders.

- In the case of a *limit order*, a minimum sell or maximum purchase price is put on the order. If you issue a limit order, you are in effect a dealer/market maker and offering liquidity to the market. If your order cannot be executed immediately, it will be added to the order book.

- In the case of a *market order*, you are giving instructions to the broker to execute directly at the best available price. In some cases the broker is given some discretion in timing and slicing up the order to improve the price. Alternatively, you can do that yourself if you are relaying the order to the exchange.

The fundamental distinction between market and limit orders is a difference in focus between execution probability versus execution price. If the bid-ask spread is high, you may be inclined to *offer liquidity* to the market by putting in a limit order. If the spread is tiny, the cost of *taking liquidity* through a market order is small, and the benefit of immediate execution may outweigh this. Note that some execution venues offer *liquidity rebates* against trading fees for parties that add liquidity. Other order types that you can give to an exchange are stop orders which will not be executed until the market price reaches a certain point. These can be used, for instance, to automatically kick in once the losses on a position cross a certain level; in that case they are called *stoploss orders*.

Systems that try to optimally route and execute orders are called *order management systems* (OMSs) and *execution management systems* (EMSs). The focus on the former is more on connectivity and communication with different execution venues. The availability of a full and comprehensive montage of quotes and order books from venues with different market models that would suit different types of trading is a necessity. The focus on the latter is more on minimizing transaction costs by intelligently slicing and routing orders and, for instance, by seeking the relation between execution probabilities and limit order prices. On the back of one trade, these systems could generate many different orders.

Order routing systems sweep the market by taking liquidity from all sources at once. Order routing is often coupled with buy-side order management systems.[17] Order management includes activities such as counter party management, inventory management, and performance reporting. Transaction analysis linked to reference data is key to attribute performance to traders' decisions.[18]

This is related to *algorithmic trading* where the algorithms are designed to seek to profit from fragmented liquidity and the way the execution venue system of coming to a transaction price is set up as well as from repeatedly observed price patterns. OMSs and EMSs have become much more important because liquidity has fragmented, and many larger institutions cross trades internally. As a result of these systems, the average trade size is shrinking, meaning higher trade volumes to clear and settle.

Implementing trading strategies that arbitrage between different markets and product types will lead to more complex trading strategies, exploiting and involving correlations between different assets (traded on different venues) in a portfolio; in this case, we get more complex orders and more complex order routing. Often either the whole order needs to go through, or nothing should happen. This is analogous to the concept of *transactional integrity* in computer science and puts demands on execution logic. If only part of the combined order goes through, it is no good, especially since the trade opportunity may be extremely short-lived. The market model and resulting set of possible order types are part of the bases for competition between execution venues. Exchanges are offering new order types such as hidden limit orders.

If you execute orders for your clients, due to MiFID regulations' best execution stipulations in the European Union, you have to assess your OMS, order routing, and overall how your connectivity to the brokers is set up so that you can track and corroborate best execution according to the definition agreed with the customers.

Special trades include very large sizes (blocks) and trades on products not yet issued. Examples of these conditional trades include the following:

- *"As, if and when issued"* trading refers to the situation in which a security is traded that is not yet issued. These transactions are normally conditional on the issue actually taking place.

- With *TBA MBS pools*, the pool properties of a mortgage pool are already defined, but the pool is not yet populated with mortgages.
- Prior to an IPO, there are already trades on the equity to be issued; the legality of this depends on the jurisdiction. This is also called the *gray market*.

A *block trade* refers to a large trade which is a significant portion or sometimes a multiple of average daily volume. Often these blocks of shares are sold by an institutional investor to a bank that has to offload it to the market without disturbing it. A bank is sometimes also asked to bid for an entire portfolio.

## Latency

Latency refers to the speed with which you can relay orders to an execution venue and how fast you are informed about this execution. In some strategies latency matters much more than in others; it depends on the number of venues that your strategy touches, on the product type, and on the liquidity.

The importance of latency and the appetite to invest in low-latency trading platforms and content depend very much on the trading strategy. For quantitative index arbitrage, the opportunities may not last long, and (comparative) low latency is critical. For value investing and long-only strategies, investments in low-latency platforms may cost more than the benefit they bring. If the market is very competitive with many players that seek to exploit price differences, latency is critical. Note that you do not need a certain absolute speed, but you need to be faster than everybody else that wants to execute the same trade idea.

Latency can be improved through the integration of real-time market data feeds and electronic trading. Collecting and feeding market data directly to trading engines shorten the real-time data supply chain. The difficulty lies in achieving the required latency *plus* addressing connectivity with the fragmentation of venues and information *plus* the data quality of the quote streams that need to be perfect if you want to act on these data automatically. Trading speed can be increased in different ways that include the following:

- Collocation, which refers to the placing of servers/communication close to exchanges;
- A thorough analysis for network latency and total order time to find out where the bottlenecks are.

## Liquidity

Liquidity is about time and place. If all trades arrive at the same time and place, no brokers or exchanges would be necessary. Liquidity is the oxygen needed to execute the trade idea or trading strategy and can be defined as the opportunity available to the trading party to implement trade ideas cheaply and quickly.[19]

Different aspects of liquidity include

- *Immediacy.* This refers to how quickly the trade can be executed.

- *Width or Breadth.* This is the cost of doing a trade, e.g., the bid ask spread plus any commissions. It gives you one of the aspects of the cost of trading—the cost of liquidity.

- *Depth.* This refers to the size of the trade that can be arranged at a given cost; e.g., 100 shares will obtain a better price than 100,000 shares. First, because the market maker will not have that much inventory, and second because the market maker will suspect that he knows less than the person who wants to move 100,000 shares so will sell that much only after adjusting the quote.

Sometimes the aspect of *resiliency* is included in liquidity. Resiliency refers to how quickly prices revert to former levels after a large order flow imbalance initiated by uninformed traders. *Uninformed* refers to those cases where traders are not acting on new information, but merely want to rebalance their position. Different players focus on different aspects of liquidity. Large traders that want to move big blocks focus on depth; impatient traders focus on immediacy and market breadth.

For larger trades, the trading costs can be high. If institutional investors deal directly among themselves, they could save costs. Systems such as Liquidnet[20] aim to facilitate this. The system looks at the trades on the blotter and checks whether it can match with someone else; if so, it then sends anonymous messages to negotiate the price.

Liquidity is part of the cost of trading. Frequent trading can erode the gains from the strategy. Together with other costs, it goes into transaction cost analysis, or TCA. Note that decreasing transaction costs is often easier and more reliable than improving portfolio selection decisions and that reductions in trading costs directly affect the bottom line.

Liquidity depends on the type of market and on the instrument. Blue chip equities and foreign exchange for OECD currencies are very liquid. Corporate bonds can be reasonably liquid; municipal bonds are often in thin supply. Exotic currencies are illiquid. In the area of asset-backed securities, for example, there is comparatively small deal flow here; the most liquid subsection would be TBA trades for MBSs, which could be in the range of hundreds to thousands of deals a week per firm; the agency-based CMOs go to the tens to hundreds a month; then they go down to deals per month, quarter, or year. In very liquid and active markets, you will tend to find more diverse market structures than in less active markets, so there will be more order types and market models to choose from when implementing a trading strategy. A good example is equity where a number of alternative trading systems have popped up alongside the traditional exchanges.

After a trade has been completed, it needs reporting with various degrees of detail. Information to be supplied to retail clients in jurisdictions affected by MiFID[21] includes, for example, the following fields:[22]

1. Reporting firm identification
2. Name or other designation of the client
3. Trading day
4. Trading time
5. Nature of the order
6. Venue identification
7. Buy/sell indicator
8. Quantity
9. Unit price
10. Total consideration
11. Total sum of the commissions and expenses charged and, where the retail client so requests, an itemized breakdown
12. Client's responsibilities in relation to the settlement of the transaction, including time limit for payment or delivery, as well as appropriate account details where necessary
13. Client's counterparty details—investment firm or any person in the investment firm's group, unless order executed through a trading system

## Other Applications

Many other applications are in place to support the *trade* step of the transaction lifecycle. One of these is *deal-capture systems* where the essentials of the trade are either keyed in or caught automatically from a trading system and then normally enriched with additional information before being passed on for processing in the clearing and settlement function. Enrichment would include supplementing the (often) summary information provided by the trading with additional information on the instrument traded, counterparty, and prevailing settlement conditions. Other trade execution-supporting activities include transactional cost analysis, cost of capital, deal definitions, and limit checks.[23] These activities help to properly price the deal and to see if the deal still makes economic sense after factoring in the risk capital needed and the opportunity costs that are incurred by using part of the allocated limit.

And, of course, trades will go into portfolios for which position keeping needs to be done. First, we will discuss the clearing and settlement processes kicked off by a transaction.

### 4.3.3 CLEARING AND SETTLEMENT

#### Introduction

A trade *clears* when both sides are in agreement and have a common understanding of all the terms of the trade. For example, for a repo transaction, both sides need to report the same notional amount, repo rate, length or term of the repo, security repoed, and price of the bond. This agreement can come about as a result of comparing trade confirms, or clearing can be done by an intermediary utility. A trade *settles* when the product purchased is exchanged against cash. A trade clears if both sides report the same terms of the trade; otherwise, it is called an *out-trade* or a *DK* (don't know).

Clearing and settlement are two different activities. Settlement is normally on a "delivery versus payment" (DVP) basis in which the security changes hands against cash. Occasionally, there is the option for settlement through "delivery by value" (DBV) where, instead of cash immediately, securities are delivered overnight and cash the next day. Settlement activities include the input of settlement instructions, the verification of verify trade details, notice of execution (NOE), and transfer of ownership. Reference data are required to support the accurate identification of securities and counterparties.[24] Settlement instructions were discussed in Chapter 3. They tell the other party where the money and securities need to go. Settlement instructions need to be periodically reviewed to check their accuracy. This can be done through a *twilighting* process, whereby counterparties are asked to reconfirm their instructions. They would have the choice between confirming the validity of the existing data on their profile or offering new information. In case no reply comes, the data can stay the same with a note that the client has been asked, or individual follow-up can be taken.

Securities and OTC products have potentially very different settlement processes. In securities there is typically a national numbering agency that assigns unique identifiers such as CUSIP, ISIN, or SEDOL codes, which makes for (relatively) easy processing and identification. This is also the case for structured products, which are effectively fixed-income derivatives masquerading as securities. Structured products fortunately have CUSIPs and settle like a corporate bond—not like derivatives, where you have to have the legal framework and master agreements established.

For the clearing of foreign exchange trades, the Continuous Linked Settlement (CLS) bank has been set up by a number of large FX trading banks.[25]

## Clearing Houses

Large clearing houses include the Depository Trust & Clearing Corporation (DTCC) and Options Clearing Corporation (OCC) in the United States and Clearstream and LCH.Clearnet in Europe. Some clearing houses clear only equity or only options instruments. Other clearing houses such as LCH.Clearnet offer a wide variety of services in equity, exchange-trade derivatives, commodities, and OTC derivatives. Sometimes, clearing houses are separate entities, and sometimes they are integrated with an exchange.[26] Table 4.1 provides an example of volumes cleared by LCH.Clearnet.[27]

Some securities transactions can be internally cleared within a bank; in this case they are offset against another transaction, and the bank does not have to go to the exchange or the clearing house to execute or clear the trade. This will save costs for the bank, but the investor will need to know a good price was received.

## Settlement Risk

The settlement function manages securities and cash and is critically important. *Settlement risk* refers to the the risk that the other party does not settle, e.g. in case of an exchange of cash and securities where you have delivered

**Table 4.1**   LCH.Clearnet Volumes

| LCH.Clearnet Transactions Cleared, Single Counted ('000) | | |
|---|---|---|
| | 2007 Total | 2006 Total |
| Equities | 314,013 | 197,620 |
| Exchange and Commodity Derivatives | 1,409,735 | 1,067,150 |
| Fixed Income | 2,913 | 2,410 |
| Swaps | 141 | 90 |
| Total | 1,726,802 | 1,267,360 |

one of them and have yet to receive the other. The longer the time period, the higher the risk. The settlement lag can, however, vary from practically zero to many weeks, and often there are confirmation backlogs when the products are new and lack standards. This was especially the case for more recent products (e.g., credit derivatives) in which the market grew very fast and for which data standards were lacking and existing infrastructure was not set up. A key development to which data products and the information supply chain in general needs to be adapted is that processes such as settlement, risk, and reporting are increasingly becoming more real time.

Sometimes there is a party in the middle to match the trades. Financial institutions can use an electronic trade confirmation (ETC) system: Both sides of the transaction submit the trade details to the trade-matching facility that crosses or matches it. This can be the depository or an intermediary. A *central matching unit* is a third party in the settlement process that sits in between the institution and broker/dealer. This is the same central model as that of a data aggregator for information gathering, of an exchange to centralize price discovery and execution, and of a central counterparty to contain settlement risk. Clearing services and central counterparty functions for OTC products have been created by the DTCC and by LCH.Clearnet among others. Example services from LCH.Clearnet include RepoClear and SwapClear[28] which have been around since the late 1990s. In a central counterparty model for OTC derivatives, the original contract between the two counterparties is replaced by two contracts with the same terms, both with the clearinghouse. The clearing service calculates all payments due at least once per day and nets them for all members. Thus, the size of the payments to be made will go down, meaning operational risk and settlement risk decrease. To minimize the risk and exposure of the clearinghouse, participants have to make an initial margin payment and, when market has moved adversely, additional margin calls will be made. Additional services that can be offered by clearinghouses include *novation*, which is the substitution of an old contract for a new one.

Operationally, the costs of settlement differ by trade. In Chapter 2 we saw that the number of cash flows resulting from a financial product is different in frequency and expected time. Settling securities transactions is fairly simple: one payment versus a title transfer of the bonds or equities. A swap trade, on the other hand, will initiate a series of cash flows which can last for many years. Many derivatives also will lead to margin requirements, meaning very frequent (possibly daily) cash flows, thereby complicating the process.

The settlement process also needs to consider the *allocation* of securities over different accounts. If an institutional investor executes a block trade for many accounts, the securities purchased have to be allocated over all the accounts with a certain price. The price achieved for every part of the block trade plays a role here, and it is important to get the (weighted) average price right and to allocate properly.

## Inefficiencies in Clearing and Settlement

There are many national monopolies when it comes to, for example, securities settlement, and often there is no choice about the settlement location. This raises the question of whether clearing and settlement are a *natural monopoly*, i.e., most efficiently organized by one central player. The same case has been made for exchanges, however, through offering different market models, (derivative) products and order types, and price-discovery mechanisms, different exchanges each offer competitive advantage to various client segments. A similar question, then, is how clearing and settlement services providers could potentially differ. Can they compete on functionality rather than on pure cost? Settlement services could potentially differ in speed, in options for automatic collateral posting, or settlement in kind if cash is not forthcoming and via the universe of products (geographic equity market, OTC derivative product types such as swaps, FX derivatives, repos) that can be cleared and settled. However, it is strongly desirable that interfaces and settlement lags are uniform.[29]

Trading in many OTC products started out on a peer-to-peer model between market participants globally and helped by the ISDA master agreements. Exchanges are rapidly engaging in cross-border consolidation. Clearing and settlement, on the other hand, often remain a national business to date. In an August 2006 report,[30] Celent claimed that less than 50% of derivatives processing in Europe were automated and that increasingly complex trades complicate STP goals. The local nature of clearing and settlement is often seen as a barrier to cost-efficient cross-border securities trading. There have been various initiatives to improve the post-trade process, including that of industry groups and regulatory-mandated groups. Settlement and automated processing of OTC derivatives remain cumbersome.

In the European Union, the main barriers to integrated clearing and settlement have been identified. A report on the European Union clearing and settlement arrangements written by a group chaired by Alberto Giovannini has identified 15 barriers to more efficient post-trade services and a strategy to overcome them. Their conclusion was that the European Union cannot be seen as an integrated entity "but remains a juxtaposition of domestic markets."[31] While there are multiple regulatory, fiscal, and legal regimes, it is impossible to be efficient.

Investors should not have to worry about the clearing and settlement arrangements. However, if different systems with different legal and regulatory regimes are involved, post-trade processing remains complex. Securities need to be treated in the same way internationally: what they are, how you own them, how you trade them. Without this, cross-border usage of securities cannot consolidate. The more systems involved in the settlement process, the higher the potential for error and the higher the cost. Specific barriers identified by Giovannini include differences in settlement periods, in issuance practice, taxation, and even legal certainty on ownership of securities: Barrier 13 refers to the absence of a uniform framework for the treatment of ownership of securities. "In modern securities markets, securities are held for others by intermediaries for which purpose they maintain accounts. These accounts are treated commercially and economically as being the focus of ownership."[32] Legally, their status differs across the EU member countries. Lack of clarity as to who has what rights when securities are held for investors by means of an intermediary's accounting records causes major complications. In some EU countries, account entries establish ownership, not so in others. There is a need for legal identity between ownership and record of ownership.

A global perspective is given by the group of 30,[33] which has published reports such as *Global Clearing and Settlement: A Plan of Action* to cut costs, reduce settlement risks, and increase the efficiency of the market. The group's 20 recommendations in this area are as follows:[34]

1. Eliminate paper and automate communication, data capture, and enrichment.

2. Harmonize messaging standards and communication protocols.

3. Develop and implement reference data standards.

4. Synchronize timing between different clearing and settlement systems and associated payment and foreign-exchange systems.

5. Automate and standardize institutional trade matching.

6. Expand the use of central counterparties.

7. Permit securities lending and borrowing to expedite settlement.

8. Automate and standardize asset servicing processes, including corporate actions, tax relief arrangements, and restrictions on foreign ownership.

9. Ensure the financial integrity of providers of clearing and settlement services.

10. Reinforce the risk management practices of users of clearing and settlement service providers.

11. Ensure final, simultaneous transfer and availability of assets.

12. Ensure effective business continuity and disaster recovery planning.

13. Address the possibility of failure of a systemically important institution.

14. Strengthen assessment of the enforceability of contracts.

15. Advance legal certainty over rights to securities, cash, or collateral.

16. Recognize and support improved valuation and closeout netting arrangements.

17. Ensure appointment of appropriately experienced and senior board members.

18. Promote fair access to securities clearing and settlement networks.

19. Ensure equitable and effective attention to stakeholders' interests.

20. Encourage consistent regulation and oversight of securities clearing and settlement service providers.

We see that many of these, including the first recommendation, are about increasing the efficiency of the information supply chain, to come to a more closely knit supply chain.[35]

### (I)CSDs

Central Securities Depositories (CSDs) hold securities to allow book entry transfer. There could be physical securities (e.g., certificates), or the securities can exist only in electronic records, in which case we call them *dematerialized*. A CSD is called an *international CSD* (ICSD) when it settles trades in international securities.[36]

CSDs are the last chain in the settlement process, keeping records of who owns what. For many countries, including Italy and Spain, CSDs are still national affairs[37] and sometimes very closely linked to a national stock market. There has been some consolidation in Europe through Euroclear, which services the Benelux, French, and UK market and Clearstream. For clients, consolidation of depositories would mean a smaller number of interfaces and room to improve processes (higher STP rate through the introduction of standards such as ISO 15022, decrease in operational risk). The introduction of the common Euroclear system could save the financial services industry substantial amounts.[38]

### SWIFT

SWIFT plays a critical role in facilitating settlement. It does this in various ways:

- Through the provision of a safe network to exchange information. This also includes the provision of member-administered closed user groups (MA-CUG) where subsets of SWIFT members can exchange information reliably and securely.

■ Through the provision and acting as the registration authority for different standards including the ISO 15022 standard discussed in Chapter 2 as well as identifications standards such as the Bank Identification Code (BIC). On the payment side, SWIFT has the BIC directory, which can be used with country and branch extensions to identify a bank's branch office. It is also the start of the International Bank Account Number (IBAN), which uniquely identifies an individual bank account.[39] To settle payments among financial institutions, countries have "real-time, gross-settlement systems" (RTGSs) in place. This is a system for settling the transaction of financial institutions. The paying bank pushes the transaction, which immediately takes effect.[40]

■ Through services such as Accord for matching and exception handling in foreign exchange, money market, and OTC derivatives. SWIFT has run a pilot whereby FpML messages were sent over the SWIFT network.

### 4.3.4 ASSET SERVICING

Securities services include *custody* (the safekeeping of securities and processing of corporate actions), *securities lending* (the temporary transfer of ownership against a fee), and *proxy voting*. These services have extended beyond administrative services, making sure the owners of the securities receive any benefits (e.g., dividends) toward more value-added yield enhancement services (lending the bonds and stocks against a fee).

Just as the information supply chain and instrument lifecycle cover many players at various stages in the chain, the transaction lifecycle is broken up in a similar fashion with many third parties offering services pre- and post-trade. We discuss various players and activities in the area of asset servicing such as custody, securities lending, collateral management, and fund administration.

### *Custody*

Traditionally, *custody*—as the name implies—refers to the safeguarding of securities in a vault, or nowadays, when most securities are *dematerialized*, the safekeeping in secure systems. In addition to this, global custody can comprise many other services, including the following:

■ Income collection and other corporate actions management. This can also include proxy voting services.

■ Cash management funding and other banking facilities for the account holders.

- Tax management through expert knowledge of different fiscal regimes.
- Reporting through periodic statements on accounts and holdings.
- Investment accounting via the track of cash inflows and outflows.
- Securities lending and collateral services. Through securities lending operations, custodians can enhance the yield on the assets the account holder has put under the administration of the custodian. The securities lending fee will be split between the security owner and custodian.
- Trustee services.
- Portfolio valuation and performance reporting.

Custody is a highly concentrated business as we saw in Table 2.13 in Chapter 2. The key metric to rank custodians is "Assets under Administration." Securities lending is a natural extension of the custody business.

Custody and corporate action processing solutions typically cover the following corporate actions processing functionality:

- Integration of corporate actions from various sources, typically custodians and commercial data vendors. This includes data collection, scrubbing, and creation of a golden record.
- Entitlement calculation and reconciliation of calculated amounts due versus those actually received based on account holdings information and events, including tax tables and cost basis calculations.
- Formatting and submitting response instructions (MT565), confirmation/entitlement payments data (MT566), and confirmation of responses (MT567).
- Workflow queues to organize and prioritize messages, facilitation of replying to elective events, and other events such as claims and class actions.
- Capabilities for custodians/account holders to give instructions on how to treat events via a portal.

Corporate actions processing solutions are essentially data integration/routing hubs that combine internal and external information with a workflow to organize the responses. There is still integration work required, e.g., to import information such as holdings and tax regimes. Some vendors[41] have a broader offering and include modules for, for example, reconciliation of securities settlement information and trades.

Benefits of these solutions are a reduction in operational risk and increased efficiencies in processing. Operational risk control should lead to fewer fails and claims and potentially also a lower operational risk charge for those institutions governed by the Basel II accord. The targeted workflow identifying and prioritizing items in need of attention should make staff more productive, hence reducing costs per trade. As custody services are typically charged for in basis points per portfolio value, this is a way to increase the operating margin for custodial business.

## Securities Lending[42]

Securities lending is a temporary transfer of securities on a collateralized basis. The word *lending* in the term is misleading because it is not a "loan" at all, but a title transfer. The duration of this "loan" can be on-demand or term. Many lenders want to preserve flexibility and loan equities on call. The economic benefits go to the borrower; however, the borrower typically "manufactures" these back to the lender.

For securities lending, the securities need to be negotiable. In the United States, you can hold securities in your own name or in "street" name; in the latter case the broker or the DTC holds them in trust, and the beneficiary owner can recommend to the broker how to vote. Transferring securities into *street name* means making them negotiable.

Securities lending deals can be seen as *metatransactions*; they often come about as a result of other transactions (see Figure 4.3). Motivation for securities lending includes the following cases:

- *Shortfalls.* Securities lending is often triggered by, for example, a failed settlement in an original trade which has led to a shortfall. Settlement needs

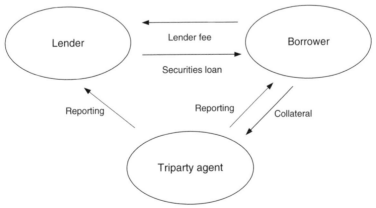

Basic securities lending flows. The lending income is typically split between the benificial owner of the security, the lender and the agent.

**Figure 4.3** Securities lending flows, securities against cash, or other collateral

to be faster because there is normally a short-term need to have these securities to cover a shortfall.

■ *Yield Enhancement.* In this case, a portfolio has been constructed with borrowed securities that yield more to the borrower than the costs that need to be paid back to the lender. The *carry* is the interest return on the securities held minus the financing costs.

■ *Tax Arbitrage.* In case two sides of the transaction fall under two different tax regimes (one side may receive tax credits), it can be more advantageous for one side to receive a dividend or an interest payment (e.g., due to a difference in withholding tax regimes).

■ *Index Tracking.* Another interesting motivation for securities lending lies in index tracker funds. There are ETFs that have to track an index very closely. They cannot take stock dividends, since this would mean a deviation from tracking the index accurately. In this case they can lend the equity, have the borrower receive the stock dividend (assuming the stock dividend is economically the more attractive option compared to cash dividend), and get it back with a cash return higher than they would otherwise have received.

The distinction between securities lending transactions and repurchase agreements (repos) is fuzzy. Generally, securities lending deals come about as a result of a need for a specific security (ISIN, CUSIP), and repurchase agreements are more to fulfill funding needs. So it is also a question of what drives the transaction; what may be a repurchase agreement to one side of the deal may be a securities lending transaction to the other party.

Typical information to be included in a securities loan transaction includes the following:

■ Transaction and settlement date
■ Term/duration
■ Security identification
■ Security price and quantity
■ Loan value and lending fee
■ Collateral and margin (top-up amount)

Note that daycount conventions differ in, for example, the United States and the United Kingdom, so the basis for interest calculation is important to determine.

Securities lending used to be more of a back-office to back-office activity but has also turned into a profit center. It is also frequently outsourced to third-party securities lending agents. As the volume of securities lending transactions has increased, there are more intermediaries who pool together supply and demand. Sometimes intermediary agents specialize in finding the right securities, just as any other broker activities but now to arrange a securities lending transaction. There are also electronic platforms to negotiate these transactions. Examples include EquiLend and SecFinex.[43] These providers offer various services including counterparty selections, matching long and short portfolios, and negotiation platforms.

Security lending fees depend on supply (availability of the relevant shares) and demand (demand for filling short positions). Sometimes exclusive lending relationships are in place where a lender makes available all its assets to a particular borrower.

## Collateral Management

In the OTC transaction space, often there will be in place master agreements on settlement and netting. In addition, collateral is often pledged to secure an exposure. Note that eligible collateral between two parties needs to be clearly defined, as well as the procedures to replace or top-up collateral and the size of the *haircut* or discount applied. There is a tendency to move beyond the relatively crude way of valuation of a collateral portfolio through a haircut to more accurate NAV calculations. This implies that good-quality pricing data are needed here as well. The size of the haircut will depend on the volatility of the collateral, proportion of the total security issue held in portfolio, and liquidity/average daily traded volume. There will be agreement on the absolute value of assets to be accepted as collateral, margin initially and to be maintained, and also *concentration limits*. This refers to the maximum percentage of an asset, e.g., below a certain percentage of average traded volume or the maximum percentage against the same issuer. Multiple bonds and equities can be pledged, but if they all refer to the same ultimate credit, there may be an undesirable level of concentration. This is closely related to portfolio management of the entire pool of collateral pledged. These limits need to be monitored against up-to-date information because the market can quickly turn or dry up. Market and credit data need to be up-to-date and accurate for good collateral management. Sometimes a triparty agent will hold the collateral. Collateral management includes the management of liquidity risk, mispricing risk, and legal risk. If there is a possible delay in selling the collateral securities, then the risk is higher. When collateral quality deteriorates because of adverse market conditions, it needs to be substituted or topped-up.

## Fund Administration

Many activities need to be performed around managing a fund that support the investment process. The fund administration function has evolved from different loose services into a full-service back-office function that does daily P&L and NAV calculations. Fund administration is frequently outsourced to third-party financial institutions that offer fund administration services to a large number of clients. Activities can include the following:

- *NAV Calculations.* NAV calculations would include dealing with all capital inflows and outflows within a fund, fund income, and fund expenses and the maintenance of the fund's financial records. We also call these activities *fund accounting*.[44]

- *Risk Management Services.* These are in operational risk, as well as fund benchmarking and attribution. This means that fund administration providers have a need for good benchmark data.

- *Reporting.* Investment products can be offshore, onshore, retail, and institutional, and for different target markets. This can mean potentially complex tax reporting. In addition, fund administration providers may also offer services around a stock exchange listing of a fund.

- *Bookkeeping for All Portfolio Transactions.* Trade and settlement date, date of receipt of broker confirmation, and allocation of transaction volume to different brokers based on settlement quality.

- *Fee Calculation.* Management fees, performance fees, and other expenses.

- *Compliance.* Investment policy compliance, mandate checks, and controls on eligible securities and markets.

- *Administrative Functions.* This includes the maintenance of the shareholders' register for the fund and transfer agency function.

Hedge funds are the primary users of fund administration services, as well as of *prime brokerage* services that typically include securities lending, financing, trade execution services, clearance, custody, reporting, risk management, and startup assistance. This leaves the hedge fund free to focus on the trading strategies, meaning it can start operations immediately once the needed capital has been raised.

#### 4.3.5 RISK, REPORTING, AND PERFORMANCE MANAGEMENT

The cumulative results of transactions are holdings in financial products that are grouped together in portfolios. Apart from measuring the return of these portfolios, part of the post-trade process consists of reporting on the risk of these portfolios, i.e., the likelihood that their value is affected by a change in drivers of that value. In this section we will sum up the various types of risk that instruments and institutions are exposed to and will then discuss various risk metrics and measures used to monitor and manage these risks. Note that the risk that is incurred typically determines the room (and indeed the appetite) for further transactions. We will also discuss benchmarking, performance, and attribution issues and end with conclusions.

## Risk Categories

Investment and trading portfolios are exposed to different categories of risk which include the following:

- *Market Risk*. This risk is induced by market price changes or changes in instrument dependencies[45] that affect the value of the assets in the portfolio.
- *Credit Risk*. This risk is induced by defaults of parties that owe the institution money or induced by a change in perceived creditworthiness of legal entities where the creditworthiness affects the price of the instrument.
- *Liquidity Risk*. The inability to fund assets or to fund the business by a reasonable interest rate impairs the success of the business.
- *Operational Risk*. This is exposure to losses because of inadequate or failed internal processes, people, or systems.

To summarize and quantify these risks, RiskMetrics, which came out of JPMorgan in 1994,[46] introduced and popularized the concept of Value at Risk (VaR). The Value at Risk of a trading position or a portfolio expresses the maximum dollar amount that can be lost within a certain time frame with a certain confidence level. For example, when the VaR of a portfolio is $12M, this could, for instance, mean that a maximum of $12M can be lost within the next 10 business days with a confidence level of 95%. Whenever a VaR measure is quoted, the time frame and confidence level always need to be specified. VaR measures are very convenient, since they summarize the risk into one dollar amount. However, note that VaR says nothing about the loss in the 5% of cases which are expected to be above $12M: They could be $12.1M or perhaps $250M. VaR was originally introduced for market risk but can also be used in the context of other risk drivers, in which case sometimes terms such as *creditVar* and *opVar* are used for credit risk and operational risk, respectively. For credit exposure, counterparty risk is also measured on a transaction basis using the concept of *potential future exposure*. This approach evaluates existing trades against possible market prices during the remaining lifetime of the outstanding transactions. Regulators officially sanctioned the use of VaR in the market risk amendment to the original Basel accord.

To calculate the VaR number, we require the probability distribution of the various risk factors that drive the portfolio as well as the correlation between them. This information is summarized in a Variance CoVariance (VCV) matrix. There are various methods to arrive at these measures, including through historical simulation or through Monte Carlo simulation. For historical simulation, the correlations between the various risk drivers as well as their volatility are retrieved from historical data. In Monte Carlo simulation, the portfolio returns are simulated for a wide number of scenarios, and the outcomes are used to find a probability distribution, which in turn gives the standard deviation and correlation. The VCV matrix can become large for diversified trading operations for which the VaR calculation requires information on thousands of risk factors. This numeric challenge has, however, become smaller due to increased computing power. Nevertheless, there are often data complications in calculating the matrix—first, because they can be very large, so they require lots of time series. Other than that, the matrix input often includes time series with stale data, or where one instrument has been proxied by another so that the correlation between them comes to 1.

Value at Risk makes assumptions that price behavior follows a normal distribution, and in the case of historical simulation, that history is relevant for the future. Some institutions use multiple years' worth of history, and it is highly questionable whether, for example, events from 3 years ago are relevant. A compromise is to weigh history and to give more recent prices a larger weight, for example, by exponential weighting introducing a decay factor. Also note that VaR is a universal risk approach; that is, it is independent of the asset class. Table 4.2 lists some Value at Risk numbers taken from the 2006 annual reports of these companies.

**Table 4.2** Example VaR Numbers

| Bank | 2006 Average VaR Number |
|---|---|
| Bank of America | $41.3M average for the market-based trading portfolio (2006 Annual Report, p. 77) |
| Deutsche Bank | €69.5M average. (2006 Annual Report, p. 80) |
| Goldman Sachs | $101M average. (2006 Annual Report, p. 59) |
| Société Générale | €25M average. (2006 Annual Report, p. 135) |

The bank's management and regulators would scrutinize the VaR numbers and compare them to the profit-and-loss figures to see how many times the VaR number was breached. The VaR number is itself the basis for a regulatory capital charge, i.e., an amount of capital that banks would have to set aside to be able to cover trading losses. To come to this amount, the regulators apply a multiple to the VaR number. The multiple depends on the confidence the regulators have in the bank's process. If the VaR number is breached much more often than expected, the multiple will be higher. VaR numbers are typically produced by products called *risk engines*. These engines can be built in-house, but since the methodology is fairly similar between institutions, many third parties offer them.[47] These engines take the aggregated positions and risk data and produce VaR reports. Banks either condense all market information into risk factors themselves or purchase ready-to-go risk factor sets.[48]

There is a lot of debate on the correct pricing models. Markets do not behave in a normal distribution, and especially not on the downside. Typical market behavior can consist of long, smooth, upward trending and once in a while a huge event downward. Pricing models based on non-normal probability distributions such as the Cauchy or Pareto distributions and power law distributions seek to address this.[49]

In addition to the measurement of VaR, which is a daily process, banks will also engage in *stress testing* (see also Section 3.5.3). Stress testing involves subjecting the bank's exposure to extreme events to gauge the effect on the portfolio's value and indeed on the bank's solvency. The data required for stress testing would consist of a set of risk factors with their evolution over the time interval of the scenario. Real-life historical events are often taken for stress test scenarios. An alternative could be to check in a historical price database for periods when volatility peaked or when correlations in the matrix suddenly changed and then to subject your current portfolio to those scenarios. Stress tests are applied for all risk domains including market, credit, and liquidity risk. In the case of operational risk, there is a special data challenge, as most of the available data will reflect small, relatively high, frequent losses. Information on the *tail*—the larger loss events—is very rare and normally consists of highly publicized loss cases. *Extreme Value Theory* is used to complement the available data and to model stress scenarios.

*Quantitative analysis* is the analysis of the sources of risk and return and the initiation of corrective action. In various areas of finance, the model assumptions will not work, and/or the data needed to model are not there. Risk management is a combination of an art and a science. Often, risk frameworks work very well in normal market conditions. But that is precisely when you do not really need them. The test is always in the unusual situations—the big market movements, unusual events, and breakdown of correlations.

## Risk Measures: The Market Risk Vocabulary

Many risk measures are specifically used in describing risks in certain asset types. Here, we will discuss the most common ones for options, equities, and fixed income.

*Options.* Option risk metrics are also known as the "option greeks." They measure the sensitivity in option price to different underlying price drivers. These are the following:

- *Delta.* The sensitivity in price based on changes in the price of the underlying.

- *Gamma.* The sensitivity in price based on changes in delta. In other words, this is the second derivative of the option price with regard to the price of the underlying asset.

- *Rho.* The sensitivity in price based on changes in interest rate with which positions can be financed.

- *Vega.* The sensitivity in price based on changes in the volatility in the price of the underlying asset.

- *Tau.* The sensitivity in price based on changes in time to expiry. So it measures the time decay.

To calculate these measures and calculate the option price, the option contract reference data, we require the current market prices of the underlying and current risk-free rate for the remaining period of the option.

*Equities.* The two measures in the equity world are *beta* and *alpha*. Beta is the portfolio's correlation with the benchmark and measures the similarity of behavior with it. Alpha is the surplus return over the index or benchmark. A number of ratios typically associated with funds, such as the Sharpe Ratio, Treynor Ratio, and Jensen's alphas, can all be used for fund ranking and comparison purposes.[50]

For equity performance, the effects of the corporate actions that took place need to be taken into account. Time series can be analyzed with or without the effects of stock splits, dividends, and other capital distributions taken into account. Some vendors deliver uncorrected historical time series, whereas others may have applied splits. Since the user requirements may also be different, this represents a challenge for common data services within financial institutions.

*Fixed Income.* Fixed-income instruments typically move in a much more systematic fashion than equities. In fixed income, two measures are normally used to indicate interest rate sensitivities: *modified duration* and *gamma* or *convexity*. Modified duration is a measure for the true life of the bond; it measures how fast cash comes back to the bond holder and takes the effect of intermediate cash flows into account. It measures the sensitivity of bond prices to changes in the interest rate. Convexity or gamma, the second order effect, measures the sensitivity of modified duration to interest rate changes. Thus, modified duration is conceptually similar to delta for options, and convexity is similar to an option's gamma with the interest rate taking the place of an option's underlying. From a data perspective, the benchmark yield curve needs to be very good because it determines the value of the bond portfolio. Note that for an MBS portfolio—unlike bonds—the modified duration cannot assume that cash flows do not change in response to yield curve movements.

*Commodities.* There are many different kinds of commodities, and not all of them have an active and liquid futures market. Every type of commodity has specific risk factors as its industrial demand and supply dynamics also come into play. One risk measure often used is that of the *basis.* The basis is the difference in price movement between two related (i.e., commodities that can be substituted for one another) commodities, e.g., crude oil and jet fuel. Other risk measures are *spreads,* which price the conversion effect of commodities at different stages of an industrial supply chain. Examples of these measures include the *crack spread* to price conversion from gas to electricity and a spread measure to price the conversion cost between sugar and ethanol. The main data source to measure against will be the most liquidly traded commodity within a group which will serve as the benchmark commodity.

### Analyzing Portfolio Returns

When the returns of a trading portfolio or fund are analyzed, the specific return measure and period over which it is measured have to be clearly defined. Apart from a simple comparing of values at the beginning and ending of the observed period, there are other return measures, including the following:

■ *Risk-Adjusted Returns.* These measures combine risk management with management accounting. These metrics measure the comparative performance of business lines and portfolios by including a cost charge for the capital used. In this way, consistency is introduced into business unit performance measurement. Measures such as risk-adjusted return and risk-adjusted return on risk-adjusted capital (RARORAC) are excellent KPIs to see how efficiently the institution's capital is put to work.

■ *Risk-Adjusted Excess Returns.* In this case the return is compared to the return of the market multiplied by the beta of the portfolio.

■ *Total Return.* This includes reinvested dividends.

Different considerations and input information as to a return measure include the following:

■ Are the returns gross or net of taxes that need to be paid (e.g., withholding tax)?

■ Are the returns gross or net of expenses and fees due to management of the fund?

■ What is the return period? Is the return a year-to-date return, is it a rolling one-year return, or is it the return of the last calendar year?

■ What benchmark is used if an excess return is claimed? Has the benchmark been consistent over the life of the fund and over the return period?

■ How does the return rank against the risk? What kind of return would be expected for the level of risk taken? In other words, what is the risk unit price per performance unit?

■ Is there a guaranteed return, for example, through an options structure? Is it possible to retrieve the price of that option construction or to replicate it via other products?

■ Are interim cash distributions from the fund included, and what are the assumptions on the reinvestment of those cash distributions?

■ Are accruals such as accrued coupon or dividend payment accrued since the last cash distribution included in the return measure?

■ Are other benefits incurred through holding this investment? If so, may they be quantified and added to the return? For example, income through securities lending operations?

■ How was the portfolio valued prior to the return calculation? Were accurate market data used? How were its illiquid assets valued? What valuation methodology was used? Was it mark-to-market, and if so, what prices were used? Was it mark-to-model, and if so, have there been independent verification of the models? Accountants have become more like bankers with the introduction of FASB 157. FASB157 on fair value accounting stipulates that three approaches can be used to revalue positions:
  • Market approach, e.g., through evaluated prices;
  • Income approach, e.g., using discounted cash flows to assess value;
  • Cost approach, e.g., by looking at the replacement costs of an asset.

  When evaluated pricing is used, it is always possible to revert to a discounted cash flow method if no quotes are available. Normally, information such as quotes, spreads, prepayment speeds, Loss Given Default measures, and so on are used to come to an evaluated price.

■ Have currency effects been taken into account? If so, have realistic exchange rates been used?

Given that to some extent the notion of return is relative, it is very important to be clear on the definition, since "return" is not just a number in a report, but also an important attribute on the basis of which consumer investment products are sold. The return number published is often the primary basis for selection of a financial product, and returns are also direct input for management fees. Prior to calculating a return, we need to establish the data requirements for analytics and attribution. The CFA Institute has defined performance presentation standards.[51] Not only does the concept of return need to be accurately defined, but it is also important to interpret what that return means. Is it good, bad, or reasonable? Typically, the return is benchmarked. The fund may have its own benchmark that it seeks to mimic or beat, in which case the *tracking error* is the difference with the benchmark. Which benchmark should be picked? Sometimes there is no appropriate benchmark. One person's tracking error is another person's alpha. If the fund has no benchmark, then the investor will still have certain expectations on return on the basis of the risk profile of the fund.

## Portfolio Performance Attribution

The *attribution* process of a portfolio checks whether the portfolio is appropriately positioned against the mandated risk factors and exposure. Good performance attribution of a portfolio will have both a tactical and strategic use and will:

■ Use a benchmark that reflects the strategy (and mandate) of the portfolio/ fund (strategic component);

■ Lead to an understanding of the relative effect each risk driver had to the performance of the portfolio;

■ Highlight the portfolio manager's skills in asset allocation (tactical component).

There are various approaches to attribution analysis. One approach is to fully reprice the portfolio with and without the effect for each risk factor. This would include the repricing of the portfolio every time while keeping one of the risk drivers constant. This approach requires a lot of data, and therefore summaries are often taken, for example, through factor models, similar to the principal components analysis discussed previously. For example, in fixed-income attribution for a government bond portfolio, the VCV matrix of yield curve changes could be computed and the principal components extracted from that market. Heuristically, the three principal components are interpreted as shifts to the curve, twists (change in slop), and changes in curvature. For other fixed-income portfolios, such as an MBS portfolio, we need to factor in prepayment factors and more factors have to be included.

Another example of risk decomposition—in this case, that of a corporate bond portfolio—is by isolating the effect on the portfolio of

- Yield return;
- Effect of changes of the yield curve (e.g., again split up in shift, twist, and curve);
- Changes in the credit spread.

This decomposition is by no means complete, since other effects would include changes in average duration (interest change effect), coupon payment effects, called/putted bond effects, other cash inflows/outflows, changes in sector allocation, dispersion of exposure over the yield curve, inflation effects, liquidity effects, and changes in option effects. Different portfolio analytics solutions providers such as StatPro[52] are creating valuation prices of non-traded assets. Tools such as Wilshire and Barra[53] are used to analyze and break down portfolio risk.

Considerations to bear in mind when setting up an attribution process include the following:

- Attribution should also reflect the purpose of the investment. For example, the purpose of holding the portfolio could be long-term growth. On the other hand, the investment can also be demand driven, such as liability-based investing for a pension fund that needs to be able to cover its disbursements to its beneficiaries every month.

- The equity and bond markets have very different performance factors, so the market that the portfolio invests in plays a role in the definition of the attribution process. Bonds are much more homogeneous in pricing compared to stocks.[54] Normally, bonds will have a smaller selection and diversification effect. Ten corporate bonds from 10 different industries are all systematically affected by the government bond curve. Ten different industries' stocks will display much less systematic price movement. Bonds are also more illiquid, often a less active secondary market compared to equities.

- Attribution against a benchmark requires knowledge of all the weights and returns of the benchmark constituents. Some benchmarks have a large number of constituents, and not all benchmarks are fully transparent. In the case of fixed income, the correct coupon amount and timing of coupon have to be taken into account for every constituent, some of which can be illiquid.

■ Equity attribution models could use different granularities from industry sectors, markets, geographies, and asset classes down to the individual stock level. Note that these attribution models do not price risk. They seek the sources of the return in order to assess the portfolio manager, but that return is not scaled by risk units through, for example, a risk-adjusted measure.

■ The interaction effect shows the dependencies between allocation and selection decisions. This effect can be large, decreasing the value of attribution models.

■ For portfolios with multiple currencies, the currency effects need to be factored in against the reporting currency.

Data needs for attribution would include the portfolio segment weights and their returns and benchmark segment weights and their returns. Good attribution means high data costs, both for gathering data internally as well as for collecting data needed externally.

## Financial Statements

The ultimate derived data are the financial statements including the cash flow statement, income statement, and balance sheet, which represent the state of the business. Internal audit and internal control need to be the watchdogs during the process of creating this information. Financial statements are typically produced quarterly and annually, and the (market) data at month end, quarter end, and especially year end will undergo additional quality checks.

## Summary Data

The risk and performance measures should give management as well as customers quick insight into the exposures and profile of the trading operations. The Risk Management Association[55] has defined a library of KPIs, which are summary measures meant to give a quick insight into the overall risk. An analogy is that of financial accounting where many ratios have been defined, meant to give a quick insight into various aspects of the business. We will discuss KPIs at length in the next chapter.

There is a large interplay between risk management and financial product innovation. Risk has become a continuum largely due to product innovation, and many generic products in the market can be used to take isolated exposure or to hedge away a certain risk factor. Thus, the number of tools at the disposal of a risk manager has grown larger. There is a general trend toward a "banking" level of sophistication in companies that used to report in less frequent or less granular fashions. Standards of measuring and reporting risk that were first developed by banks have spread to pension funds and also to, for example, other companies heavily involved in trading, such as energy companies. Investment managers are using more stringent EOD processes for their NAV and introducing more risk-based performance measures. The same holds for pension funds where many have become more active investment managers and have become active in a much broader set of asset classes. Some pension funds used to predominantly invest in fixed income but have diversified into equities and commodities and are undertaking derivative strategies to enhance yield or for portfolio (risk) management reasons. This has meant that their risk systems and portfolio reporting standards in terms of accuracy, frequency, and use of VaR-like measures needed to increase as well.

### 4.3.6 CONCLUSIONS

The measures of risk determine the room left for new transactions through their impact on trading limits. So, although financial reporting and risk reporting are to some extent the end of the transaction lifecycle, they also determine which new transactions can be initiated.

An important question is how the information supply chain of the instrument lifecycle *facilitates* or *impairs* successful processing? In many institutions various parts of the transaction lifecycle are decoupled in the sense that they do not only occur in different departments or divisions, but are typically left to specialized third-party providers which fulfill a significant part of the post-trade part. The general trend to invest in the front office where the trade ideas are born and executed and to leave the post-trade processing and support to specialized providers has meant that it can be more challenging to manage all aspects of the transaction lifecycle. This means that metrics on each step of this cycle are critical.

## 4.4 Processes Under Scrutiny: Regulation and Audit

### 4.4.1 INTRODUCTION

The main business processes we discussed around the transaction lifecycle are in reality not so much a single flow, but more like a river with many concurrent branching channels. Because of the propensity of data degradation, these processes are under increasing regulatory scrutiny. Requirements include increased retention of records, redundant channels and sources to secure business continuity, speed and automation in relaying information to reduce the number of points of failure due to good data, establishment and retention of data lineage, accessibility of audit information, and quality controls at every juncture in the supply chain where information is processed and potentially changed or enriched. Consequently, compliance is gaining in budget, in headcount, in status, and in prominence on financial institutions' orgcharts. Compliance officers have become quite powerful and are not provoked with impunity.

### 4.4.2 TOWARD A ZERO TOLERANCE FOR SLIPPAGE: EDP AND SAS BEST PRACTICES

There have been various initiatives to set up standards for sound processes. The Information Systems Audit and Control Association (ISACA) published the CobiT.[56] Standards such as the Committee of Sponsoring Organizations of the Treadway Commission (COSO) address the process that leads to accurate statements. The COSO enterprise risk management framework[57] addresses aspects such as internal environment, objective setting, event identification, risk assessment, risk response, control activities, information and communication, and monitoring. The enterprise risk framework aims to help set strategic focus and make tactical choices and encompasses focal areas such as the following:

- Aligning risk appetite and strategy.
- Enhancing risk response decisions. How does the institution deal with the risk? Responses can vary between risk avoidance, risk reduction, sharing, or acceptance.
- Reducing operational surprises and losses.
- Identifying and managing multiple and cross-enterprise risks.
- Improving capital deployment.

Electronic data process (EDP) audit is basically the ICT side support of the accounting function. It concerns itself with information and application security, but also with the correct implementation of business rules. For example, it could look into all information streams that go into the pricing of a complex derivative or the generation of the financial statements and risk figures. It focuses on the information technology and data flows that should safeguard the accuracy of the statements. EDP would look at how information is kept. In a database, local or central? In text documents, notes, scribbles, spreadsheets? In people's heads? Is it backed up? How can it be retrieved after 1 month, 1 year, 5 years?

EDP is also about vetting new processes or vetting modifications to processes, e.g., checks that controls cannot easily be circumvented through collusion of actors or in any case that circumventions and loopholes are monitored and violations tracked and reported. EDP should identify weaknesses in infrastructure, ensure the reliability of reporting, and identify potential risk events.

Another source of best practices in audit is the standards issued by the Auditing Standards Board of the AICPA.[58] A well-known one is Statement on Auditing Standards (SAS) 70, which lays down how an auditor evaluates the internal controls of a service company. Service organizations include data centers, ASPs, and clearinghouses, all of which are companies highly relevant to the financial industry. Service auditor reports come in two types:

- *Type I* gives the auditor's opinion on the accuracy of presentation of description of controls that are in effect, combined with an opinion on how suitable those controls are to attain their stated (control) objectives.

- *Type II* includes the Type I information but also includes an opinion on how effectively the controls were operated during a specific period of time, the review period.

SAS 70 reports include the role of information technology in the control environment. If part of the securities value chain is outsourced, the auditors also have to assess the internal controls of the service organization. The reason is that FSIs can outsource many functions and activities but cannot outsource their liability and the regulations to which they have to comply.

### 4.4.3 REGULATORY FOCUS

There was an increasing discrepancy during the 1990s between the financial risks taken and the information about these risks that was covered in the financial statements. Many derivative products such as swaps used to be off-balance sheet. This meant that the value of financial statements for investors as a means to understand the health of the company deteriorated. Financial reporting scandals led to an increased emphasis on control. This regulation made the controls over financial reporting even more important. There has also been a move to more fair value accounting. FASB 157 refers to fair value measurement and defines a framework to measure it, and it implies a need for more transparent securities pricing.

Whereas some of the earlier regulations to hit the financial services industry addressed specific issues (a credit risk measure, a market risk measure, fine-tuning of credit risk, an operational risk measure, investor protection), Sarbanes-Oxley covers all processes.

The financial reporting processes of most organizations are driven by IT systems. Few companies manage their data manually, and most companies rely on electronic management of data, documents, and key operational processes. Information technology plays a vital role in internal control: "The nature and characteristics of a company's use of information technology in its information system affect the company's internal control over financial reporting."[59]

For a bank, good quality market data are necessary for accurate financial statements. The Sarbanes-Oxley Act in the United States for publicly listed companies has given internal controls even more prominence than they already had. This legislation especially stresses controls on the overall process that leads to financial statements and emphasizes separation of duties, clarity on who changed what when and why (audit trail). Sarbanes-Oxley is more *qualitative* (i.e., you must have and be able to prove a solid process) rather than *quantitative* regulation, such as CAD 2, proscribing so many days' worth of historical data, a specific confidence level, and a specific holding period.

One key part of Sarbanes-Oxley is paragraph 404 ("404: Management's Reports on Internal Control Over Financial Reporting and Certification of Disclosure in Exchange Act Periodic Reports"), which addresses internal controls on financial reporting:

- Sarbanes Oxley comes down to a requirement to be able to back up all the published numbers and, by implication, also all price, curve, and reference data items that can have an effect on stated earnings or forecasts. This means that audit, security, and accuracy of information are enormously important.

- Regulators/auditors will review how secure, accurate, and auditable the interfaces and data infrastructure are.

In general we can conclude that

- A weak data process/infrastructure has knockvon effects.

- There is a need for the ability of "peeling the onion" in drilling down into the data management and quality assurance process, going back through the various steps, and tracking back to the ultimate source.

- Implementation of the G30 recommendation on implementing reference data standards[60] is slowed down due to the absence of a global owner.

### 4.4.4 COST ALLOCATION OF INFORMATION AND BUSINESS LOGIC

From the user side (applications, business processes, departments), costs of data supply are apportioned back to the consumers in various ways, including the following:

- The number of end users;
- The number of primary sources used (i.e., directly correlated with content spend);
- The number of consuming applications (i.e., correlated with the internal system integration work);
- The number of files (correlated with data sourcing effort).

Thus, we see that it can be either through identification of exact use and matching that to costs or through using a proxy for usage and then use a cost attribution formula. Sometimes the allocation process is done in a very crude way. Note that the metrics mentioned here allocate total costs based on efforts of specific steps in the supply chain, i.e., sourcing, content spend, and system integration work.

Because of the difficulty of quantifying the costs of data, an adequate assessment of value of serviced solutions such as BPO, outsourcing, and also of internal software solutions, central data warehouses, and cross-reference content offerings is often hindered and business cases remain fuzzy for all but the largest institutions that can collect statistically meaningful results by themselves.

## 4.5 Use Cases

### 4.5.1 INTRODUCTION

In this section we will discuss various use cases on how data access leads to productivity gains and which aspects of data are important for different activities in the transaction lifecycle. In short, it always comes down to a browsing problem. If reliable data were available instantly, productivity would soar. The common thread in this discussion is that the combination of and cross-linking between different categories of information improve decision making. The use cases cover the various main stages in the transaction lifecycle that we discussed previously. In this section we will discuss the following use cases:

- Risk management
- OTC derivatives valuation

- Commodity trading and pricing
- Some miscellaneous cases for front-office information access and counter-party data processing

### 4.5.2 RISK MANAGEMENT DATA CHALLENGES

The adage that historical results do not predict the future holds also for correlations; they also tend to change very abruptly. What could appear to be a nicely constructed, well-optimized hedge on day one can become a serious risk on day two. Sources of risk in (derivative) instruments include currency risk, commodity basis risk, yield curve risk, sector concentrations in credit and equity, default risk and correlations between different risks such as credit, equity and interest rate risk. In this section we will look at some information challenges in market, credit, and operational risks, respectively.

*Market risk* data challenges include the following:

- Dealing with sometimes different quoting and *dateroll* conventions. Dateroll refers to the treatment of days when they fall on a weekend or bank holiday. For example, when a 1-month deposit is traded on October 27, it would settle on October 29 and expire 1 month later, on November 29. If this day is on a weekend or on a bank holiday, expiration would be on the first business day following the 29th. Exceptions can occur in this case as we cross over into a new month. There are various ways of dealing with this: either going into the month, sticking to the 29th, or going back to the last business day before the 29th.

- Agreeing on sources for the most accurate prices, for example, the brokers that are most reliable and the execution venues that are most liquid.

- Agreeing on curve sources, for example, the zero curve for OECD countries using deposits, swaps, forward rate agreements, money market futures, and bonds as available. Decide which products to use and maintain the source lists with these products as bonds mature and futures expire. Create short zero curves for some emerging markets using deposit rates snapped from broker pages (see Figure 4.4).

- Deciding on the curve methodology to be used. There are many flavors of bootstrapping and interpolation methods.

- Deciding on which validation functions to apply to screen the data used and data produced. If you are too loose, you will miss bad data; if you are too strict, you will incur high operational costs. Special treatment will normally be meted out to data on end of month, end of quarter, and especially end of fiscal year dates.

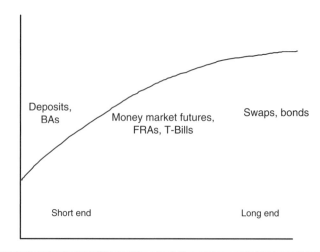

**Figure 4.4** Zero curve with different instrument types as sources for different sections of the curve

■ Addressing a numerical calculation problem of producing a VCV matrix and VaR number fast for the CFO and the Head of Trading, and also to be able to calculate the marginal effects of new trades on the institution's risk position so that the remaining risk capital can be deployed most effectively.

■ Creating your own benchmark as a linear combination of market indices or on the basis of a basket of instruments. Create a correlation matrix for the index constituents.

*Credit risk* data challenges include the following:

■ The ability to cross-reference ratings from the different agencies, the ability to define a proxy rating (e.g., in case the issuer is not rated, reverting to the rating of a linked bond). This is an example of making use of the issuer-issue links.

■ The content and financial markets provide various measures of credit, all of which can be used to contribute to the overall credit assessment. Matching rules need to operate to combine these various credit assessments, such as credit default swap curves, corporate bond price history, corporate data, ratings, dividend history, earnings, and interpolated dividend forecasts.

■ Sovereign risk is a special credit area and relies on, for example, an internal economic bureau that researches macroeconomic and political analysis.

■ Keep a historical set of internal ratings, probabilities of default, earnings at default, and loss given default numbers as required for the Internal Ratings Based approaches under Basel II.

■ Additional credit risk challenges include the linkages of guarantors to obligations, and to account for other credit protection and enhancement measures in the risk assessment, recognizing former legal names, rolling up to the ultimate global obligor through the tracking of a legal hierarchy, unique unambiguous identification of legal entities.

*Operational risk* presents its own content challenges. One issue is sourcing it and getting staff to report on losses. You have to get the definition right and determine how you will group and classify operational losses, plus decide what constitutes a loss and what is an expected cost of doing business.

Unlike market and credit risk, the cause of operational risk is often internal[61] and quite specific for the organization. It is a cultural challenge for many organizations to get people to report on their own errors. Apart from this, there is a data scarcity problem; operational risk events have the typical distribution shown in Figure 4.5.

To get sufficient representation of big losses, you need to also use either artificial internal data produced by theoretical stress tests (hard to get this right) or to combine your own data set with external data. This has been done through various pooling consortia.[62] But, by the definition of operational risk, loss events are closely linked to a unique institution because they are the result of failures in people, systems, and processes; so the question becomes how to map them to your own financial and cultural situation. A loss event for a

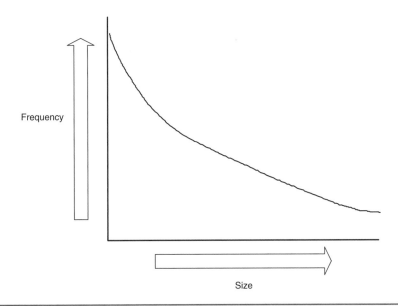

**Figure 4.5** Operational risk losses distribution

Japanese broker or German insurer may not be that useful for a French investment bank. Even if you are comparing apples and apples, there are differences and complications in scaling. Suppose there is a reference loss that occurred at a Dutch fund manager with $200 billion AUM, and you are a Dutch fund manager with $100 under management. How should you treat the loss? Take it unchanged or halve it? Note that these loss collection problems presuppose an operational risk measurement process that used the actuarial loss distribution approach (LDA); other loss VaR modeling methods present their own unique data challenges.

### 4.5.3 (OTC DERIVATIVES) VALUATION POLICIES

There is the question of determining the valuation policy. This can become a thorny issue because the choice of execution venues and therefore the number of potential sources from which to draw a revaluation price increase. This selection problem due to the fragmentation of liquidity means you have to keep tabs on many more venues, e.g., to be able to perform selections such as "three most liquid venues" even assuming you have a uniform and workable definition of liquidity. Besides, the market models of the various venues may also differ. Following are some options:

- Pick the most liquid value; look at the traded volume and the average size of the transactions taking place at that venue. Check periodically whether that venue is still the most liquid.
- Look at the highest and lowest price point from several venues.
- Look at the bid-ask spread on the best available quote from all venues.
- Look at the last traded price on all venues.
- Use a VWAP measure, either on one venue or on a selection of venues. The selection can be based on the venues on which the institution normally trades, or it can be identical to the set of venues agreed with the originator of the trade, e.g., as per the best execution policy agreed with the client.
- Take the price from the local exchange or execution venue.
- If the bank is *internalizing* (or crossing) transactions, take the trader's mid-price verified against one or more external sources.
- Convert prices in case of multiple available execution venues that list the product in different currencies. Take up-to-date foreign exchange prices to do this.

Note that these kinds of price consolidation functions (selecting the best valuation price from a series of sources based on criteria such as date, time, venue, volume, and internal policy) are an integral part of the information supply chain. This process used to be done in-house, but some content providers also started to offer these services. These companies would have access to the raw data available already and would manufacture a tailored set of valuation prices as per the client's instructions.

When evaluated prices are used to revalue positions in illiquid products, this task is often done by looking at "like" or comparable securities. This means that when a price cannot be found for a product, pricing for a comparable security is used. *Comparable* can mean comparable in terms of type, (sub)sector of industry of the issuer, quality, cash flow structure, and possibly comparable in terms of duration, convexity, average life, weighted average maturity, and so on. These will typically not be fully economically equivalent—i.e., responding in the same way to the same fluctuations in risk drivers—so a basis risk is introduced.

For adequate OTC derivatives processing, extensibility of a data model is a must-have, as the number of terms can always grow. The constant flow of new products means that if you can keep up from a processing perspective, there are also significant benefits in being first to market. Time-to-market advantages and the higher margin made on these products to some extent can justify the higher processing costs and even manual processing for a while, until rising volumes lead to a paper crisis and cause a processing backlog that increases settlement risk. If OTC derivatives are not accurately priced, the institution could also suffer from *adverse selection*: Counterparties will select the institution as a trading party and continually ask it for quotes with the hope of mispricing. In that case the institution can become the fool of the market if its quotes are accepted the whole time.

Let's consider a specific example in credit derivatives: that of a first to default note (FDN). The buyer gets a premium on taking the risk on a basket of credits. If any credit in the basket undergoes one of a predefined set of credit events, the buyer will get bonds of that entity against the proceeds of the FDN. The most common form of this structure is a 5-year FDN with five credits in the basket. To calculate the price of the structure, we need the credit spreads, but also the default correlation between the various components of the basket. In case of a high correlation, the price of the basket will be like the largest credit spread. If the correlation is low, pricing is like a weighted average spread. The difficulty in valuing this structure lies in measuring the default correlations with little available historical data. In information terms, the problem is similar to using a Basel II IRB advanced approach.

### Mutual Fund Repricing NAV Process

Two distinct processes are used in calculating the NAV. The first process is to update the previous night's NAV for any trading activity, as well as any daily expenses, shareholder purchases and redemptions, and income earned. The second process is updating the NAV for the change in market value on the securities the fund holds. This cannot be completed until the market closes. This pricing process occupies the late afternoon for the entire accounting department and is the busiest time of the day. There are other responsibilities, including researching and resolving bank balance variances and other items. Finally, maintaining the monthly general ledger reconciliations and expense accruals fall under this category.

Recalculation of the NAV of a fund is not as easy as it looks. Apart from the issues listed previously in securing reliable prices, there are other factors that need to be taken into account. In short, someone responsible for determining the NAV needs to:

- Include payments made on holdings such as dividends;
- Include daily purchases and redemptions of fund units by holders of the funds;
- Include money extracted to pay fees to fund managers, brokers, custodians, etc.;
- Include changes in holdings;
- Take new updated prices;
- Use business logic to create a price if none exists;
- (optional) Include costs made for margin calls and revalue liabilities, for example (in case short sales are allowed).

To take away the effect of cash inflows and outflows, we can also use participations in the fund and calculate a *Unit Value* for each participation. For fund performance on NAV, we can calculate the internal rate of return (IRR): The interest rate that a savings account would have needed to give us to come to the same value at the end of the reporting period based on the same cash in- and outflows.

#### 4.5.4 DATA CHALLENGES IN COMMODITY TRADING

### Market Landscape and Development

Over the past years, commodities have become an integrated product line for many sell-side institutions and a more ordinary asset class to invest in for the buy-side. More products have been offered by investment banks or have become listed on exchanges which have trended toward screen-based trading. New primary products have been created as power exchanges are adding emissions to their portfolio of products, and emissions are now part of the overall energy portfolio. Because investment managers have added commodities to diversify, the proportion of fund holdings in commodities has grown. Banks are offering power-based or emissions-based risk products, and more hybrid or structured products (i.e., products linked to indices such as the Goldman Sachs Commodity Index (GSCI)) can be expected from the banks to accommodate institutional investors and retail individuals. Because of these developments, commodity-based financial products are no longer fundamentally different from other products in trading and to some extent processing. The main system providers in risk and portfolio management have fully integrated commodities into their product lines, which means that the data supply to these systems should keep pace, too. Nevertheless, specific data management challenges remain, and they include the following:

- Energy commodities are very volatile. This means that data quality has a different dimension here and that access to accurate and independently verified price and curve data is essential.

- It is necessary to look at the whole group within a commodity complex. For example, there is a large set of grades of oil, only a couple of which have a forward market (e.g., WTI and Brent Crude). Often you need to proxy the physical with one of these grades, or you have a product sitting between two other products (e.g., ethanol is the middle product in the market between oil and sugar). When one product is hedged with another (related) commodity, the basis risk has to be carefully monitored.

- Because the long end of a curve is often very illiquid, the bid-offer spread and illiquidity of longer-dated contracts should be included into measures of VaR and stress testing. The high transaction costs incurred to roll over futures positions or to hedge longer dated exposures also need to be accounted for in the risk measure.

- In energy markets, typical model assumptions such as that returns follow approximately a normal distribution are violated; energy markets are particularly non-normal!

- Commodity prices are exposed to a very large set of risk factors that combine such items as diverse as event risk, cash flow risk, basis risk, legal/regulatory risk, operational risk, tax risk, and geopolitical/macro and weather risk.

The political situation often determines the relative rarity and supply risks that impact the price. In addition to this, price volatility is caused by fundamental factors such as supply/demand and—for soft commodities and energy commodities—the weather. More data, including macroeconomic data, will need to be integrated to get to the full picture. Also, some commodity prices are correlated with the business cycle and some not. All this translates into more data needs from potentially other and more heterogeneous sources than those traditionally used for financial products.

- Because of the enormous variety of grades and developments in structured products, new data elements need to be added frequently to deal-capture and processing systems to cater for descriptions of all current and future product varieties. The required information will also vary by jurisdiction and company type. In the case of utilities, for example, it is necessary to include tax relief applicable to the use of biomass fuels and costs of emissions (e.g., the use of coal versus the use of natural gas).

## The Forward Curve

The forward curve is the foundation of any commodity product pricing and risk assessment and therefore a core ingredient to any rates system. However sophisticated the derivative pricing model may be, if the forward curve that is put into the calculation is inaccurate, the resulting errors will overshadow any value the complex pricing model has to offer. A common error in a valuation process is to focus on pricing exotic products, while the foundation of the whole process—the forward price curves that affect the valuation of the whole portfolio—are inaccurate to begin with, thereby rendering the whole pricing exercise of the exotics useless. In terms of derived data and analytics, the forward curve presents the following challenges:

- Detecting or correcting seasonality. Seasonality effects differ between products. For example, WTI has no seasonality, whereas heating oil exhibits seasonality and electricity has two seasonality factors during a year. Historical temperature data may need to be contrasted with an observed forward price curve to forecast.

- Deriving data from primary and daughter commodities such as the calculation of different spreads (for example, crack spread, dark spread, spark spread, and unit of measurement conversions such as rebasing prices from a CAD/Gigajoule to a USD/million British Thermal Units basis). See also Section 4.2.

- Different data representations may be necessary for different purposes, so flexibility in viewing data is required. For example, in some cases a forward curve should be presented with the maturity expressed as actual calendar days and in other cases as different offsets from today's date (1M, 2M, 6M, 1Y, 2Y, and so on). Another example would be different representations of volatility smiles and surfaces in delta points[63] or in absolute dollar terms.

■ Validation functions that operate on the data may check for day-to-day consistency and may also check the curve at time T against the curve at time $T - 1$ in terms of the percentage change, the absolute shift, the expected jump of long end versus the observed jump at the short end, and so on.

■ A capability to compare data from different sources. Examples of this case would be to compare the WTI curve built out of trader assessments against the WTI constant maturity futures curve built out of New York Mercantile Exchange (NYMEX) futures. Another example of this case would be to compare the NYMEX curve versus the Intercontinental Exchange (ICE) curve: The ability to detect if anything significant happened during the ICE close and the NYMEX close is imperative prior to using the curve.

The data issues and potential benefits that can be achieved when information management is done properly can be summarized as shown in Table 4.3.

### 4.5.5 MISCELLANEOUS

Apart from these three cases, two other concise examples are discussed in this section for front-office data access and for the treatment of counterparty data in the internal supply chain.

#### *Front-Office Data Access*

For front-office decision support and the generation of trade ideas, a lot of time is wasted through inefficient browsing of information. Indeed, we would claim that easy access to data is one of the largest untapped productivity improvement opportunities left to financial institutions. Highly paid staff waste time on more mundane data collection work—especially for more time-critical trading strategies where the opportunity costs of *not having access* to data are often literally prohibitive.

Examples abound. In the case of arbitrage, a hedge portfolio needs to be constructed. For example, in index arbitrage you would have the index on one hand and constituents (or a major subset of the constituents) on the other hand. You need to keep prices up to data on both. Easy access to related

**Table 4.3**   Benefits and Objectives from Improved Information Management in the Commodity Trading Example

|  | Front Office | Mid-Office | Back Office |
|---|---|---|---|
| Control | ■ Determine curve methodology without influencing the daily mark to market prices | ■ Segregation of duties<br>■ Apply logical validation of data<br>■ Apply solid controls<br>■ Reduced dependency on Excel | ■ Increased accuracy of price and curve data<br>■ Transparency of data lineage to trace back to sources |
| Efficiency | ■ Improved price capture interfaces<br>■ Establish a single source of data across all business lines | ■ Automation of curve generation and validation reduces manual work<br>■ Single internal authoritative source of price data<br>■ Reduce manual work in reconciliations | ■ Single data flow enables STP efficiencies<br>■ All price and curve data in one place<br>■ Workflow to route exceptions to relevant locations |
| Growth | ■ Enables insightful cross-product analysis<br>■ Improved risk and profit and loss process helps decision making<br>■ Flexible modeling for new products and local context | ■ Improved efficiency enables more capacity for data volume<br>■ Underpins mark-to-market and risk measurement processes | ■ Improved efficiency enables growth |

instruments can explode productivity and insight. For example, the ability to link from an equity directly to all the (ATM) options. For fixed-income securities, look up other Euro government bonds around a certain point on the curve to do research on z-scores, for example, or other cheap/dear analysis. Compare the credit spread of bonds against other measures in the credit market such as CDS so you can generate trading ideas much faster. Collect basic statistics on top performances, and for behavioral finance, track the overshooters and undershooters. An example of structured finance is the selection problem when creating a CDO, looking for bonds with right characteristics. In all cases, the rapid *deployment* of information is critical and the absence of timely accurate information carries significant opportunity costs. The science and art of financial engineering are the conversion of risk from one form to another. If you identify the price drivers correctly, you can separate them and bundle them together in different mix to produce tailored offerings for your clients.

## Counterparty Data Processing

In managing and processing counterparty data, there are some special aspects to consider.

Apart from the identification of the security or contract, the counterparty of the trade is also part of the required settlement information. In general, complications in the area of counterparty and legal entity data management include the following:

- *Larger Variety of Sources.* A larger variety of sources for legal entity data including chambers of commerce, rating agencies, court proceedings, news feeds, direct research, websites, and data aggregators.

- *Internally Sourced Information.* A larger proportion of data is sourced internally because some information is proprietary, for example, internal ratings, client profiles (e.g., MiFID customer classification and best execution agreement), and reporting hierarchies.

- *Diversity in Content Licensing.* There is commercial content as you have in security master and in streaming pricing information. However, some legal entity information is public (e.g., financial statements of public companies), whereas other information is sourced peer-to-peer through business relationships (SSIs), and other information would be confidential (limits, client profiles, holdings, internal credit ratings, and exposures). Contrast this with, for example, security master or pricing data, which are much more homogeneous as far as sensitivity and sourcing are concerned. This means specific challenges for access rights and data protection.

■ *More Politics as to Ownership of Data.* Compared to relatively neutral security master data, counterparty data may be more politically sensitive. After all, with the ownership of the client data could come the ownership of the client relationship.

■ *Different Data Quality Assurance Process* driven by integration rather than comparison and the lack of identifiers, which makes for a different matching process. The national numbering agencies do not cover the legal entities in their jurisdiction; as a result there are more proprietary identification standards (IBEI 16372, starting to be issued by some vendors; some standards are in place but have not been set up to serve as unique identification of an entity necessitated by regulation—for example, BIC code: there are multiple per entity, but this is more an office identification and no strict correspondence to a legal structure). In the data integration process, unlike security master, you will not have a lot of redundant sources in use to cross-check vendors or to ensure business continuity; the process will be more about completing the jigsaw by sourcing complementary data sets (financial information, research information, relationship information). So the data management process is more about integration than comparison, and the matching process is typically fuzzier (on strings), since there is a lack of identification standards, meaning matching will take place on many different attributes (e.g., legal form, country of incorporation, sector, string matches) or on internal identifiers, and you will need to put more business value-add in your cleansing rules.

In Chapter 5, we will build on the anecdotal material presented in this section and discuss in more general terms quality aspects—fitness for purpose— together with KPIs that allow you to assess and measure that quality.

## 4.6 Conclusions

In Chapters 2, 3, and 4, we have dissected and discussed the matrix of trade and instrument lifecycle versus the information supply chain.

We have looked at content types, at the financial instruments, and at the processes in the trade lifecycle. In the next chapter, we will take a closer look at the many metadata aspects that play a significant part. This will conclude the information process discussion. We will end Chapter 5 with a set of conclusions for the design and setup of these processes and how content and quality measures of content can best be fitted to the different business processes and workflows that rely on them.

Getting the matrix of information supply chain right across products and processes is what information and process management is all about and is a determining factor in competitive advantage. Understanding your users' needs not just in information terms (what they want), but just as importantly in meta-information terms (where, how do they need it, how fast, what quality checks, what is the marginal value versus cost of a second pair of eyes to check it, another source to cross-compare, another execution venue, etc.), is critical input to setting up your trade processes and information supply chain. Only when you have done that can you look to another issue: Which parts of the trade lifecycle and information supply chain do you make your business and which parts do you leave to other parties? If you cover many different markets and arbitrage between numerous products and venues, information integration is a key competitive differentiator. If you specialize, you can outsource more but will invest, for example, in the lowest latency.

Pressure has been put on traditional processes to accommodate an increasingly diversified set of products and disparate downstream information needs. Instead of local solutions and quick fixes, strategic investments into information infrastructures are required to set the foundation for growth. Because of the fragmentation in financial products and processes, the trend we see is that the vendor community is growing and that home-grown solutions will be options only for the largest or most specialized financial institutions. In an ideal world, high-quality data on instruments, counterparties, and prices would be available instantly and as easily as utilities such as power, natural gas, and water. In this kind of household, productivity would soar.

Access to information is a critical basis of competition between the various categories of players within the financial services industry. If you know your risk measures and your portfolio attribution, you know what you are doing. If you know your clients and the effects of your actions better than the neighbors, you can also more accurately price a transaction. Regulation on solvency, on investor protection, on sound processes, and on financial reporting plays a large role as well. Ultimately, however, more insight into the products and industry participants that you deal with is not a regulatory matter; it provides you with a foundation on which to do subsequent business.

## Endnotes

[1] The formula to convert between forward prices and deposit rates is $F = S * [(1 + rf * (n/d2)] / (1 + rUSD * (n/d1)) - 1$ where $F$ = FX forward rate, $S$ = spot rate,

rUSD = deposit rate for USD (base currency), rf = deposit rate for foreign currency (quoted currency), and n = number of days between the spot and forward dates.

[2]Proxies are not confined to time series. They are also used in the area of credit ratings. If an issuer is not rated, the issuer rating could be proxied by taking the rating of the senior debt.

[3]For the original article, see Nelson, C.R., and Siegel, A.F. (1987), Parsimonious modeling of yield curves. *Journal of Business*, *60*, 473–489.

[4]An example of a company active in this space is Human Inference, http://www.humaninference.com/.

[5]See, for example, numbers on IT spent in reports from research firms such as TowerGroup, Celent and Aite Group.

[6]Players in this space include SunGard—Adaptiv 360 (http://www.sungard.com/Adaptiv/default.aspx?id = 4195), Advent—Geneva (http://www.advent.com/solutions/fund_administrators/geneva), Macgregor XIP (http://www.itg.com/offerings/macgregor_xip.php), DST—HiPortfolio (http://www.dstinternational.com/HiPortfolio.asp), Eagle Pace (http://www.eagleinvsys.com/products/eagle_pace.aspx), Princeton PAM (http://www.pfs.com/solutions/overview/overview.asp), Summit from Misys (http://www.misysbanking.com/Misys_Banking_Family/Summit/index.html), and Reuters—Kondor + (http://about.reuters.com/productinfo/kondorplus/).

[7]Players active in this area include GLTrade (formerly FNX at www.fnx.com), Sierra Treasury, and Wall Street Systems (www.wallstreetsystems.com/). Specialized companies focus on forecasting techniques such as 4CAST (http://www.4castweb.com/).

[8]Pre-trade analytics/analysis providers include SunGard—Front Arena (www.frontarena.com/), Sybase—Risk Analytics platform (www.sybase.com), Vhayu—Velocity (www.vhayu.com/velocity.html), and Quadrus (www.quadrus.com).

[9]Sample providers of generic reporting functionality include products such as Business Objects Crystal Reports (www.businessobjects.com), Microsoft Analysis Services/Report Services, and Excel.

[10]A specific area is that of Event Stream Processing, which operates on streaming data and can filter out anomalies or patterns. Companies in this space include Aleri (www.aleri.com) and StreamBase (www.streambase.com).

[11]See, for example, Credit Delta from UBS on www.ubs.com and other prime brokerage activities.

[12]Services such as the Lipper Tass database (http://www.lipperweb.com/products/tass.asp) provide classifications. Typical style epithets include long/short equity hedge, event-driven, emerging markets, multistrategy, fixed-income arbitrage, global macro, managed futures, equity market neutral, and convertible arbitrage.

[13]See http://www.hedgefundresearch.com.

[14]See www.hedgefund.net/publicnews.

[15]*Source:* http://cisdm.som.umass.edu/research/pdffiles/benefitsofhedgefunds.pdf, p.6.

[16]See http://www.newstatesman.com/200607310033.

[17]Players include Lava colorbook (https://www.lavatrading.com/) and RealTick (www.realtick.com).

[18]Players in this area include Advent Moxy (http://www.advent.com/solutions/prime_brokers/moxy), Charles River Development (http://www.crd.com/hom.php), Murex (http://www.murex.com/home.php), INDATA Precision Trading (www.indataweb.com/), Linedata LongView Trading System (http://www.ldsam.com/longview_trading.html), Sungard Decalog (http://www.sungard.com/decalog/), Eze Castle Traders Console, and Macgregor Financial Trading Platform (www.ezecastlesoftware.com).

[19]For an excellent discussion on liquidity, see Harris, L. (2003). *Trading and Exchanges—Market Microstructure for Practitioners*, Oxford University Press. The terminology used here is based on that discussion.

[20]See www.liquidnet.com.

[21]This includes the 27 European Union countries plus Norway, Iceland, and Liechtenstein.

[22]Taken from MiFID level 2 text, February 2006.

[23]Players with solutions that do some or all of these activities include Advent (www.advent.com), Charles River (www.crd.com), Fidessa LatentZero (http://www.latentzero.com/), Selero (http://www.selero.com/), and FlexTrade (http://www.flextrade.com/).

[24]Players in clearing and settlement systems include SunGard—STeP intelliSUITE (http://www.sungard.com/STeP/default.aspx?id = 38), Findur—Open Link (www.olf.com/), Kyriba (www.kyriba.com), PFPC (www.pfpc.com), DTCC, and many national clearing houses.

[25]See http://www.cls-group.com/cls_bank/index.cfm. CLS currently settles in 15 currencies.

[26]Clearstream and Deutsche Boerse are examples of the latter category. Euronext and LCH.Clearnet are examples of the former category.

[27]*Source:* www.lchclearnet.com. DTCC cleared and settled a daily average of $4.5T in securities value in 2004; *source:* www.dtcc.com.

[28]The SwapClear service clears USD, EUR, JPY, and GBP swaps up till 30 years maturity and a number of other OECD currencies up till 10 years in maturity. See www.lchclearnet.com.

[29]Equity markets are still, for the most part, at T+3; Germany is at T+2.

[30]See http://www.celentPress.com/Releases/20061010/EuroPostTrade.htm.

[31]See *Second Report on EU Clearing and Settlement Arrangements*, The Giovannini Group, Brussels, April 2003, http://ec.europa.eu/economy_finance/giovannini/clearing_settlement_en.htm.

[32]Ibid.

[33]See www.group30.org.

[34]Reproduced from http://www.issanet.org/pdf/G30-01-2003.pdf.

[35]Specific trade organizations that have also advised on making clearing and settlement more efficient include the International Organization of Securities Commissions

(IOSCO at www.iosco.org), European Central Securities Depository Organization (ECSDA at www.ecsda.com), and Committee on Payment and Settlement Systems (CPSS at www.bis.org/cpss/index.htm). CPSS and IOSCO have issued recommendations for settlement systems and for central counterparties.

[36]DTCC and Euroclear are some of the largest ICSDs. Other examples include SIS SegaInterSettle (www.sisclear.com/).

[37]In Italy, it is Monte Titoli, part of Borsa Italiana group (www.montetitoli.it/). IBERCLEAR is the Spanish CSD (www.iberclear.es).

[38]Estimated at 300 million Euro per annum. See the white paper "Euroclear Business Model Implementation Update Paper—Single Platform Implementation Plan," March 31, 2005, at www.euroclear.com.

[39]The term IBAN is not used in the United States where the term ABA (American Bankers Association) number is used.

[40]Examples of RTGSs include Fedwire in the United States and CHAPS in the United Kingdom.

[41]For example, SmartStream (http://www.smartstream.com).

[42]This section draws from the following text which I found very helpful: *An Introduction to Securities Lending*, by Mark C. Faulkner which is available at http://www.bba.org. uk/bba/jsp/polopoly.jsp?d=130&a=3311.

[43]See www.equilend.com and www.secfinex.com.

[44]Note that the phenomenon of hard and soft dollaring is a result of fund accounting. For a fund, it is better to keep expenses low (so limit the hard dollars) and to get all ancillary services (e.g., research) on the back of trade execution commissions. Commissions are not expenses but depress investment returns.

[45]Such as a change in correlation that renders what was a good hedge into a more risky position.

[46]See www.riskmetrics.com for more background.

[47]Third-party risk solutions include Kamakura (www.kamakura.com), Murex (www. murex.com), Sophis (http://www.sophis.net/index_v8.html), Mysis's Riskvision (http:// www.misysbanking.com/Misys_Banking_Family/Risk_Vision/index.html), SunGard Corporate—Adaptiv market/credit risk (http://www.sungard.com/Adaptiv/), Algorithmics (http://www.algorithmics.com/EN/solutions/ integratedmarketrisk/1-integrated.cfm), Calypso ERS (http://www.calypso.com/risk.html), and DSTi's Risk Solutions (http://www.dstinternational.com/Solutions/Investment_Management/ Risk_&_Performance_Solutions/).

[48]For example, that provided by RiskMetrics (www.riskmetrics.com), which came out of JPMorgan in the 1990s. Note that banks that are market makers and specialists in certain countries would be better positioned to create the risk factors but could still choose to rely on independent risk factor sourcing.

[49]For great discussions on this topic, see, for example, Mandelbrot, B.B., and Hudson, R. L. (2006). *The (Mis)Behaviour of Markets: A Fractal View of Risk, Ruin and Reward*, Perseus Books Group; and Taleb, N.N. (2005). *Fooled by Randomness: The Hidden Role of Chance in Life and in the Markets*, Random House.

[50]The alpha/beta paradigm can be found mostly in plain vanilla products, such as cash equity portfolios, and is also often used in marketing material. Unlike some other measures, alpha and beta are purely statistical. The simplicity of the alpha/beta paradigm contrasts sharply with the difficulty of attribution and performance analysis.

[51]See http://www.cfainstitute.org/centre/ips/.

[52]See http://www.statpro.com/data_hub.asp.

[53]See www.wilshire.com and www.mscibarra.com.

[54]An exception would be junk bonds, which would be highly dependent on the unique nature of the borrower; in that case a junk bond trading at a deep discount will behave more like an equity.

[55]See http://www.rmahq.org/RMA/.

[56]The *Control Objectives for Information and Related Technology;* see www.isaca.org/cobitonline/.

[57]See http://www.coso.org/Publications/ERM/COSO_ERM_ExecutiveSummary.pdf.

[58]See http://www.aicpa.org/.

[59]See PCAOB's Auditing Standard 2, www.pcaobus.org/Standards/Standards_and_Related_Rules/Auditing_Standard_No.2.aspx.

[60]See www.group30.org/.

[61]For the BIS operational risk classification, see, for example, Table 2 in *Operational Risk Data Collection Exercise—2002*, http://www.bis.org/bcbs/qis/oprdata.pdf.

[62]See, for example, the Operational Risk Exchange Association on www.orx.org.

[63]*Delta points* refers to the moneyness of an option; *100% moneyness* would be at-the-money. A strike price could be represented in a relative manner, i.e., as an offset to the at-the-money level through, for example, 110%, 120%, or 70% or in absolute dollar terms.

# Chapter 5

# Metrics and Criteria for Success in Infrastructure

## 5.1 Introduction

So far we have looked at the instrument lifecycle through a discussion of products and markets; at the information supply chain through a discussion of the steps in creating content and the various categories of content; and at the transaction lifecycle from trade idea to execution, settlement, asset servicing, and reporting. Tying these strands together and having everything operating smoothly means the difference between a well-oiled operation that allows for opportunities to *scale* in terms of new clients and products or an information jungle that has users drown in irrelevant information and endlessly wonder about the presence and trustworthiness of the information on which they depend.

This chapter focuses on aspects that can be used to define quality and fitness for purpose of information and on the metrics by which the efficacy of information sourcing, processing, dissemination, and generation can be assessed. We will discuss criteria with which to judge the quality of information used throughout any process and discuss how to arrive at a well-managed information architecture. We will present examples and discuss benchmarks, key performance indicators (KPIs), early warning signs, costs involved, and the balance between operational risk and cost of a process. Due to ongoing product development and growth in data volumes, process efficacy erosion is a fact of life. Processes can be hard-wired into an organization, and since the rest of the world evolves, what normally happens is that the process is tweaked at the edges (e.g. through the use of spreadsheets and manual workarounds) or abused (forcefully fit in new information into a data standard) and becomes increasingly less transparent.

Section 5.2 discusses the typical state of information architectures in large, diversified financial institutions—that of high entropy—and what the challenges are to introduce common data services to streamline the information supply chain. Section 5.3 covers various aspects of information quality. The topic of Section 5.4 is the content manufacturing process in financial institutions, and Section 5.5 aims to quantify the quality of a process through metrics and service-level agreements reflecting the maxim "what you cannot measure you cannot manage." After having discussed KPIs in depth, we will return to the trade process model of wholesale versus retail in Section 5.6 and see whether these two could ever be reconciled in information management terms. In this section we will also discuss what constitutes success in information management. Section 5.7 contains the conclusions of this chapter. We will weigh the different criteria for the various processes discussed. In addition, we will make the case for common data models and business logic because that is how the four main types of content discussed in Chapter 3 can come together, interact, and enrich one another. We also will discuss what the future holds for financial content and the way it is sourced and distributed. Combined with a discussion around best practices and what aspects of information management are important where, we finally will draw lessons for data sourcing and distribution architectures.

## 5.2 The Information Entropy Situation

### 5.2.1 THE NOTION OF INFORMATION ENTROPY

In information theory as well as in probability theory, *entropy* refers to the level of surprise and amount of uncertainty in information presented. In a financial infrastructure context, we can apply the concept as a measure of the efficiency of the information supply chain.

Many different steps in a supply chain are often necessary before it reaches a place where an end user or system actually acts on it with regard to business decision making. This, combined with the sheer number of different departments, locations, and so on, provides an indication of data quality and hence of the trust that users can have in it.

Often an information supply chain is likened to a game of "Chinese whispers," with increasing uncertainty on the accuracy of the information as the number of places where it is touched grows. Product proliferation and regulatory demands continuously foster the need for new vendor content and software products. These need to be integrated with existing infrastructures in turn. This is one of the reasons why, if we look at an institution's data architecture from a bird's-eye perspective, it can look like a clogged-up river delta. Data flows branch out and come together. Some channels run smoothly from source to destination, but others are clogged up with silt, causing backlogs and flow to come to a standstill.

Emergency Excel sheets are often used to intervene because they at least give users the illusion of control. This observed system, spreadsheet and database jungle, and high entropy are also the result of all the past mergers and acquisitions. To some extent, the stratigraphy of acquired companies can be observed in the information infrastructure. The reason that forensic accountants and EDP auditors have to act occasionally as amateur archaeologists is that it is *very hard* and *very costly* to get the information supply chain perfect, and it is also often risky to touch processing which has (more or less) run for many years. Users will always be reluctant to cede control.

Let's list some factors that qualify the extent of the entropy, of the uncertainty in the data, or in other words of the chance of unpleasant surprises. The extent to which information is dissipated around an institution determines the effort it takes to create a coherent and comprehensive picture of the state of the business. The entropy depends on a large number of variables.

Entropy indicates the overall complexity and cost magnitude. Through looking at the different elements that went into creating it, we can investigate the potential for improvement. The mitigating factors will not be a big surprise at this stage. It's all about knowing what you are doing, doing it in a consistent way, sharing information, and also avoiding redundancy. Having two security masters does not *double* the work, it *triples* the work, because you also need to reconcile between these two data stores. Mitigating factors that can reduce the data uncertainty and improve the efficiency of information lifecycle management include the following:

Factors that contribute to the overall information entropy in an institution:

- The number of independent data streams coming in
- The volume of transactions
- The range of products traded
- The dispersion of users across geographies and time zones
- The dispersion in human languages, units of measurement, and file formats
- The number of independent data stores
- The number of intermediary actors and steps in process flows

- Use of single data standards to solve the incompatibility and interpretation issues
- Additional staff doing reconciliations
- Separation of duties
- Controls and operational risk reporting framework
- Insurance against major operational risk events[1]
- Metrics and dashboards to monitor changes in quality and to spot trends

How to go about implementing these mitigating factors depends on the way the business is organized and whether it is organized on product lines; as a matrix organization whereby product lines, geographical areas, and client segments, for example, all have functional owners; and whether there are cross-vertical shared services which can drive standards and common services (see Figure 5.1).

Even the best information architecture designed and set up from scratch will—to a greater or lesser extent—be a reflection of the business requirements *at that moment*. Because of changing needs, it will be tweaked, abused, and retrofitted. The label *future proof* applied to applications is more a marketing term than anything else. Even in the case of a sound underlying architecture, people will tend to take shortcuts. This is just one reason why *metrics* are important: to keep everyone on the right path.

A separate set of products has evolved as a result of this entropy: extract, transform, and load (ETL) tools. Whether these are a symptom or cure remains debatable. When things keep breaking down, do you keep on buying and applying glue and band-aids? At what point will you question the material that breaks? Things break for the following reasons:

- They are too brittle (bad designs, misuse of formats, operationally complex, use of applications for new things without proper testing).
- The stress is too high (volume, tweaking of formats).

The extent to which mitigating factors such as data standards and overall metrics can be centrally driven depends on the type of organization and the clout of central functions such as finance and risk. A central function could push standards thereby facilitating upstream reporting and integration, a decentralized matrix organization could lead to a range of occasional cross-departmental but primarily local initiatives which means corporate wide reports need to be pieced together in many (possibly widely) differing ways.

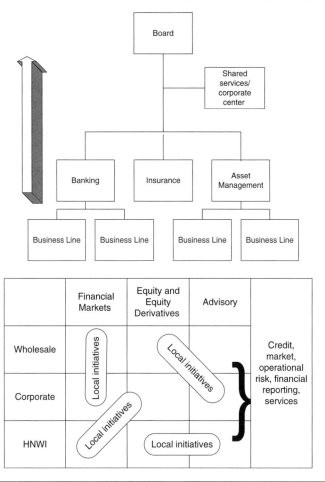

**Figure 5.1**    Various organization charts of financial institutions

▪ Patches that were applied earlier do not work or are no longer relevant to the new situation.

Often, all three reasons are in place simultaneously. Some integration solutions focus on extracting, uploading, and transporting sets of information; other solutions focus more on dictionaries, business rules, mappings, and cross-references. Some integration products have grown out of consulting companies that have productized their integration methodologies.

### 5.2.2 IMPEDIMENTS TO STANDARD DATA SERVICES

Think about the second law of thermodynamics: If you do nothing, entropy will only increase. The only way to stem and reverse the pull toward data degradation is to invest energy into the system. In the financial service industry, energy is money, and the overhaul of an information supply chain is often a costly process.

There are many different aspects to integration, and software packages are just one tiny piece of the puzzle. Other technical components comprise protocols, message format standards, and well set-up data flows and workflows. The most important is, however, the organizational aspect. The organization chart detailing responsibilities and mandates must be clear to all involved, since political islands can kill a project easily. There are, in short, many reasons why it is difficult to create enterprise standard data services. There are challenges in the following areas:

- *Licensing costs* are an issue. Getting enterprise-wide rights to the content and systems. Vendors of both software and content will aim to preserve additional commercial opportunities by putting in place limitations of use. Financial institutions that aim to achieve this face potentially very large upfront license costs.

- There are *political challenges*. There needs to be acceptance of a dedicated service team decoupled from individual business lines. The political situation in an institution needs to accommodate that. Organizations typically have managing directors for lines of businesses, and everything is organized vertically. There are not often interesting career opportunities when looking horizontally cross-business, and that is the political challenge. Plus, there is the issue of trust: Users need to let go in some cases and hand control to a separate data function.

- Users need to agree on *common terminology*. There will be different types of services in terms of extensiveness of coverage (which attributes), frequency (real-time or batch data), and quality (manually validated, automatically checked, or just passthrough from the vendor). But even so, opinions may differ within one institution on, for example, asset type or industry sector classification.

- Users need to agree on *ownership* of content. When ownership of content passes to a dedicated central department, that department has to carry enough clout and be credible enough in terms of budget and staff to gain acceptance. When ownership is decentralized, it can fragment along product, matrix, or client segment dimensions. Unfortunately, these different lines of segmentation can intersect. Furthermore, politically it can be difficult to determine ownership of customer data, as this is directly linked to a commercial relationship. More neutral information such as business holiday calendar information would be easier to centralize. Security master information would be somewhere in the middle. It is not as sensitive as client data, but there can be differences of opinion on certain hybrid products that determines under whose remit they fall (e.g., hybrid equity/debt, convertible bonds).

- It is *time consuming* to get sufficient users and systems to tap into these data services even if you get acceptance of what they should be. Data integration solutions are inherently sticky: It takes a long time to get them into place, but to get them out of place can take just as long. The organization needs to be willing to invest for a prolonged period of time, and there needs to be sufficient pickup of the data services downstream to justify the investment.

- *Market and product development is fast.* This means it will be a challenge to keep the content of the services up-to-date. The level of maturity of the downstream systems that do the processing will also differ. Cash equity, for example, is a bulk volume low margin market, and the downstream system world and trading infrastructure will be set up to accommodate bulk deal flow; there will consequently also be standards in place. For high margin OTC (e.g., commodity) derivatives, a lot of the pricing work will be Excel-based or in any case proprietary, and settlement and clearing and trading will also be on a one-off basis. Product development in these areas is so fast that central data services may find it hard to cope, even provided there is reliable external vendor data.

- There is a *technology challenge* of dealing with a heterogeneous downstream architecture with applications on different platforms. There are also often legacy systems that embed their own data model, which in some cases just does not fit with the envisaged common service.

## 5.2.3 ROI ASPECTS

Note that the higher the information entropy, the higher the potential return on investment (ROI) when you clean up and streamline your "content act." Reducing the entropy means reducing the opportunity for bad data and reducing the opportunities for data defects. This will mean lower costs in retrieving the information, higher productivity, and easier compliance. Other inputs to the ROI calculation should include the following:

- *Cost avoidance through regulatory compliance.* Good data processes will mean a lower operational risk and can lead to lower capital adequacy requirements.
- *Time to market and opportunity costs.* A highly complex decentralized infrastructure means that there is nothing in place whenever a new product line or trading desk is created. Common services, on the other hand, can expedite the introduction of new products and services.

The prevalent decentralized information management makes it difficult to estimate spending and to attribute costs to use of the data.[2] From the world of management accounting, we can borrow concepts such as Activity-Based Costing (ABC) to allocate costs of a data management function. Usage has to be very well defined to make this work, but note that this concept would also favor applications that request only what they need. Therefore, ABC could also work against efficient data infrastructures because it would stimulate keeping local copies of data to minimize calls on data, and this would increase entropy!

# 5.3 Aspects of Information Quality

Asking people how to define and measure quality can cause a lot of hazy looks and in any case triggers lengthy philosophical and often heated discussions. In this section, we will list a number of factors that pertain to different elements of quality because obviously quality depends on the needs of the people at the receiving end; the dimensions on which you measure it will vary from department to department and from data type to data type. Metadata—data about data—may well be just as important as the data itself.

To illustrate these different quality criteria, we will present real-world examples. The following is by no means an exhaustive list (see also Figure 5.2):

- *Speed.* The time dimension of data. When can you act on it? What is the decay factor in the value of it? See the latency race in real-time information where an opportunity exists for a microsecond. This discussion includes timeliness, i.e., getting information to the right place at the right time. It can refer to, for example, the time taken to service a client, to set up a new account, to reply to an IOI, and so on, where an overly long delay can lead to loss of business.
- *Accuracy.* When do you need to be 100% sure of the accuracy, e.g., precise spelling, precise coding of something? For example, ascertaining the full legal name underlying a CDS from an authoritative data source.

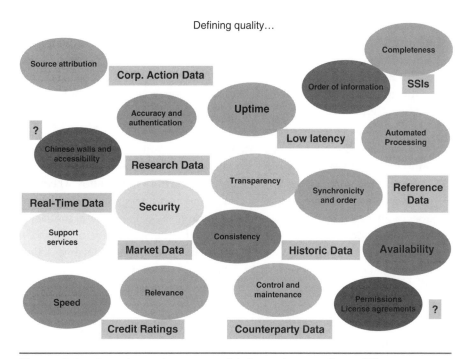

**Figure 5.2** Overview of aspects of information quality—different aspects determine fitness for different purposes

■ *Consistency*. This can be internally; e.g., if you have different trading books for risk purposes, you want to use the same exchange rates. Similarly, are you treating your various clients consistently or some more favorably than others? Institutions will want to present one voice to the external world, not just from a corporate marketing perspective. Globally active, diversified financial services institutions can have many product lines that all serve the same customer.

■ *Authentication*. Has the source of the information confirmed the validity? Is a quote indicative or actionable? Has the trade been confirmed? Are there liability ramifications if the price, settlement instruction provided, etc., prove to be wrong? Is there a "twilighting" process in place to reaffirm validity periodically?

■ *Transparency*. To what extent is the complete data lineage clear? For example, what information was used at what point around the decision making to take on a new client? For example, in the content of best execution reporting requirements. What elements went into a price used to revaluate a position?

■ *Synchronicity and Order.* Are you preserving information for regulatory reporting in the right order, even if it happens at the microsecond level? Also, if you have to piece together a report and rely on cut-and-paste information and queries from various repositories, chances are your information is not obtained at the same times and may be out of sync immediately.

■ *Completeness.* Is the full picture on an instrument available? For example, you can have 25 covenants in a loan or bond, but you could have 100% accurate but nonetheless incomplete information if you report only 24. Another example on completeness can come from legal entity information where you will want complete information on the legal structure, guarantees, and liabilities of an entity. It is much easier to start the entity data provision for the on-boarding process of a customer which maybe requires 10 to 15 fields. The compliance function will need more information on audit and documentation. There can be different levels of completeness of information depending on the function; for example, in the case of information on a legal entity, it could be

1. Research ready; a subset of information is present.
2. Compliance ready; a potentially different subset of information on the entity is present.
3. Trading ready; the complete set of attributes is available and has been checked.

Different information-consuming workflows have different requirements.

■ *Relevance.* Is information filtered in useful ways? You do not want to be cluttered with useless information and want the useful bits extracted out of the torrent. Ways to address this could be to filter out the relevant updates only; to alert users only on a real update; or to prioritize or filter information offered by *held securities*, by the top 25 exposures, by credit rating, by price volatility, or by complex product exposure. The concepts of *inherent* and *pragmatic quality* are also sometimes used in this context. Inherent quality refers to all quality aspects of a piece of information looking at it in isolation. Pragmatic quality first determines which quality aspects will ever make a difference in usefulness of that information.

■ *Control and Maintenance.* Spreadsheets and macros represent the democratization of IT but can lead to dramatic control and maintenance issues. Macros and spreadsheets have put strong IT tools in the hands of the masses, but without a management framework for version control, sharing, reusing, etc. Also, too much power can be concentrated in whoever understands the 80MB spreadsheet.

■ *Accessibility*. Do data reside on local desktops? Can everybody who needs data access it? Are access permissions, Chinese walls, and separation of duties in line with content licensing terms, conflict of interest rules (for example, between research and advisory functions, between corporate finance and sales and trading), and data protection legislation. Data protection and privacy laws would especially be areas of attention when outsourcing or offshoring the collection or processing of customer information. Are the data (or access to it) leaving the building, leaving the country, or leaving the organization? Each of these acts may or may not be allowed. Another aspect of accessibility is how easily the information lends itself to automated retrieval and processing.

■ Information may be lurking *somewhere* in the institution, but there are often no yellow pages in place directing you to the relevant department. Which people have *backdoors* allowing them direct and privileged access to data stores, e.g., database administrators, IT staff, and management? If the number of people with backdoor access is fairly large, the controls put in place for other users will become meaningless.

■ *Usage Restrictions*. Is the organization abiding by the content licensing terms in the contracts? This can well be an operational risk.

■ *Security*. Both in terms of abiding by content licensing terms (operational risk), but also as the flipside of accessibility. Is unauthorized access prevented? Is information being encrypted? Are the standards of the institution with regard to security level of information (from public to confidential and shades in between) being adhered to?

■ *Service and Support* around data. If you want to change something, what are the flexibility and turnaround time? If you have an issue with it (query, error, or enhancement), what is the turnaround time in addressing it from your vendor, from your internal data management team? Another aspect of data services is the availability. Can you always access the data? Is there an uptime target such as *four nines* or *five nines*.[3]

What these different quality aspects really say is that information can be fit for purpose in different ways. Whether you, as a user, rely on those data for revenue-generating capabilities, cost controls, or compliance leads to radically different perspectives on quality. Furthermore, various subsets of these quality criteria are more relevant depending on the type of data (pricing or static, equity or commodity, counterparty or corporate action). For example, information quality aspects associated with the quality of order execution would include measures on effective spread, rate of price improvement or decrease (versus a benchmark), fill rate of the order, and speed in turning it around. There is no single right answer to the quality question. When it comes to defining standard data services, different users will want to embed different combinations of the preceding factors in their service-level agreements and assign them different weights.

## 5.4 The Content Manufacturing Process

### 5.4.1 SUPPLY CHAIN MANAGEMENT: THE MANUFACTURING OF CONTENT

The end of the information supply chain described in Chapter 2 is *new information*. Financial institutions are essentially *information-processing endeavors*. Based on the execution of the processes fed by the content types described previously, new information is put back to the client, counterparty, marketplace, and authorities. Since financial institutions are information-generation enterprises, the costs (for commoditized products) and speed (for higher margin bespoke products) of pushing all the raw information through to produce new content are the critical measures. Complementing the sourcing strategies discussion, we need to evaluate the effectiveness with which an organization produces content itself. Quality aspects of information produced internally also strongly depend on the function of that piece of information—for example, whether it is to be used as

- Indication of interest;
- Indicative quote;
- Trade confirm;
- Report to regulator;
- Invoice to client.

The analogy of supply chain management can help to give a broader perspective here. What else is a set of automated processes and information flow but a conveyor belt of information? Also, it is a useful analogy both because the number of suppliers of content is very large and because certain parts of that supply chain or of the trade lifecycle (post-trade) will have been serviced by third parties. Less direct control over the various steps in the supply chain translates into a greater need for clear metrics to go into service-level agreements. These metrics may help us judge the effectiveness of the information supply chain in fulfilling the needs of its customers that need to process/initiate the instrument and transaction lifecycle processes. It may help us define quality in terms that translate to business benefits for the users.

In classic supply chain management analysis, there is a distinction between bulk ("standardized") and bespoke ("customer") products and services. The *Customer solutions* product concept includes aspects such as customization, product focus, low volume, complex, and high margin. The *Standardized* product concept includes characteristics such as a high level of standardization, process focus, high volume, relatively straightforward processing, and low per unit margin. In financial services terms, this translates, for example, to different processing needs for bespoke OTC derivatives and cash equity, respectively. Bottlenecks in processing information are typically access to information (links, cross-references) and lack of confidence in the information presented, leading to manually checking it before continuing to take action. Note that this same distinction between highly automated and ad-hoc processing of information is also found at the reporting end. The distinction between standard, regularly produced reports (e.g. account statements, daily risk reports, financial information) which are all produced in a highly procedural and often fully automated way and ad-hoc information (research, analysis) which often involves a lot of manual work and cuts across laterally across different information types and stores.

For financial content, given the typical information entropy situation encountered, the term *information supply chain* may be flattering. In reality, it is often better characterized as a supply web where the different filaments have various strengths, depending on the disparity in sourcing and distributing. In the following section, we will discuss the applicability of manufacturing supply chain management concepts and their associated metrics to the information supply chain.

We can visualize a layering of information from content, to metacontent, to different ways of summarizing and managing this. Corrective actions at the end should influence data-sourcing decisions leading to a continuous feedback loop to the start of the process (see Figure 5.3).

## 5.4.2 THE PHYSICAL SUPPLY CHAIN ANALOGY

Just as in physical supply chain management, the right balance between service and cost is the key question in (information) supply chain management. A key concept is that of *inventory*, which has various meanings in financial information management. In the financial markets, inventory can refer to

- A position in a financial product, which can refer to either
  - *Physical securities.* When there are imbalances, either the institution can experience settlement shortfalls, meaning it has to borrow securities, or it

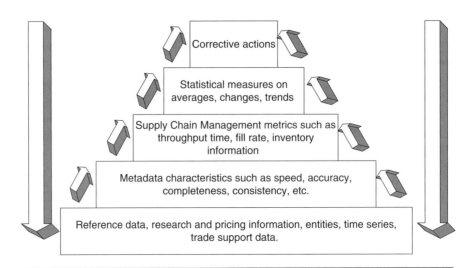

**Figure 5.3**   Content pyramid and continuous feedback loop

can retain too much exposure on its books, in effect taking unplanned directional bets on market movements.

- *Contracts* (e.g., options) that are cash settled. Here, there will not be physical settlement constraints, but the focus will be on risk management of the position.

■ Managing the financial product inventory in the case of trading means adhering to limits and using the available capital in an optimal way; managing the financial product inventory in a market-making content means turning the inventory as frequently as possible.

■ Contractual inventory with regard to usage permissions of content and software. There may be an inventory of a certain number of named or concurrent users that data or software content licensing agreements allow for. Sometimes an institution pays for usage rights that are not taken up.

■ Data management inventory of *finished goods*: the number of financial objects such as instruments and counterparties which are maintained in the company's databases. Similar to physical goods, data will degrade. Especially in the case of price data, you can make golden copy prices, but they will lose their value if not kept up-to-date.

Just like in the physical world, lean inventory can keep costs low but can lead to opportunity costs. Inventory also provides for options. In commodity data, this is referred to as the *convenience yield*. Unlike the physical world, when you have a stock-keeping unit (SKU) in information management, the number of clients that you can serve with it is limited only by the terms of the content licensing agreements signed with the owners of the information. The marginal costs of adding SKUs (e.g., unique financial objects) to an inventory can be appraised as follows:

- *Content Costs*. These do not really scale when content is sold on a per item basis. When sold in bulk, marginal costs will decrease.
- *Staff and Infrastructure Costs*. There is a high fixed cost involved in staffing a department and putting IT infrastructure in place. So the costs for the first financial object are enormous; then they go down very quickly. Exceptions are when specialized content needs to be processed for which new skill sets are needed, necessitating the training or hiring of staff.

The information supply chain is a supply chain of intellectual property rather than physical property. Compensation for the owners of the goods is not always in a Delivery versus Payment way, and usage of goods is sometimes harder to determine, especially in a high-entropy situation in which it is not always clear where data ends up. This explains efforts on the side of the content vendors to standardize billing[4] for financial information and to track information dissemination periodically through audits. Contrary to physical goods, in the case of manufacturing information, the cycle time is very short. Information products degrade very quickly in the financial space. They are like oysters: best consumed fresh, and when not can lead to problems of similar nastiness. The supply chain management challenges are therefore also different.

- Instead of a shipping date, we talk milliseconds or hours tops.
- The number of SKUs would be unique financial objects and can potentially run in the millions.
- The safety stock or inventory buffer contains, for example, instruments that are likely to be traded in the near future; for instance, you may keep all domestic-listed companies on record.

The supply chain can also be worked backward when it is demand driven. "Built to order" information supply kicks in the whole supply chain in reverse: from the request of an end user or application for a piece of information to retrieving the source data from multiple external vendors. This is feasible when the sources of the content provide online access or keep their information up-to-date in real time. Facilitating this "just in time" sourcing is difficult and also requires automation of aggregation, cross-reference, and validation. In *Vendor Managed Inventory*, the supplier is kept abreast of what supply the financial institution requires. This implies that a supplier is given insight into potentially competitive information; e.g., a hedge fund with an event-based trading strategy would not necessarily want to let third parties know its watch list.

# 5.5 Quality Metrics: Information Management KPIs and Their SLA Context

## 5.5.1 INTRODUCTION

In this section we will discuss a number of metrics and key performance indicators (KPIs) borrowed from the world of physical supply chain management. These are helpful analogies in measuring the effectiveness of the information supply chain and could be input for a service-level agreement (SLA), either internal or with the BPO partner. These concepts from supply chain management could be applied not just to the quality of the information supplied, but also on the success by which the instrument and transaction lifecycle are managed and by which new content is produced by the institution. We will then discuss various statistics that could be applied to it, best practices in picking KPIs, and how to monitor them.

## 5.5.2 SUPPLY CHAIN MANAGEMENT METRICS

### Throughput

*Throughput* refers to basic volume and can refer to the scalability of an information infrastructure. How many messages can be processed per second? How quickly can information be loaded and retrieved? What is the speed with which orders are filled?

### Fill Rate

The *fill rate* metric can refer to the percentage of customer orders that can be filled out of inventory immediately. In information management terms, it could also refer to the proportion of queries from users and downstream systems that can be answered immediately from the golden copy information inventory (security master, counterparty, corporate actions, etc.) in the repositories. The questions that cannot be answered (unfilled orders) result in a query to external parties. The costs of keeping an item on inventory and keeping it fresh have to be measured. Content costs can often be directly attributed; a portion of hardware, staff, and overhead cost need to be allocated on usage. This leads to requirements on data usage tracking. Often a financial institution is not fully aware of what content has been bought and what information is available where. This means that there can be unused content inventory available.

## Balanced Scorecard

*Balanced scorecard*[5] refers to qualitative metrics to measure the efficacy of the information supply chain. An example of a balanced scorecard in the area of information management could look like the one shown in Table 5.1.

The balanced scorecard—as the name suggests—forces a much more comprehensive way of looking at a business function, balancing, for example, costs and benefits. It offers a high-level perspective which can sometimes be very refreshing for data supply chain practitioners who can get bogged down in details or lengthy discussions of standards.

## Cycle Time

*Cycle time* is the time that elapses between a downstream system or end user requesting a certain piece of information necessary for a process and receiving it. It is closely related to the *fill rate*. The target average cycle time will be set at different levels for different business processes. When you are trading or responding to a client query, turnaround needs to be fast. When answering to a query from a regulator or tax office, you normally do not need to be able to recover the information online. However, from a cost perspective, what counts are the most stringent requirements. If one department wants to keep the rough rice futures online and in the golden copy database, for example, this means overdelivery on the cycle time to the other departments, which leads to an interesting cost attribution question: Who will bear the cost of this? The required cycle time can vary from microseconds in quantitative trading

**Table 5.1**   Example Balanced Scorecard

| Financial aspects | Internal aspects |
|---|---|
| ■  Costs of inventory | ■  Department budget |
| ■  Ad hoc costs | ■  Planning/new content |
| ■  Savings/ROI | Training aspects |
| Customer aspects | ■  Knowledge level of data management |
| ■  Scoring on KPI metrics | department |
| on SCM | ■  Capability to take on new types of |
| ■  Customer satisfaction | content, new products to process |

**Table 5.2** The Turnaround Time Spectrum

| Fast | Algorithmic trading |
|------|---------------------|
|      | Distribution of quotes and orders to execution venues and confirmations |
|      | Output of quant models to price an OTC product for a client |
|      | Lookup reference data (e.g., SSI and security master) for trade confirmations |
|      | Historical data, correlations for VaR, EAD, LGD, PGD models for credit risk |
|      | Corporate actions processing |
|      | Lookup of quotes/transactions for regulatory reasons from, e.g., 4 years ago |
| Slow | Preparation of annual report and financial statements |

strategies to hours or weeks when preparing financial statements. Table 5.2 gives some indication on data types versus response times.

The concept of *manufacturing cycle time* is the time spent between receiving the last bit of needed raw or untreated data from the content supplied and the delivery or update of the golden copy master information. Note that normally the infrastructure can also be set up so that the most frequently requested items will have the fastest cycle time.

### DPMO

*DPMO* is a concept from the six sigma process improvement methodology; it refers to "defects per million opportunities." The $6\sigma$ goal is 3.4 DPMO maximum.[6] DPMO is defined as follows:

(Total number of defects / Total number of opportunities for defects) *

   1 million.

In the case of data management, we can define the number of defects quite straightforward in an SLA: define a set of financial objects and a set of attributes to be tracked for those objects. Whenever the value of one of the fields delivered either on request or as part of an agreed daily delivery turns out to be wrong at that time or delivered too late, this is a defect. What is more difficult to measure is the number of opportunities for defects. Accounting for the number of disparate data formats, lack of standards, overall entropy, number of sources, and often lengthy supply chain means that for the financial information supply chain, the number of opportunities is huge. Probably, six sigma is not good enough by far for the financial markets. Let's illustrate this by making a ballpark estimate of defect opportunities. Consider a typical architecture with representative numbers:[7]

- 7 ultimate sources;
- 3 redistributors;
- 3 input channels in a bank;
- 4 security masters;
- 5 export formats;
- 16 downstream interpreting systems;
- 1 million instruments + 200 thousand clients and counterparties + 500 thousand corporate actions.

Assuming we update each bit of information once per day, this set of numbers would lead to 1.7 million $* 16 * 5 * 4 * 3 * 3 * 7 = 34{,}272$ million opportunities for a defect. Taking the six sigma goal of 3.4 DPMO would lead to no fewer than 116,500 defects.[8]

### Perfect Order Measure

The *perfect order measure* is roughly the error-free rate at each stage of the order where we interpret an order in information management terms. An order is a query of a user or downstream application that will act on the data. The term *perfect order measure* hence refers to the error-free rate at each stage of the supply chain. Note that it is often very difficult to measure the quality at each stage, partially because you do not have the complete information picture, partially because various formats and identification standards cloud the picture. If you do have some of it in place, though, you can confront your external and internal sources with the score and report cards. The information on this perfect order measure can be collected through information from the consolidation and validation process, plus by feedback from the users on defects they report. It also includes technical defects earlier in the cycle which caused, for example, files not to be loaded (see Figure 5.4).

Note that there will be special "critical items" in the set of financial objects that you give extra special sourcing and validation treatment because you *cannot* afford to be wrong or off-market on these—for example, the EURUSD

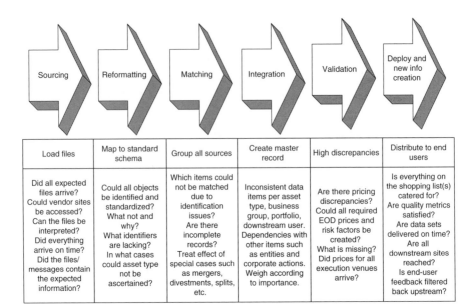

| Load files | Map to standard schema | Group all sources | Create master record | High discrepancies | Distribute to end users |
|---|---|---|---|---|---|
| Did all expected files arrive? Could vendor sites be accessed? Can the files be interpreted? Did everything arrive on time? Did the files/ messages contain the expected information? | Could all objects be identified and standardized? What not and why? What identifiers are lacking? In what cases could asset type not be ascertained? | Which items could not be matched due to identification issues? Are there incomplete records? Treat effect of special cases such as mergers, divestments, splits, etc. | Inconsistent data items per asset type, business group, portfolio, downstream user. Dependencies with other items such as entities and corporate actions. Weigh according to importance. | Are there pricing discrepancies? Could all required EOD prices and risk factors be created? What is missing? Did prices for all execution venues arrive? | Is everything on the shopping list(s) catered for? Are quality metrics satisfied? Are data sets delivered on time? Are all downstream sites reached? Is end-user feedback filtered back upstream? |

**Figure 5.4** Information supply chain with quality questions asked at each stage

exchange rate, the government bond curve, and blue chip equities. The specific critical items depend on the institution's business.

### Inventory Turns

In supply chain management, the term *inventory turns* is defined as the number of times inventory is shipped out ("turned") during a given time period. In the context of data, we can relate this to data usage. How often is something *shipped* out of the golden copy database, and what portion of the sourcing/validation work is never used? This information can be used in turn to drive internal cost allocation.

### COPQ

An interesting metric is the *cost of poor quality* (COPQ) of information. These are the costs that would vanish if systems, processes, and data content were perfect. COPQ is the main number to be estimated for any business case for information quality improvement projects. Direct costs on staff, redundant repositories, and content are relatively easy to measure. As we have seen in some of the use cases earlier, if opportunity costs are woven into the equation, the number would become very high.

## Other Measures

Many other measures could be used for metrics in SLAs. They include *performance to promise*, which measures adherence to the terms of the SLA. *Material value add* is the measure of value added in the process and is normally expressed as follows:

$$(\text{sell price} - \text{material cost})/\text{material cost}$$

If we look at the ratio of total cost over the whole information supply chain divided by content costs, then we will see content represents only a fraction. Even if we leave out the costs of actually uploading content in applications, the amount spent within an institution to treat the content is higher than the price paid for the content. We can interpret these *freight costs* as the costs of the data distribution infrastructure including interfaces and mappings—the cost of putting a piece of content through the supply chain. Latency is also called *transit time* in SCM metrics terms. In information terms, we also need to check how much history is kept online and what level of audit is kept on the information. This will depend on how often you have to satisfy (ad hoc) historical data requests for risk, audit, and client queries.

KPIs can also measure the number of disruptions in the information supply chain—for example, when we have unknown instruments, unknown customers/counterparties, or unknown settlement locations or when there are no prices for an instrument. This information has to be fed back to the information supply chain infrastructure and perhaps down to the content supplier if that is where the break occurred.

## Link with Operational Risk

If you closely study KPIs, you may also be able to deduct the potential for process failure. This means you will be one step ahead of the occurrence of the loss. Failed processes will lead to losses; KPI dashboards can help show you when a process is about to break. More likely, the process of putting together these dashboards will give you a lot of insight into where processes are brittle and can lead to improvements directly. Historical data on the metrics need to be tracked to spot trends and to be able to deduce performance and costs balance. Supply chain management is all about the balance between costs and quality. Theoretically, it will perhaps be possible to reach 100% accuracy of information, but this could well be at the cost of going out of business.

The metrics collected on the information supply chain will form a significant portion of the input to an operational risk data collection process. Operational risk has to be quantified for institutions governed by the Basel II

The Bank for International Settlements categorized risk for different business lines; they are as follows:

- Corporate finance
- Trading and sales
- Retail banking
- Commercial banking
- Payment and settlement
- Agency services and custody
- Asset management
- Retail brokerage

Metrics collected could be broken up along these lines. Note that the bulk of operational risk losses occur in information mismatches such as failed trades and are therefore catered for by metrics such as the ones discussed here.

accord. "Operational risk is defined as the risk of loss resulting from inadequate or failed internal processes, people and systems or from external events. This definition includes legal risk, but excludes strategic and reputational risk."[9] Three of the main operational risk event types (clients, products, and business practices; business disruption and system failures; and execution, delivery, and process management) are directly related to the information supply chain.[10]

There can be various approaches to measure and report on operation risk if the institution reports under the Advanced Measurement Approach (AMA) of Basel II. Whether the methodology chosen is top-down or bottom-up, the measurement method will determine what data are required. In case of the Loss Distribution Approach (LDA) which is similar to the Value at Risk approach for market risk measurement, this will be heavy on data collection, and you will require large histories of losses per business line and loss type for the information to be statistically meaningful. A Bayesian approach requires a detailed analysis and understanding of the business processes.

### 5.5.3 STATISTICS

It is of the utmost importance to clearly define the relevant metrics and then to be willing and able to act on deviations from their target levels. Normally, the numbers collected through the preceding measures will be subject to statistical analysis. Relevant statistical indicators will be applied to KPIs such as DPMO

Standard statistical numbers include measures such as the following:

- Minimum and Maximum Value
- Historical Volatility
- Mean Reversion Level
- Spread Adjusted Mean Reversion Level
- Mean Reversion Speed
- Mean Reversion R-Squared
- Standard Deviation of Values
- Skew and Kurtosis of Values
- 5% Percentile 95% Percentile Value
- Skew and Kurtosis of Log Returns
- 5% Percentile and 95% Percentile Log Return
- Minimum and Maximum Log Return
- Mean and Standard Deviation of Log Values
- Skew and Kurtosis of Log Values
- 5% Percentile and 95% Percentile Log Value
- Minimum and Maximum Log Value
- Mean Reversion Normal — Mean Reversion Speed

or fill rate, and alerts will be set based on thresholds. This is also the basis for trend and operational risk analysis.

These statistics could be applied on the supply chain management metrics discussion previously and on metrics of costs; defects; number of instruments; settlement delays; latency rates; fill rates of orders; responsiveness of counterparty; limit utilization; internal rating; credit quality of a loan portfolio; response times in requesting new instrument setup; changes in asset correlation; tracking error with regard to an index; deviations in cost per transaction; numbers of fails and claims; volume of various trading desks or of a brokerage operation; collateral quality and composition; custody metrics such as timeliness; and accuracy of corporate event information, user satisfaction, and so on.

## 5.5.4 DEFINING AND MONITORING KPIs

### Introduction

We already discussed different quality aspects of information. Different areas in a financial institution worry about different things. Traders need information around price behavior, drivers, and arbitrage margins; custodians need clear identification and timely details on events such as dividends; investors need to know about controls and fair pricing; regulators need to know about

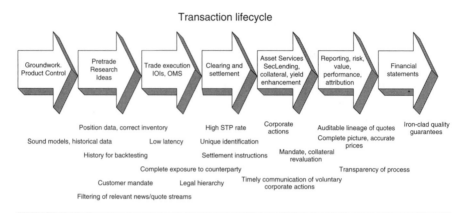

Transaction lifecycle

**Figure 5.5** Different information interests at different stages of the transaction lifecycle

transparency; and back offices need to know about smooth operations and low cost per transaction.

KPIs can be set at various points in the instrument lifecycle and corresponding supply chain. They can be set in different post-trade stages such as STP rate, calls, cash management/funding costs, missed corporate events, and also for the information supply chain: ambiguous instruments and counterparties and wrong valuations. KPIs will be of interest not only to the firm's management, but also to industry analysts and company rating agencies that want to compare different companies and to regulatory agencies that want to check the soundness of control procedures. In Figure 5.5, we list various information interests at different stages of the transaction lifecycle.

### KPI Best Practices

When selecting KPIs, you must keep in mind many things. Some best practices are as follows:

■ KPIs should be *compared* to those of your peers or other departments, if only to see where you can improve most for a minimum effort. There are consultancy companies to help do that.[11] They would pool data from multiple companies that share a common KPI methodology, make sensitive or proprietary data anonymous, and send back a comparison on how you do relative to your peers. This benchmarking can be done *internally* from department to department or externally with a peer group.

■ Take great care in choosing the right indicators that reflect the operational efficiency of *your business* rather than copying a set of indicators from the neighboring financial institution. KPIs are, after all, a classic statistics problem: You want to condense information as efficiently as possible without losing the big picture and the main trends (similar to principal components analysis mentioned in Section 4.2). In data terms, if you measure parts of the information supply chain, for example, you would expect the KPIs to reflect the important *quality* aspects discussed previously, or in any case put emphasis on the right mix.

■ The selected KPIs should reflect the *purpose* of the specific relationship (in case of outsourcing to a third party) or purpose of the measurement. The purpose could be customer satisfaction—through metrics such as the response time for ad hoc queries or percentage of portfolios adequately serviced with pricing/models, e.g., 100% accurate NAV, nothing contested, number of mispricings, STP rate for settlement. The purpose could be cost—e.g., in $/transaction. Or, it could be the support of higher volumes through metrics such as the uptime of systems such as *five nines* availability,[12] number of new instruments set up, number of corporate events processed, number of portfolios serviced, latency, throughput in messages per second, and so on. Similarly, it is important to understand what the result of improving on the current values of the KPIs will be. Will this be happier clients? More revenue? Lower costs? All the above?

■ Do not collect *too many* KPIs. KPIs can be strongly correlated, so too many do not necessarily provide additional information. Furthermore, KPIs should be easily collected, ideally in a fully automated fashion. If collecting them is costly or time-consuming, this will not (always) happen, and you will either have an incomplete picture or will have an imprecise picture because people will rush to deliver something and interpret the data to be delivered in different ways. Reports with hundreds of KPIs will not be acted on in an appropriate and efficient way and will probably not even be read; people will not be able to see the forest for the trees.

■ Make the definition of the KPIs *consistent* among the various processes that need to contribute them. Inconsistent KPIs can never be rolled up into aggregate information or be the basis for operational risk charges allocation to business divisions. Consistency can also help operational risk reporting and will definitely benefit the regulators that need to interpret and compare these reports.

■ The KPIs should be under the *control* of the responsible party or of the party to which this process is outsourced. For example, if an external party that manages the data is measured on lead time in setting up new instruments or customers in the systems, it could be that the lead time heavily depends on the financial institution's own risk control procedures.

- KPIs should *support root-cause analysis* and predict trends.
- KPIs should have *owners* who are responsible to reach a certain value with the KPIs. There should be a feedback loop back to responsible people who can *act* on the KPIs.

### What to Do with KPIs?

Another concept from six sigma is that of the "DMAIC" approach: define, measure, analyze, improve, control. The same process should be applied for KPIs on the financial information supply chain and supported processes. After KPIs are defined and measured, they should be collected and exposed. We will define the terminology of BPM and BAM and their relevance to financial process metrics.

*Dashboards* present a collated view of various KPIs to provide quick insight into the overall health of a process. *Business Process Management* (BPM) refers to the control and transparency of various steps in a business process and is at the crossroads of the fields of management and information technology. It addresses the process aspects of enterprise architectures.[13] *Business Activity Monitoring* (BAM) refers to the definition of certain metrics that need to be maintained and conditions for alerts and actions. Compared to a dashboard, BAM is typically more real time and driven by events and oriented around business processes. *Business intelligence* (BI) refers to historical analysis and data mining to uncover trends that BAM would (ideally) expose in real time. Dashboards, BAM, and BI are all techniques to gain insight into (how to compare) processes and all feed off KPIs. Traditionally, BI reports run on a scheduled basis, and are not event-based-driven by triggers and exceptions. BAM could, for instance, be used as inventory management in cases where proactive alerts can be created, such as the following:

- Limit breaching or approaching limits, which could in turn lead to securities lending operations when shortfalls need to be covered or swaps/other diversification/mitigating transactions;
- Cash balances in accounts, real-time inventory of specific instruments;
- Collateral portfolio quality, e.g., when certain credit or industry concentration limits are reached, triggering collateral top-up or substitute calls;
- Market-making inventory, leading to adjustments in quotes and size quoted or direct buy/sell orders to change the inventory level;
- Margin calls, triggering cash transfers;
- Checking of outstanding corporate events where deadline approaches and sending of alerts to account holders to inform them to make a choice.

BI could be used in a more post-fact reporting and analysis environment. For example, it could be used on STP rates to investigate which accounts and which products cause the largest number of breaks and invest in the data quality of those areas.

Initially, BPM and BAM will show only the symptoms, but if well set up, they should lead to diagnosis. Diagnosis should lead to prescriptions, and prescriptions should lead to a cure. In practice, however, the patient may not always be that well behaved and not always rational. The best practices for KPIs discussed here should mitigate these risks. Note, however, that any logic and value in the tools used can never be a substitute for intelligence that is needed in configuring and using them.

### SLAs and the Continuous Feedback Loop

SLAs define the expectations between two parties for a service provider relationship. They define what is being promised by the service provider, possibly the acceptance criteria of a service's deliverables, how it will be measured, how it will be priced, and what the effects of deviations from the service are. KPIs are useful tools to have clear and concise agreement on measures in place and to summarize the expectations. Since more and more services are provided either by common services departments within institutions or by third parties, it is important to set the expectations right from the start.

SLA metrics apart, data management groups always need to retain upside flexibility. They need to be able to handle ad hoc and special orders where time to market has a big business impact. This flexibility will have its price in any SLA. KPIs should not just be used as a reflection of the status quo. They present an opportunity to drill down into the root causes to improve the processes. Frequent feedback is needed from observed values in KPIs to scrutiny of processes and improvements in the sourcing, processing, and distribution of information. The feedback on quality needs to travel the opposite direction from the direction of the information supply chain. Without this, there will never be any improvement. Ideally, the continuous feedback loop will look something like that shown in Figure 5.6.

## 5.5.5 CONCLUSION

Dashboarding and corrective actions on KPIs are the logical conclusion of collecting quality aspects of the information supply chain. The process starts with identifying which content is required and what the required service levels are for the processes that depend on that content. Setting up KPIs is the next step. As we have seen, the relative weights of each of the quality dimensions will vary by business function. Also note that data quality elements can represent competitive

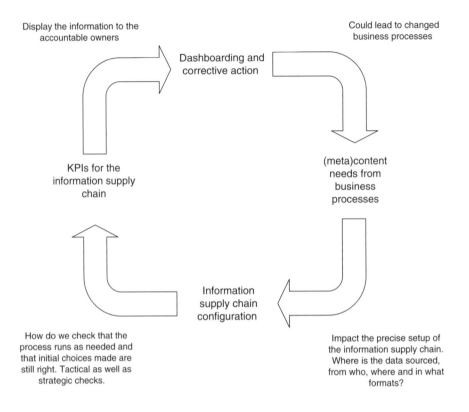

The continuous feedback loop requires an an-depth understanding
of process and of the quality aspects that are tracked

**Figure 5.6** The continuous feedback loop in the information supply chain

advantage; it may not be the goal to reach a certain *absolute* level of quality, but
you may merely need to be *relatively* better than everybody else. If that is the case,
you will have a competitive advantage even with far-from-perfect quality data.

## 5.6 What Constitutes Success in Process and Content Management?

As far as information management is concerned, it seems obvious to centralize
what you can centralize. After all, in the end there will be only one balance
sheet, one income statement, and one cash flow statement. Centralization
reduces operational and compliance costs and can also provide a foundation
for more nimble processes. If business applications do not have to worry about
information needs, they can focus on business logic and value add. This will

allow the organization to compete on volume or price and to be able to focus on product innovation.

We discussed the basic distinction between an infrastructure that needs to cater for a high deal volume low margin and an infrastructure that has to allow for low deal volume high margin. In the first category, cash equity trading leads the way in infrastructure. It is the most developed market in terms of data provision, transparency, price discovery options, and regulation. A result is that trading in this market is also most suited to automation and hence also to algorithmic trading.[14] The second category requires more technology-savvy users and has higher costs per staff. This stems from more specialized back-office staff who need to be able to deal with new situations and new products and potentially more vendor solutions. We can make a similar breakdown between data needs for *processing workflows* and for *revenue-generating workflows*—the classic back-office and front-office dichotomy.

Productivity and success measures for these two business processes will be measured in different ways:

■ The back office is about operational efficiency. Tracking of metrics and KPIs can mean the difference between red or black numbers, given that the margin is very thin. The process is set up for high volume throughput and control and requires high-quality reference data and settlement data. The key KPI would be costs per transaction.

■ The front-office world is opportunity driven. Since opportunities do not last, ideas need to be powered with new data sources fast. In product innovation, we have the case of low "unit processing" high margin. You want to invest in ultra low latency data, in price models, in quantitative models that would need access to cross-sectional data, and in securing exotic data not easily to be found via the standard aggregators. Complex instruments need to tap into multiple databases to collate all the information required; this is costly and time-consuming. Disparate sources need to be linked together to find new patterns and to generate new trade ideas.[15]

These two processes also translate into a "wholesale" and "retail" flavor of information management. In terms of different quality dimensions of data, the wholesale needs are in the areas of transparency, control, security, accuracy, synchronicity, and order. The retail needs are in the areas of relevance, completeness, accessibility, and speed. Consistency is equally important for both. The retailers also have to loop back and provide feedback to the wholesaler.

A well set-up information management process without the jungle of information streams will create a lot of strategic options for the company—not just through scalability options for new clients, products, and services, but also options to decouple bits of the information supply chain or of the transaction lifecycle management. If an institution understands how its processes are implemented, understands the (meta)content needs of its businesses, and is capable of measuring their operational effectiveness (through well-chosen and well-monitored KPIs), it is able to consider

- Outsourcing part of the information supply chain such as the integrating, consolidating, and validating of content, or part of the transaction lifecycle including execution management, reporting, and asset servicing.

- Replacing one third party in the transaction lifecycle with another. With this, we mean coming to the essential pluggability of, for example, execution venues and clearers—because the execution and clearing options will multiply as, increasingly, the different segments in the transaction lifecycle will be decoupled and serviced by many players.

In fact, the institution is able not only to consider this, but, more importantly, to adequately *price* these various options because it will be aware of baseline costs in detail. This means the ability to use price differentiation for products and clients.

## 5.7 Conclusions

### 5.7.1 INFORMATION SUPPLY CHAIN REQUIREMENTS

What will bring these different types of content and distribution together? What will enable it to be integrated and presented to people/systems who can act on it within needed time frames? In our opinion, that will be standard services to request content—common data models.

The required information supply chain and information management function will serve the high volume side of the instrument lifecycle business, as well as low volume niche products. For new OTC structures, ad hoc requests will need to be accommodated. In this case, information management will be much more about digging for information; there is far less pre-trade transparency, a far more difficult price discovery process, and a higher asymmetry of information, and therefore higher bid/ask spreads. Although this bit is more difficult to automate, common standards and a common data model can help and will provide for stability and common ground.

In summary, the information supply chain should allow for the following:

- Coverage of all instrument types and associated information on counterparties and corporate actions;

- Ability to manage various frequencies of data;
- Enterprise-wide consistent data standards;
- Quality and completeness of data via validation rules;
- Enriched data via application of various calculations;
- Flexible and extensible data model to cater for new product and regulatory developments;
- Reformatting of data to feed internal/external applications;
- Easy reporting and disclosure of data to downstream users;
- Robust security and audit functions;
- Scalability to meet enterprise requirements;
- Easy definition and collection of summary statistics and KPIs.

There are many reasons why this is easier said than done:

- Finding a home for data in the agenda of the management team is difficult.
- For all data centralization projects as with all infrastructure issues, to make the business case, you have to take a high-level approach. You need to be able to either make money directly or save enough (or need a regulatory imperative). Plus, you always require critical mass in downstream pickup to make the business case work.
- It is difficult to assess the impact of centralized solutions because of constant organizational reshuffles which make for difficult cost analysis and cost attribution.
- The existing infrastructure is sticky. An information infrastructure is normally incredibly sticky. Changing it is very hard because changes are costly due to the vested interests in the people who look after it (not just vendors of content and software, but also the internal staff that have built up all the knowledge which will become worthless when it is gone).

## 5.7.2 OUTSOURCING AND SERVICE OPTIONS

The potential for outsourcing can be marked on a scale from relatively high for data interfaces to gradually lower, moving down from mapping, sourcing, and cleansing to data enrichment where a financial institution adds most value. Apart from offshoring and outsourcing, and the traditional and still most common *onsite delivery* of content and application software, we see different service models come into place to service the information supply chain and instrument and transaction lifecycles. These different service solution approaches will all require different KPIs. The most common ones are as follows:

- *Data Service Providers* (DSPs) refers to the provision of information management services. These providers differ from data vendors in that they are not directly aggregating and publishing data, but seeking to position themselves in between content vendors and application software to take on part of the information supply chain problem.

- *Software as a Service* (SaaS) refers to software services over the Internet. The application is hosted centrally. Software is not customized, and the client manages its own content. This can work for end-user applications but is rare as part of a core business process in financial institutions. SaaS can lower the hurdle for institutions because costs can move from a CapEx budget to an operating expenses model. It can also lead to a change in departmental charge-backs and different attribution of costs.

- An *Application Service Provider* (ASP) is the hosted version where the applications software is run by a third party—often the supplier of the software. This can imply that proprietary content leaves the building. If a separate instance of the software is hosted for every client, customization of the service is still possible.

### 5.7.3 FOR THE VENDORS

Content products need to be set up and delivered with the anticipated workflows of the content in mind. How users across the institution consume the information needs to be accounted for in the product. There is a need for new content products that also cover the metadata/quality aspects up to that point of the information supply chain. The content products should be clearer and more explicit *about what happened up to that point*. It should be transparent how a supplier came to this information, and if the vendor cannot tell you, how will you ever know? This can include information on the confidence the vendor has in the accuracy and completeness, plus also time stamps on when the content item was originally picked up.

There are also challenges for application vendors, not just for content vendors: They should become more open and flexible with regard to the ability to take in information, conform to standards, and allow for metadata handling, that is, the ability to calibrate actions on quality markers.

There are also opportunities for content providers to move downstream in the information supply chain. This means offering integration and data enrichment capabilities that currently typically happen *within* a financial institution. Given the outsourcing and offshoring trend, the time may be ripe for that. This could include offerings such as the following:

- *Combining Data.* Not just offering bid/ask prices from many venues, but offering consolidated prices as per a client's instructions, leading to mass-customized products.

- *Deriving Data.* Not just offering prices, but directly offering the piece of information the customer needs to value its books and measure its risk. So not only offering FRA quotes, SWAP quotes, deposit quotes, bond prices, and futures prices, but offering the set of constituents together or, even better, providing a zero curve as per a client's instructions on parameterization sourced through, for example, a web portal.

- *Providing APIs and On-Demand Data.* Proactively sending out notices when something changes, for example, the rating agencies and news services that can give alerts on predefined business-critical events.

- *Ensuring Content Talks to Logic.* Legacy systems sometimes find it hard to communicate among themselves. They also often have data models hard-wired into them so that it's hard to decouple data from application logic.

### 5.7.4 FOR THE FINANCIAL INSTITUTIONS

Information supply chain improvement projects should not be sold internally on regulatory grounds. It is not so much "because you have to," but far better to present the revenue-generating opportunities and take the "because you want to" angle.

Infrastructure products switching costs are very high. They are very sticky, precisely because of the entropy and sheer number of point-to-point connections. This has meant that organizations are often locked in for substantial periods with solutions that they are not really happy about. Conversely, vendors may not be sufficiently incentivized to provide world-class service, since their clients have little choice. Therefore, when setting up projects to smooth and reorganize the information supply chain, make sure to always address at least one immediate business need instead of painting lofty blue-sky pictures. When data quality improves, there is more room for automation as the number of potential points of failure goes down.

Generally, clean up decrepit formats of older products that have not aged well. Some formats are like uninvited guests to a wedding who somehow get hold of the rings and can ruin the whole affair. Ultimately, tuning the information supply chain to the specific transaction lifecycle management needs of the financial institution is not a technology issue, but about addressing business requirements. Be sure to be part of the trend to go from data processing to data management. With this, we mean not just processing but actively managing how and what you process through various KPIs.

Some predictions as to the future challenges of information management are easy: more volume, lower latency, more regulation, and larger geographical spread between different links in the financial transaction processing chain. If data quality is a comparative advantage, it is also a moving target because the average quality and thus the benchmark shifts and the bar is raised continuously. One constant is that risk will always end up where you least expect it because there will always be information discrepancies, and less sophisticated investors will keep biting off more than they can chew. As transferring risk becomes easier and easier, the financial products that carry these risks also become more sophisticated and more difficult to price and process. Risk procedures and data needs will increase, but this will, in itself, not be enough. The seller will always know more than the buyer, and risk—whether market risk, credit risk, or operational risk—will remain a slippery concept.


# ▌ Endnotes

[1]This is swapping one cost for another; it can be seen as a fixed-for-floating operational risk swap.

[2]This lack of transparency also complicates the strategic options an institution has, e.g. in bringing in new service providers or outsourcing part of its securities processing.

[3]Refers to 99.99% and 99.999% uptime, respectively.

[4]For example, through the use of VRXML; see also Chapter 2.

[5]The term was originally introduced by Robert S. Kaplan and David P. Norton in the early 1990s.

[6]Stemming from the background of six sigma: six standard deviations.

[7]These are numbers based on an A-Team survey on the number of security masters typically in place, plus experiences of author when talking to clients, plus the number of instruments typically tracked in these security masters, see www.a-teamgroup.com.

[8]Note that we are not even talking about transactions here. Consider 5,000 trades per day during 240 days in the year, so 1.2 million trade tickets. If there are only 1.2 * 3.4, this would be 4.08 defects in total, fine. But the number of opportunities for 1 trade ticket is not one; there are possibly hundreds of opportunities for defects in a convoluted information supply chain.

[9]Basel Committee on Banking Supervision, *International Convergence of Capital Measurement and Capital Standards*, November 2005, p. 140. See http://www.bis.org.

[10]For event breakdown, see, for example, Basel Committee on Banking Supervision, *Sound Practices for the Management and Supervision of Operational Risk*, February 2003, p. 2. See http://www.bis.org.

[11]For example, KPI Benchmarking Services; see www.riskbusiness.com.

[12]Meaning 99.999% uptime or about 5 minutes maximum unscheduled downtime per year.

[13]The question is whether you can ever migrate a large diversified enterprise to an architecture redesigned from scratch or whether that would mean suspending all operations for a year or more. The enterprise architecture can be seen as a yardstick against which to evaluate new initiatives, rather than a project deliverable.

[14]Note that this is spreading to the trading of other asset classes wherever data availability and liquidity allow it.

[15]For example, weather data can be linked to the CDD/HDD futures, to the soft commodities to energy prices, to sugar/ethanol, to the BRL/USD exchange rate, and so on. You want to uncover secondary and tertiary effects to create trade ideas.

# Chapter 6

# Concluding Comments

We have surveyed and charted the information supply chain and various products and processing in the instrument and transaction lifecycles. If you depend on data, you cannot afford to ignore any of its aspects. Market information is the raw material which has to flow into models and to be processed, to be mingled with, and to produce proprietary information. We have looked not only at data consumption, but also at new content production. Data become valuable when used. Data are not just a *byproduct* of doing business, but a *corporate asset* in themselves.

If these processes are robust, the end result should be fit for purpose. The difficulty is that the purpose can be manifold, depending on the step in the transaction lifecycle and, indeed, the type of business and even the instrument type processed. We saw that the typical infrastructural situation in financial institutions is not so much a chain as a spider web. In the information supply chain, the data model is critical because it is the foundation upon which the software applications are going to be built. If you tweak it, then independent stores can pop up left and right. Data maintenance and entitlement rights need to be restricted to a central team to control who has access to what efficiently.

Whether data feeds are a hodgepodge of different elements or whether they can be easily processed and acted on by users and applications because of clear formats and identification makes an enormous difference in sourcing information. We have looked at various outsourcing options. Institutions need to decide whether they want to be in the data collection business and determine which of their content needs are *fungible* (so that it can be serviced through packaged distribution) and which are not (proprietary information that needs a more bespoke approach). A good infrastructure brings you the organizational flexibility to change the structure through providing outsourcing and decoupling options. Outsourcing options can really be considered only when an institution fully understands its information supply chain and understands what the KPIs are that go with their specific business needs.

We have discussed various data standards. In a discussion about standardization, it is illuminating to consider how hardware has been standardized (see Table 6.1). The software industry is following with different development methodologies, coding standards, and essentially standardization on one of two platforms.[1]

Low levels of information standardization have been the cause of high-entropy situations—the costly and messy infrastructures described in Chapter 5. Although the content business is still lagging, switching costs of applications could well be decreasing because applications and databases are becoming more data agnostic due to the introduction of XML and web services.

**Table 6.1** Different Standardization Levels

| Layer | Level of Standardization |
|---|---|
| Hardware | High standardization. Hard-wired standardization |
| Software | Becomes more embedded. More rigid development methodologies. CMM standards. |
| Information | Some standardization in niche domains. Semantics problems. Many standards competing. |

We have discussed the need for horizontal roles across the traditional vertical-siloed business lines. Simply put, siloed companies do not share best practices. The financial services sector is undergoing continuous change, and in a merger, data governance has so far always been a luxury. Although some institutions have appointed Chief Data Officers, the question is whether this is a police role or a driver role. Does this represent the function of a steward, or is it someone who can veto projects and control budgets?

If an institution wants to attain a pristine, 360-degree view of financial information and its supply chain, continuous investment is needed. It is not possible to do solid and secure infrastructure on a shoestring. The success of process improvement initiatives will be limited if they do not include enterprise content management. Feedback loops where KPIs are fed back and acted on upstream are essential. Information that is hard to find will lead to breaks. But whatever is hard to find will be hard to find for the competition as well and therefore valuable as a basis for competitive advantage. The key challenge for any information supply chain is how to simultaneously resolve data needs, e.g., for STP, cost reduction, vendor and system rationalization, while at the same time providing added value, for example, for complex derivatives, structured products, and flexibility for the demands of the front office.

The key theme is data liquidity and agility: getting the information that is needed fast and at low cost. This requires substantial data integration, the breaking down of silos, a common data model, and the distribution into the hands of end users and business applications. The percentages of back-office budgets spent on IT are on the increase.[2] The underlying consulted content needs to be in sync for all steps of a transaction, and the availability of one *master view* of an instrument, a corporate action, or a client will significantly bolster productivity.

As we move from blind processing of information to more intelligent managing of information, more insight into the information supply chain will be created. We will see a trend and a tendency to push standards up the information supply chain upstream. This means that the problem is pushed closer and closer to the originators of the data and to get it in the right standards from the start.

Content products and information services will become more user-friendly and adapted to end-user workflow. Underlying data standards in terms of format, but especially in terms of semantics and (ISO) standards on unique identification, are a prerequisite. Information constraints for decision making will be reduced as data and data quality become an enabler rather than a blocker for new products and services. Financial institutions are recognizing more and more the criticality of knowing and managing the information supply chain—not so much for regulatory and cost-control reasons, but to establish a solid foundation for growth.

## Endnotes

[1]Windows/.Net on the one hand and Unix/Linux/J2EE on the other hand.
[2]Perhaps also because personnel costs decrease after outsourcing.

# Index